D1439115

An
EDINBURGH
Alphabet

An
EDINBURGH
Alphabet

J. F. BIRRELL

1980

JAMES THIN
THE MERCAT PRESS, EDINBURGH

James Thin
The Mercat Press
53–59 South Bridge
Edinburgh

ISBN   0901824 62 3

Printed by John G Eccles Printers Ltd,
Henderson Road, Inverness

INTRODUCTION

"All our beauty might have been preserved without the extinction of innumerable antiquities conferring interest and dignity. But reverence for mere antiquity, and even for modern beauty, on their own account, is scarcely a Scotch passion." (Lord Cockburn, *Memorials of his Time*, (1856), 174).

    This is not my book — it is not even my idea. The notes for it were collected initially by my father during World War II and were added to in manuscript jottings until his death over 25 years ago. These proved a useful source of reference when topics arose during conversation with family and friends, but my lack of historical, antiquarian and architectural knowledge, and, worse, lack of interest, meant that I did not add much to them after my father's death. Since my retiral they have stimulated me to read widely and to investigate on foot the remains of the Old Town and the changes effected in the New Town.

    Training in my profession taught me that articles and books of value were well documented, and that before writing on any subject the available literature should be studied. So many books contain sentences beginning 'Grant says . . .' or 'Cockburn describes . . .' without any reference to the title of the book or the page where the quotation is to be found. My father's annotated notes appealed to me and encouraged me in the belief (which I am certain that he held) that they might form the basis of an acceptable book, basically one of reference, but containing notes to encourage further reading. My first task was to check the accuracy of his references and, by further exploration, to add to them and bring them up to date. This has more than doubled the original notes and has brought to light the paucity of published information about the history of the changes in Edinburgh during the past century.

    One of the interesting sidelights which has emerged was the discrepancy in dates accorded to certain events in different publications, and a number of possible explanations arise. The first is poor proof-reading, which, at the best of times, is a tiresome chore. Another is the reliance placed by some authors on previously published work without any reference to it, and one can sometimes recognise sentences or even paragraphs in books taken from previous ones without any acknowledgment. A third possible explanation is that authors writing on a particular topic may have conducted their research in original documents not previously consulted, and which offer different dates or alternative explanations. In this book the references will show such differences, even if only of a year or two, and this may encourage the reader to make use of the library facilities to read the varying accounts.

Occasionally the discrepancy in dates is such as to arouse greater interest, and perhaps some reader may be able to resolve the longevity of Peter Brusche. He is reported as being the German engineer who placed a lead ball in Cannonball House in 1609 to show the height of the water supply which he hoped to bring from the Pentland Hills. Peter Brusche, a German engineer, is said to have brought water from Comiston in 1632. Peter Brauss, a German engineer, is reported as having brought water from Comiston in 1674; while Peter Bruschi, a Dutchman, is credited as having brought water from Tod's Well in 1720, and having fled when the water did not arrive at the opening ceremony!

While nearly every statement in this book is annotated some bald remarks occur without any reference. The source of these is from a small book called *Greater Edinburgh*, written by my father and published anonymously by Anderson of Edinburgh in 1946; from the extramural courses conducted by B. C. Skinner and E. F. Catford; from answers to specific questions put to various authorities or societies or in conversation with knowledgeable friends; or from the satisfying source of walking in Edinburgh.

I am greatly indebted to the *Scotsman* Publications for their permission to quote from the small paragraphs headed 'The Scotsman 100 (or 150) years ago', and from articles in the *Scotsman* and its allied papers, past and present. It will be apparent that this book owes its being to the authors and publishers throughout the years from whose works I have taken the various references, and I am indebted to the publishers of those books where copyright exists who have allowed me so to do.

This book is intended primarily as a source of quick reference on many aspects of Edinburgh, while for those who may wish to enlarge on the basic facts presented it is hoped that the references given may provide a stimulus to further reading.

EDINBURGH, 1980

J.F.BIRRELL

The drawings are by John Mackay, who is well-known for his ability to capture something of the feel of Edinburgh, past and present.

The plates are reproduced from Swarbreck's *Sketches in Scotland*, 1845. His own captions have been retained, in order to preserve the 19th century atmosphere of the plates.

The jacket illustration is, of course, also from Swarbreck. "This view presents itself on entering Edinburgh by the New London Road. The bold and craggy eminence, on which stands the residence of the jail governor, forms a striking feature in the scene; which, with the castle in the distance, and the noble North Bridge, and part of the Old and New Towns of Edinburgh, invariably arrests the attention of the stranger."

Adew, Edinburgh! thou heych tryumphant town,
Within quhose boundis rycht blythful have I bene,
Of trew merchandis the rute of this regioun
Most reddy to resave Court, King and Quene!
Thy polecye and justice may be sene:
War, devotioun, wysedome, and honestie,
And credence, tynt, thay mycht be found in thee.

Sir David Lyndsay
The Complaint of Papingo, 1530.

ABBREVIATIONS

O.E.C. = *Book of the Old Edinburgh Club.*

R.C. = *Royal Commission Inventory of the Ancient and Historical Monuments of the City of Edinburgh.*

'Abbey Lairds' see also Sanctuary.
Debtors and bankrupts, and even common criminals before 1560,
living in Holyrood Sanctuary (Maxwell, 253). They dwelt in and
around Holyroodhouse under the care of the Bailie of Holyrood, an
official appointed by the Hereditary Keeper of the Palace of
Holyrood.

Abbey Strand or **Girth**
The boundary between Canongate and Holyrood Abbey, marked
by three 'S' signs spanning the Abbey Strand beyond which lay the
Sanctuary of Holyrood (q.v.). The Abbey Strand has recently been
renovated.

Acheson House, 146 Canongate — south side.
Home of Sir Archibald Acheson of Glencairney (Wilson, II, 103), of
Glencairnie (Grant, II, 27), of Abercairny (Chambers, 314), of
Clonekearney, Co. Armagh (R.C., 166), Secretary of State for
Scotland in the reign of Charles I. The lintel above the door bears
the date 1633.
1633 Built in Bakehouse Close (q.v.) (O.E.C., XI, 6, gives 1622; XVII,
28; Chambers, 314; Grant, II, 27).
1935 Bought by Marquess of Bute (R.C., 166). Over the rear gateway
from Bakehouse Close is a lintel dated 1679 and taken from
Elphinstone House, South Gray's Close, in 1927 and incorporated
in 1938. Over the entrance from the Canongate is a lintel dated
1699, taken from Anchor Close (q.v.) in 1932 and erected in 1937
when the Marquess of Bute restored the house.
1949 Opened as Scottish Craft Centre (Keir, 707).

Adam Bothwell's House, Byre's Close (q.v.).
1593 Adam Bothwell died (Grant, I, 220). He was Bishop of Orkney and
Commendator of Holyrood, and he conducted the marriage
between Mary, Queen of Scots, and James Bothwell. His house
was at the foot of Byre's Close, and may be seen from the
neighbouring Advocate's Close. The house was also associated
with Sir William Dick of Braid who accumulated great wealth,
supported the Covenanters in 1641, gave Charles I £20,000, and lost

9

Adam Bothwell's House, Byre's Close, as seen from Advocate's Close.

the remainder when he was seized by the English Government. He went to London to recover his money, was imprisoned, and died in 1655 in extreme poverty (Wilson, II, 8-11; Williamson, 220). See Grange House.

1650 Oliver Cromwell occupied Bothwell's House (Chambers, 99).

Adam Square

Adam Square lay in the east of what is now Chambers Street.

1770 Square formed (O.E.C., XI, 6) by two houses, built by Robert Adam, on the north side and the Old College on the south (Grant, I, 379).

1821 Edinburgh School of Arts, later, in 1851, the Watt Institute and School of Arts, founded in one of the houses (Grant, I, 379).

1854 Statue of James Watt erected in the Square (Gilbert, 125).

1869 Adam Square demolished for the construction of Chambers Street (Smeaton, (a), 318; Gilbert, 146, says 1870).

Adam House in the present Chambers Street is so called because it stands on the site of the family house of the Adam brothers, and it was erected by the University of Edinburgh in 1947 (Stewart, 33).

Advocate's Close, 357 High Street — north side.

It took its name from Sir James Stewart, Lord Advocate 1692-1713, whose house the Close contained at the foot, on the west side, immediately before the steps (Cochrane, 88). It is thought to date from before 1544 (R.C., 86). The Close contains two lintels on the east side, both dated 1590. It is described in Scott's *Guy Mannering* in which Andrew Crosbie, advocate, who lived there before

10

moving to St. Andrew Square, is portrayed as Councillor Pleydell (Williamson, 222).

1884 Lower part of the Close demolished (O.E.C. I, 7) but the upper part still communicates with Cockburn Street.

Advocates' Library, Parliament Square.

1680 Advocates' Library planned (Maitland, 416; Smeaton, (a) 183) to lie at right angles to and west of Parliament Hall.

1682 Library founded by George Mackenzie of Rosehaugh ('Bluidie MacKingie', q.v.) (O.E.C., II, 10; Arnot, 295; Grant, I, 123).

1689 Library opened (Keir, 910).

1700 Fire in Parliament Square; library moved to the Laigh Parliament Hall (Keir, 911).

1710 Library entitled to a copy of every book published.

1925 Library transferred to the nation to become the National Library (q.v.) (Keir, 912), but the legal section remains as the Advocates' Library.

Air Transport

1947 Turnhouse aerodrome, used by the Royal Flying Corps and the Royal Air Force since 1915, became the civil airport for Edinburgh (Keir, 428).

1952 Ministry of Civil Aviation and Air Ministry agreed to joint ownership and air traffic control.

1956 Terminal building opened for civil air transport.

1977 New terminal buildings and extended runways opened.

Albert Institute, Shandwick Place.

1876 Institute of Fine Arts built (Grant, II, 209).

1880-90 Methodists worshipped in the Hall (Keir, 184). Now only occasionally opened for exhibitions.

Alison Square

1750 Built between Nicolson Square and Potterrow (O.E.C., XI, 6; Chambers, 358).

1876 Marshall Street constructed through the Square (Grant, II, 332; Chambers, 358, f. n.).

Amenity Associations

1875 Cockburn Association, Albyn Place (the subtitle The Edinburgh Civic Trust was added in 1968) — concerned with preservation of Edinburgh's amenity.

1931 National Trust for Scotland, Charlotte Square — places of historical interest or beauty.

1936 Saltire Society, Atholl Crescent — Scottish life and culture.

1956 Scottish Georgian Society, Forres Street — to protect listed
buildings.

Anchor Close, 243 High Street — north side.
In Anchor Close were Dawnay Douglas's Tavern (see Inns), the
meeting place of the Crochallan Fencibles, and the printing office of
William Smellie, founder of the Crochallans to whom he
introduced Robert Burns. Smellie printed the Edinburgh edition of
Burns' poems which were published by William Creech
(Pennycook, 37), after proof-reading by the poet in 1786-7; and the
first edition in three volumes of the *Encyclopaedia Britannica* in
1771.

The Close was the residence of George Drummond, six times
Lord Provost, who was highly influential in the conception of the
New Town (Wilson, II, 28; Grant, I, 235; Youngson, 3; 15).

A shield with the date 1699 stood at the northern entrance to
the Close until 1932 (R.C., 90) when it was transferred to the
Scottish Craft Centre (see Acheson House).
1859 Close partly demolished during the construction of Cockburn
Street into which it still opens.

Archery
1603 Archers shot on Leith Links for the Musselburgh Silver Arrow
(Marshall, 10).
1676 Company of Archers formed (Maitland, 323; Grant, II, 352;
Smeaton, (a), 331).
1677 The Queen's Prize presented by the Privy Council (Keir, 153).
1704 Royal Company of Archers incorporated by Queen Anne (Grant,
II, 353; Smeaton, (a), 331; Maitland, 324, says 1713).
1709 Edinburgh Silver Arrow presented (Maitland, 324; Arnot, 359).
1776 Archers' Hall built (Arnot, 276), 'near Hope Park end' (Grant, II,
354), 'at the head of the Boroughloch Lane' (Smeaton, (b), 357).
1798 Part of the East Meadows given to the Royal Company as a
shooting ground (Keir, 151).
1822 Royal Company became the Sovereign's Bodyguard in Scotland
(Keir, 150).
1900 Archers' Hall enlarged and modernised by R. Rowand Anderson
on the same site in Buccleuch Street (Keir, 152).

Architecture, see also Carving and Early Houses.
c.1437 In James I's reign "the dwelling houses were rarely more than two
storeys in height, and were usually constructed of wood brought
from the forests of the Boroughmuir." (Smeaton, (b), 18).
c.1500 From the time of James IV "dates that Franco-Scottish style of
architecture which became so common in Edinburgh during the

succeeding century." (Smeaton, (b), 54).

1535 "The houses erected at this time and during the next eighty years, before religious austerity began to regard architectural beauty as a weakness of the flesh, were in the highest degree picturesque and romantic." (Smeaton, (b), 59).

1560-1660 "The style which dominated building for the nobles and lairds . . . is generally referred to as 'Scottish Baronial'; the building of the same date in towns — familiar, for instance in the Royal Mile . . . has no popular name." (Smout, 180).

c.1800 "We must . . . remember that the period at the end of the eighteenth and beginning of the nineteenth centuries is a byword for lack of architectural taste." (Williamson, 148).

1809 Abercromby Place, begun in that year, was the first instance in which the straight line was voluntarily departed from (Cockburn, 287).

1815 The peace of 1815 brought improvement in architectural taste. "There was a period during which feudal war created striking castles and Popery glorious temples: but when the operation of these ceased and internal defences became useless, and religious pomp odious, we sank into mere convenience, which we were too poor to associate with architectural beauty or grandeur." (Cockburn, 285).

1853 "The city began to extend steadily south-westward, the estates of Grange and Merchiston being laid out in streets for detached villa residences, a new departure from the heavy style of city mansion that had been adopted in 1776, when laying out the streets of the New Town." (Smeaton, (b), 137).

Argyle Square

1730 Square, named after the Duke of Argyle, built on land now covered by Chambers Street, west of Horse Wynd (q.v.) (Grant, II, 271; Minto and Armstrong, in the Introduction, say c.1746). It incorporated on its east side the Trades Maiden Hospital (q.v.), founded in 1704 in a building in the Square.

1766 Meeting House for Scottish Baptists in the Square (Grant, II, 274).

18th century Minto House (q.v.) in the Square.

1861 Royal Scottish Museum (q.v.) built on the site of the Square (Smeaton, (b), 341).

1867 Square demolished under the Improvement Act (q.v.) for the building of Chambers Street.

Arms of the City

1562 Figure of St. Giles removed from the Coat of Arms as idolatrous, and replaced by a thistle (Wilson, I, 94).

1732 Arms patented.

13

1774 Arms recorded in Lyon Court with the motto *'Nisi Dominus Frustra'* (Keir, 286).

Arthur's Seat
An extinct volcano, 822 feet (253m) high, surmounted by a view-finder; it is named either from King Arthur or from the Gaelic *Ard-na-Saigheid*— the height (of the flight) of arrows (Maitland, 152; Grant, II, 305).

c.1430 St. Anthony's Chapel built (Smeaton, (a), 247). "Ruins of what was once a chapel, or hermitage, dedicated to St. Anthony the Eremite." (Scott, *Heart of Midlothian*, chap. 15). A light used to burn in the tower (Smith, I, 3). The ruin is still to be seen on a spur overlooking St. Margaret's Loch (*vide infra*).

1540 Arthur's Seat added to Holyroodhouse grounds by James V.

1688 Beacon to announce landing of William of Orange (Grant, II, 306).

1744 'Guttit Haddie' — a rift in the west slope caused by a water-spout (Grant, II, 307) or by a cloudburst during a great storm (Keir, 967).

1778 Mutiny of Macraes (Seaforths) encamped on Arthur's Seat (Boswell, 108, f.n.; Grant, II, 307).

1820 Radical Road (q.v.) built (O.E.C., XVIII, 182; Grant, II, 311; Smeaton, (a), 247; (b), 261).

1825 Complaints of over-quarrying Salisbury Crags (q.v.) (O.E.C., XVIII, 181-210). "Salisbury Crags will bear the marks of insensate folly [of the Hanoverian age] for all time." (O.E.C., XVIII, 210; Cockburn, 307).

1843 Queen's Park (see Holyrood Park) under Commissioners of Woods and Forests (Grant, II, 312).

1843 Queen's Drive laid out for Queen Victoria (Grant, II, 312) and was completed in 1847 (Scotsman, 29-5-1847).

1857 St. Margaret's artificial loch formed (Malcolm, (a), 96).

1862 St. Margaret's Well (q.v.) moved from Restalrig to Arthur's Seat (Grant, II, 312).

Assemblies, see Dancing Assemblies.

Assembly Hall, Mound Place — see Churches and Religion.
The Assembly Hall houses the General Assembly of the Church of Scotland in May each year, attended always by a Lord High Commissioner acting on behalf of the Sovereign, and, since 1834, living during the Assembly in the Palace of Holyroodhouse. In 1960, 1969 and 1977 Queen Elizabeth attended in person, being the first monarch to do so since the Union of the Crowns in 1603.

A brief history of events in the Church of Scotland is given below.

1560 Reformation. The Church of Scotland arose from this, but from

14

1560-1689 Presbyterianism was the authorised religion for only 57 years compared with the 72 years in which Episcopalianism was authorised.

1690 Certain members withdrew to form the Reformed Presbyterian Church in Scotland (J. T. Cox, *Practice and Procedure in the Church of Scotland* (1964 edition), 362) after the Act of Settlement established Presbyterianism 'for ever' in Scotland, because they feared that what had been established by Act of Parliament might later be disestablished. They worshipped in the Lady Lawson Street area.

1733 Secession. Secession Church in Scotland formed (Cox, loc. cit., 362) because the General Assembly upheld the 1712 Patronage Act.

1761 Certain members withdrew to form the Relief Church in Scotland (Cox, loc. cit., 362).

1842-4 Church of Scotland Assembly Hall built, designed by Gillespie Graham and Augustus W. N. Pugin (O.E.C., XIV, 168, f.n.; Grant, I, 90); it was known as the Victoria Hall from 1844 until 1929 and is now the Highland Church, Tolbooth St. John's.

1843 Disruption. Over one-third of the members withdrew from a General Assembly held in St. Andrew's Church, George Street, on the question of patronage, and, under the leadership of Dr. Thomas Chalmers, headed to Tanfield Hall (q.v.) to form the Free Church of Scotland (Grant, II, 145; Cox, loc. cit., 362). Free Church Assemblies were held in Tanfield Hall until 1856 (Grant, III, 88) when they moved to the Assembly Hall.

1843 Free Church opened its Theological College in George Street (Grant, II, 96) — closed in 1850.

Entrance to Assembly Hall and New College.

1846-50 New College and Assembly Hall, designed by William Playfair, built by Free Church on the site of Mary of Guise's Palace, Castlehill (Grant, II, 97; Chambers, 25, f.n.; Keir, 917) for training theological students. Church of Scotland students were trained at the University of Edinburgh.

1847 Secession and Relief Churches joined to form the United Presbyterian Church (Cox, loc. cit., 363).

1851-61 Offices of Free Church designed by David Cousin built on site of half of James's Court (q.v.), Lawnmarket (Grant, II, 95).

1876 Free and Reformed Presbyterian Churches united (Cox, loc. cit., 363).

1883 Free Church New College buildings extended by demolishing Somerville's Land, built in 1602 on the north side of the junction of Castlehill and the Lawnmarket (Cruft, 4).

1896 Statue of John Knox by John Hutchison erected in New College quadrangle (Smeaton, (a), 164; Williamson, 205; Cox, loc. cit., 363).

1900 Free Church and United Presbyterian Church formed United Free Church of Scotland.

1911 Church of Scotland opened offices in 121 George Street (Keir, 1009).

1929 Union between Church of Scotland and United Free Church with the result that the combined Church of Scotland used the Free Church's Assembly Hall for General Assemblies and its New College for theological training. (See Free Church below).

1930 Faculty of Divinity of University of Edinburgh transferred to New College (Stewart, 18).

1935 Buildings beside New College adapted for library use, and the library of General Assembly, formerly housed in the present Tolbooth St. John's Church (its Assembly Hall) was split up in the 1960's, the manuscripts being lodged in the Register House and the books going to New College Library (Keir, 917).

Free Church

Certain members of the United Free Church did not take part in the Union of 1929 and since 1907 (Keir, 178) this body has used the offices built in 1861 in North Bank Street. This building contains Free Church of Scotland College for theological training and considers itself historically continuous with New College. The Free Church of Scotland holds its annual General Assembly in May in Free St. Columba's Church, Johnston Terrace (Keir, 178).

Assembly Rooms, George Street; see also Dancing Assemblies.

1787 Assembly Rooms, designed by John Henderson, built by public subscription (Youngson, 95).

1818 Portico added (Youngson, 253).

1843 Music Hall, designed by Willaim Burn, added (Grant, II, 150; *Edinburgh — An Architectural Guide* says 1834).

The Assembly Rooms and Music Hall were bought by the Town Council after World War II (Keir, 306).

Auld Reekie

The name conferred on Edinburgh in the latter half of the 18th century (Maxwell, 256). The name may have originated in Fife on account of the smoke screen seen across the Forth over the city in the evenings (Chambers, 152, f.n.) but Keir (946) suggests that it arose from the foul odour of the streets (see Street Cleanliness).

Baberton House

1623 Built by John Murray, Master of Works to James VI (Geddie, 105) and may have been used by that monarch as a royal residence (Grant, III, 319).

1765 New wing added.

1830 Charles X of France lived in the house (Grant, III, 319). It is still used as a family house, beside the golf course entering from Westburn Avenue.

Back Stairs

A massive flight of stairs leading from Parliament Close to the Cowgate (O.E.C., XII, 130; Smeaton, (b), 193).

1828 Partly demolished.

1844 Site cleared for erection of Law Courts (Grant, II, 245). Back Stairs should not be confused with President's Steps (q.v.).

Baijen Hole, High Street — north side.

A baker's shop opposite the Old Tolbooth. The name comes from the French *béjaune* — freshman or greenhorn (Chambers, 155, f.n.); c.f. 'bejant', the name given to a first-year male student at St. Andrews University.

Bailie Fyfe's Close, see Heave awa' Land.

Bailie MacMorran's House, see Riddle's Close.

Bakehouse Close, Canongate — south side.

Was formerly Hammermen's Close, reached from a pend near Huntly House (q.v.) which the Hammermen owned. The entrance from the Canongate is surmounted by a lintel, bearing the date 1699, removed from Anchor Close in 1932 and erected in 1937.

1633 Acheson family (q.v.) lived in the Close (Grant, II, 27).

Bakehouse Close — and Huntly House — a magnet for artists.

1647 Canongate magistrates granted a Charter for a house to the Hammermen of the burgh (Chambers, 313).

1832 Partly owned by the Incorporation of Bakers who established their Guild in the Close.

1968-9 Restored with Huntly House (q.v.), retaining its original form.

Bank Street, see Mound.

Banks

1695 Bank of Scotland chartered (O.E.C., XII, 61; Maitland, 324; Arnot, 530; Grant, I, 176; II, 93; O.E.C., II, 13, says Old Bank, later Bank of Scotland, was founded in 1697). The Bank was in Parliament Square and then, after destruction in the fire of 1700, in Old Bank Close (q.v.).

1727 Royal Bank of Scotland founded (O.E.C., II, 13; Maitland, 351; Arnot, 532; Grant, II, 94). Opened in Ship Close, High Street.

1740s Coutts Bank, a private bank, in existence (Youngson, 24; D. Young, *Edinburgh in the Age of Sir Walter Scott*, (1965), 22, says 1723).

1746 British Linen Company founded to merchant linen (Maitland, 324; Arnot, 533; 592;, Wilson, II, 213); became a bank in 1906.

1769 Edinburgh Branch of Ayr Bank opened (O.E.C., XII, 94). The Ayr Bank collapsed in 1772 (Smout, 229).

1805 Bank of Scotland building on the Mound, designed by Robert Reid (Dunlop and Dunlop, 103; R.C., 102, says 1806).

1806 Leith Bank, Bernard Street, built (Grant, III, 239).

1810 Commercial Bank founded (Cockburn, 251). The original office was at the corner of Picardy Place and Leith Walk. Founded mainly by Forrest Alexander, bootmaker, Robert Cox of Gorgie and others who found existing banks too independent to do their business as and when they wished (Livingstone, (a), 65). In New Assembly Close 1814-47.

1824 Speculative mania in the city (Gray, 99).

1825 National Bank founded (Grant, II, 170).

1825 Royal Bank bought Dundas House, St. Andrew Square (q.v.) (O.E.C., XXII, 28).

1836 Edinburgh Savings Bank founded as the National Security Savings Bank of Edinburgh (Grant, II, 95; Keir, 578 says 1814). Now the Trustee Savings Bank.

1843 Union Bank of Scotland formed (O.E.C., XIV, 150, f.n.).

1843 Commercial Bank built on site of College of Physicians in George Street (O.E.C., XXIII, 9). The building, designed by David Rhind, was completed in 1846 (Grant, II, 147; Scotsman, 11-7-1846).

1852 Bank of Scotland premises on Mound redesigned by Thomas Hamilton (R.C., 103).

1868 Bank of Scotland on Mound enlarged, architect David Bryce (Grant, II, 95; R.C., 103, says 1865).

1875 Institute of Bankers in Scotland formed (Keir, 578), now in Rutland Square.

1877 Royal Mint in Edinburgh (see Cunzie House) demolished (O.E.C., XII, 84; Grant, I, 268).

1924-39 Royal Bank purchased share capital of Glyn Mills, Deacons Banks (Keir, 577).

1952 Bank of Scotland acquired Union Bank (Keir, 577).

1959 National Commercial Bank formed from merger of Commercial and National Banks (Keir, 577), and was later taken over by the Royal Bank of Scotland.

1971 Bank of Scotland merged with British Linen Bank whose share capital had been bought by Barclay's Bank in 1919 (Keir, 577).

1977 British Linen Bank re-emerged as a Merchant Bank.

Barnton
Formerly called Cramond Regis because it was a royal hunting seat (Grant, III, 316).

1508 Overbarnton belonged to Sir Robert Barnton (Grant, III, 317).

1691 House in large grounds bought by Lord Ruglen (Geddie, 36).

18th century House passed to the Ramsay family (Grant, III, 317).

1926 House a ruin (Geddie, 36).

The grounds are now extensively built upon and include the Royal

Burgess and Bruntsfield golf courses.

Barras (Barres or Barreres)
Barras = burrows, formerly tournament grounds (O.E.C., XIV, 103) where King's Stables Road meets the Grassmarket (Fraser, 56), or = Baresse, later Livingstone's Yards, near the West Port (Maxwell, 89).

Baxter's Close see Upper Baxter's Close.

Bawbee see also Coinage.
1 bawbee = ½ penny Scots.

Bearford's Parks
The land on which the earliest building of the New Town took place (O.E.C., XIII, 79–92; Grant, II, 115). Also called Barefoot's Parks and Lochbank (O.E.C., XXII, 174; XXIII, 6, f.n.). Embraced 30 acres (12 hectares) of land between the Lang Gait (q.v.) and the Nor' Loch (q.v.).
1716 Town Council bought the Parks (O.E.C., XXIII, 6; Malcolm, (b), 15, says 1717).

Bedesmen
Also known as Blue Gowns, they were privileged beggars (Chambers, 102; Wilson, I, 244). An excellent example is Edie Ochiltree in Scott's *The Antiquary*. The name Bedesmen applied from the telling of their beads as they walked from Holyrood to St. Giles (Chambers, 102, f.n.).
 An almshouse for bedesmen, founded by Michael Macquhen (Fraser, 64) stood near the Magdalen Chapel (q.v.) in the Cowgate (R.C., 41).
1863 Last bedesman died (Dunlop and Dunlop, 84, f.n.).

Bedlam
A lunatic asylum in Bristo where Robert Fergusson died in 1774. It stood near the sites of the present New North Church, Darien House and the Charity Workhouse, and it was removed in 1842 (Robertson, 297; Grant, II, 324, says 1871).

Beechmount House
Built on the southern slopes of Corstorphine Hill, east of Beechwood House. The House was bequeathed to the Royal Infirmary by the then owner, Sir George Anderson, Treasurer of the Bank of Scotland (Geddie, 50). It was used by the Infirmary as a radiotherapy convalescent house before World War II (Turner, 337)

and is now a general convalescent home.

Beechwood House

On the southern slope of Corstorphine Hill, it was reputed to have been praised by the Duke of Cumberland in 1746 (Grant, III, 104), but as the present building was erected in 1780 (R.C., 229) there must have been a previous house.

The Scotus Academicus School occupied the house until 1977, and the house and grounds may be used for property development.

Bellevue House, Drummond Place.

The villa of General John Scott (Cockburn, 171) built for him, after the demolition of the house of Lord Provost Drummond, who gave his name to Drummond Place, by Sir Laurence Dundas following a gambling loss (Steuart, 181). It later became the Custom House and then the Excise Office (q.v.) (Grant, I, 217).

1846 House demolished during the completion of the tunnel in Scotland Street for the Edinburgh and Leith Railway (see Railways) (Grant, I, 217).

Bell's Mill

An ancient village on the Water of Leith below the present Belford Bridge (Wilson, II, 210).

Bell's Wynd, High Street — south side.

Contained a hospital and a Chapel called the Maison Dieu (R.C., 126) which was converted into private property at the Reformation (Grant, I, 149; II, 261).

The *Edinburgh Gazette* was printed in Bell's Wynd.

1756 Dancing Assembly opened (Chambers, 46, f.n.; Wilson, II, 32; Grant, I, 245, says 1758).

1784 Building became a tavern when the Assembly Rooms opened in George Street. Later was a children's shelter and is now a playground which is entered from Old Assembly Close.

Bible Land, 187-197 Canongate — north side.

1677 Built by Incorporation of Cordiners (R.C., 177) and the entrance is surmounted by an open scroll of the first verse of Psalm 133. Some consider Bible Land as synonymous with Shoemakers' Land (q.v.) because cordiners were shoemakers, but R.C. (177) gives a different number in the Canongate to each.

1954 Bible Land reconstructed into flats but there is no plaque to explain the scroll to visitors.

Bickers

A street conflict among boys (Chambers, 189; 245).

Birth Rate
Statistically, per 1000 of the population, the birth rate fell from 35.5 in 1861 to 17.7 in 1961 (Keir, 101), and to 11.9 in 1977. Illegitimate births in the same period, expressed as a percentage of all births, dropped from 9.9% in 1861 to 5.7% in 1961 (Keir, 103) but has increased to 9.6% in 1977.

Bishop's Close, High Street — north side.
Here was born Henry Dundas, Lord Melville (1742-1811), 'the uncrowned king of Scotland between 1784 and 1793' to whose memory the column in St. Andrew Square was erected.

Lady Jane Douglas, remembered for her part in a lengthy legal case, lived here (Chambers, 238; Maxwell, 220 and Grant, II, 349, date the case 1762-7; Steuart, 64, says 1749-69).

In this Close was the school of Louis Cauvin where Robert Burns learned French.

It is now closed by a locked gate and appears deserted.

Bishop's Land, High Street — north side.
A doorway in Carrubber's Close (q.v.) states that the house of Archbishop Spottiswood stood here (Chambers, 269).
1578 House built; 1813 house burned down; 1864 house rebuilt. It is now a public house.

Black Friars (Dominicans)
See article in O.E.C., III, 13-104
1230 Black Friars came to Edinburgh under Charter from Alexander II (O.E.C., III, 24; Maitland, 181; Wilson, I, 7; II, 265) and established a Friary in a large area to the south of the east end of the Cowgate (R.C., 125).
1528 Monastery in Cowgate destroyed by fire (Grant, II, 285). "During the long period of 330 years [1230-1560] our local Black Friars sounded the diapason of the Christian religion in the public streets of our city; and it may be asserted that it was largely upon their religious and ethical teaching that the social fabric of these stormy days was supported and maintained." (O.E.C., III, 76).
1559 Friary destroyed by a mob (R.C., 125).
1656 Curriehill House in Black Friars' Land given to the Deacons of the College of Surgeons (O.E.C., V, 78).

Black Turnpike, High Street — south side.
1461 Black Turnpike built (Grant, I, 204); R.C., 128) east of St Giles Church and opposite the Guard House. It was the town house of Sir Simon Preston (Williamson, 231) and later of the Earl of Home (Nimmo, 79) and was a sumptuous edifice (Wilson, II, 34).

1567 Mary, Queen of Scots, imprisoned in the house after her defeat at Carberry Hill (Wilson, II, 35).

1788 Black Turnpike pulled down to make room for Hunter Square (q.v.) (Wilson, II, 35; Grant, I, 206; Dunlop and Dunlop, 132; R.C., 128).

There is a plaque, erected in 1894, on the west side of Cockburn Street at its junction with High Street denoting the site of the house, but it has been said that the plaque once stood on the west side of the entrance to the Royal Exchange as Preston's house was opposite and to the east of the site of the entrance to that building.

Blackford Hill

1884 Hill (539 ft. (166 m.) high) bought by city (Smeaton, (a), 342; Gilbert, 162).

1895 Royal National Observatory built on Blackford Hill (Smeaton, (a), 143; 342) aided by a donation from the Earl of Crawford who gave the basis of the finest library of books on astronomy in the world (Keir, 922). The professor of Astronomy is the Astronomer-Royal for Scotland.

On the south side of Blackford Hill is a rock declared in 1840 by the Swiss geologist Louis Agassiz to have been polished and grooved by ice during the Ice Age (q.v.).

Blackfriars Wynd, High Street — south side.

The Wynd led to the Cowgate and was so named because it led to the Dominican Friary of 1230 (O.E.C., XXIV, 240).

Here lived William St. Clair of Roslin, Cardinal Bethune (Beaton) (q.v.) and, reputedly in 1564, the Regent Morton whose family house (q.v.) may still be seen and is now used by the University of Edinburgh as an examination hall (Stewart, 17).

1507 First Scottish printing press of Walter Chepman and Andro Myllar was at the foot of the Wynd (R.C., xlviii). Chepman lived at the top of the Wynd (Steuart, 68).

1520 'Cleanse the Causeway' (q.v.).

1668 Attempt on the life of Archbishop Sharpe of St. Andrews in the Wynd (Arnot, 148).

1847 Dr Thomas Guthrie's Industrial School in the Wynd (Grant, I, 264; Smeaton, (a), 141).

1867 Blackfriars Wynd demolished (Grant, I, 264) under the Improvement Act (q.v.) and is now Blackfriars Street.

The buildings on the west side are largely cleared away and those in the middle third of the east side are boarded up.

Blair Street, Hunter Square, opening south to Cowgate.

1788 Street built (Grant, I, 245). Named after Lord Provost Hunter Blair who printed Bibles there.

Now largely evacuated as a housing area, but contains a long-established pen-making firm.

Blue Blanket
A flag worked by Queen Margaret (Dunlop and Dunlop, 148) and granted to the citizens by James III in 1482 (Maitland, 9; Chambers, 183; Maxwell, 78; Smeaton, (a), 50). It was the symbol of the exclusive rights of the craftsmen of Edinburgh, and was kept by the Convener of Trades (Chambers, 183). "The incorporated trades, in recognition of their loyalty, were presented with a banner or standard which, from its colour, received the name of the 'Blue Blanket'." (Smeaton, (b), 46).

The Blue Blanket was placed for safe keeping in the National Museum of Antiquities in 1850 (Fraser, 43) and a 17th century replica is preserved in the Trades Maiden Hospital (q.v.) (O.E.C., X, 82; Grant, III, 55; Fraser, 43).

Blue Gowns see Bedesmen.

'Bluidie MacKingie' or 'Bluidy Mackenzie'
Sir George Mackenzie of Rosehaugh was King's Advocate in the reigns of Charles II and James VII (II), a patron of learning and founder of the Advocates' Library (q.v.). His nickname of 'Bluidie MacKingie' or 'Bluidy Mackenzie' was given by the common people in detestation of his acting as an instrument of the hated English government. He lived in Strichen's Close (q.v.) (Chambers, 223; Grant, I, 264; Williamson, 234) and is buried in Greyfriars Churchyard (Grant, II, 382).

Bodle see also Coinage.
1 bodle = 2 pence Scots = one-sixth of an English penny.

Bonnington
An old mill on the Water of Leith. Remnants of the old village may still be seen.

Booths see Luckenbooths and Shops.

Borestone see Burgh Muir.

Borough Loch see South Loch.

Boroughmuirhead
This is the area of the present Churchhill (see Burgh Muir).

Borthwick's Close, High Street — south side.
The Close took its name from the Borthwick family (Grant, I, 242).
Napier of Merchiston owned a house in the middle of the Close
(Grant, I, 242). One of Heriot's Free Schools lay between
Borthwick's and Old Assembly Closes.

Presently the only communications between High Street west
of Hunter Square and the Cowgate are Stevenlaw's (Stephen
Loch's) Close, Old Fishmarket Close and Borthwick's Close.

Boswell's Court, 352 Lawnmarket — south side in Castlehill.
A 17th century court which formerly contained the house bought
by Dr. John Boswell and backed on to the Duke of Gordon's 17th
century mansion (Chambers, 18; Grant, I, 90) between Brown's
and Blair's Closes, on the site of Castelhill School, built there in
1887.

Botanic Garden
1656 Surgeons planted a physick garden at Curriehill House in the land
of the Black Friars where botany and pharmacy were taught
(Guthrie, 9).
1661 Gardener of Heriot's Hospital was instructed to plant part of the
grounds "with all sorts of physical, medicinal and other herbs"
(Scotsman, 31-3-1950). The earliest public botanic garden was a
small piece of ground belonging to Holyrood Abbey (Scotsman,
31-3-1950).
1676 Old Physic Garden was near Trinity College Church (q.v.) (Grant,
I, 362) in the valley of the Nor' Loch extending from the foot of
Halkerston's Wynd (q.v.) to the site now occupied by the
foundations of the General Post Office (Scotsman, 31-3-1950). The
Garden was created by Sir Andrew Balfour who added to his own
collection the botanical garden of Patrick Murray of Livingstone
(Grant, I, 362). Sir Robert Sibbald, whose main interest was to find
herbal cures, began his botanical collection in 1670 and moved it to
the Physic Garden (Fraser, 127). The Town Council appointed
James Sutherland, formerly in charge of the Abbey Garden, as
Keeper of the Physic Garden (Turner, 32). A plaque was unveiled in
1978 in the Waverley Station to mark the approximate site of the
Physic Garden.
1689 Garden inundated during the partial drainage of the Nor' Loch, and
many plants were lost from deposited mud (Grant, I, 363).
1699 James Sutherland was the first Professor of Botany in 1695 and
became King's Botanist, appointed by William III, in 1699.
1710 Queen Anne reissued the Warrant for the Regius Professor of
Botany although Sutherland had retired.
1766 Physic Garden removed to Leith Walk (Arnot, 418; Grant, I, 362)

when it was called the 'Botanical' (O.E.C., XXIII, 54).

1774 Inverleith House built. In 1881 it became the residence of the Regius Keeper of the Botanic Garden (Grant, III, 97) who was also the Regius Professor of Botany. The house contained the Scottish National Gallery of Modern Art from 1960 (Keir, 875).

1823 Botanical Garden moved to Inverleith (Cockburn, 411; Grant, III, 96; Smeaton, (a), 299).

1858 Large Palm House erected (Cruft, 81).

1881 Arboretum opened (Grant, III, 97; Smeaton, (a), 299).

1898 Conservatories constructed (Cruft, 81).

1967 Further glasshouses for plant propagation.

Bowfoot Well

1681 Built in the Grassmarket at the foot of West Bow (Wilson, II, 166; Grant, I, 310; II, 233), but the inscription on the Well says 1674 which was the date of bringing water from Comiston (see Water supply).

Bowls

"A much more prevalent amusement than now, being chiefly a favourite with the graver order of citizens." (Chambers, 247).

Bowling greens existed behind the Excise Office in the Cowgate; in the grounds of Heriot's Hospital, where there were three; in the Canongate near the Tolbooth; on the opposite side of

Bowfoot Well.

the Canongate; immediately behind Holyroodhouse (the oldest green) where the Duke of York (later James IV) played; and others were scattered in the outskirts (Chambers, 247).

1552 Town Council petitioned to make more ground available for bowls.

1581 Sunday bowling declared illegal.

1769 Society of Bowlers founded (Arnot, 362; O.E.C., XXIX, 185) which drew up laws for the game.

There are now many public and private outdoor and indoor greens in the city.

Boyd's Inn, Boyd's Close, Canongate — south side.
At the head of the Canongate, it was originally called White Horse Inn, St. Mary's Wynd, and the site is marked by a plaque on the wall in St. Mary's Street. When Boyd's Close became the name of the Wynd the name of the Inn was altered (Stuart, 112). There was obvious confusion with White Horse Inn at the foot of the Canongate (q.v.).

1635 White Horse Inn belonged to James Hamilton, stabler (O.E.C., XIV, 129).

1773 Dr Samuel Johnson arrived at Boyd's Inn (O.E.C., XIV, 129; Boswell, 11).

1868 Inn demolished when St. Mary's Street was built.

Braid Hills

1298 Edward I camped there (O.E.C., X, 59; Grant, III, 41).

1650 Cromwell camped on Braid Hills (O.E.C., X, 200).

1889 Braid Hills (675 ft. (207 m.) high) acquired by Town Council for a golf course — 'the father of muncipal golf courses'.

Brewing
"One of Edinburgh's most important and oldest industries. It goes back at least to the 12th century, when the Monks of Holyrood Abbey made the most of the excellent springs nearby to brew their beer." (Keir, 629).

By a statute of James I one full quart of the best beer or ale was to be sold for one penny, and two quarts of small beer for one peny (Scotsman, 1-9-1877).

In the late 18th century the City levied an impost on ale over and above the Government tax, and this was an inducement to brew in Holyrood which was then outside the city (Keir, 629).

Other breweries arose in Fountainbridge and Craigmillar, and many of the best-known brews came from Edinburgh.

Monks brewing ale.

Bridewell see Calton Hill.

Bristo Port
Bristo Port, also known as Greyfriars Port, was a gate in the Flodden Wall situated near the site now covered by the New North Church in the angle between Bristo Place and Forest Road (see Town Walls).

1845 During widening of the street from Bristo Port to the junction of Lothian Street with Teviot Row the old city wall was replaced by a modern one (Scotsman, 27-12-1845).

Bristo Street
Mid-eighteenth century tenements, the earliest large-scale urban development outside the Town Wall. Burns' 'Clarinda' lived in General's Entry here and Robert Fergusson died in Bedlam (q.v.) near Bristo Street (Grant, II, 324; 327; Minto and Armstrong, 48).

Here stood the Woolpack Inn which existed from c.1741 and was so named in 1823 (Minto and Armstrong, 47). It was a favourite with students until the street's demolition along with Charles and Crichton Streets in the late 1960's for the building of the University of Edinburgh's Student Centre in 1970.

1741 The Bristo Seceders occupied a building in Bristo Street through which a pend led to their meeting place (Cruft, 41).

British Legion
The British Legion (Scotland) was founded in 1921 at a meeting in

the Usher Hall of various ex-servicemen's organisations (Keir, 555).

Brodie's Close, 306-310 Lawnmarket — south side.
1570 Mansion of William Little of Liberton was in the Close (Chambers, 76), when it was known as Little's Close.
1780 Residence of Deacon William Brodie (Chambers, 76), Deacon of the Guild of Wrights (cabinet-makers), whose crimes began in 1786 when he used keys, forged from putty or clay impressions, for robbery.
1788 Brodie arrested in Amsterdam whither he had fled after robbing the Excise Office in Chessel's Court (q.v.), and was hanged at the Tolbooth (O.E.C., XII, 60; Chambers, 91; Wilson, I, 222; Grant, II, 23; Smeaton, (a), 171).
1836 Mansion taken down under the 'improvements' (Chambers, 76).
1962 Brodie's Close was restored and houses the Celtic Masonic Lodge.

Broughton
1143-1560 "The lands of Broughton, together with the Burgh of the Canongate, formed part of the possessions of the Abbey of Holyrood." (O.E.C., XVIII, app. 14; Wilson, II, 208).
1392-3 Broughton raised from a barony (see Burgh of Barony) to a regality (q.v.) (R.C., lx).
1568-87 Period of Adam Bothwell's superiority of the Barony of Broughton (O.E.C., XVIII, app. 14).
1630 Charles I bought lands of Broughton (O.E.C., XVIII, app. 16).
1636 Heriot's governors obtained the lands of Broughton (O.E.C., XVIII, app. 16; Grant, II, 181).
1636 Town Council purchased part of the Barony of Broughton (Smeaton, (b), 103).
     The Town Council "obtained the long-coveted superiority of the whole of Leith and the regality of Broughton. In this they were indebted indirectly to Heriot's legacy, for two of the principal debtors to the jeweller, the King and the Earl of Roxburghe, unable to repay the great sums they owed, gave up to the Town . . . the superiority of the regality of Broughton, which included the burgh of the Canongate, North Leith, Pleasance and parts of South Leith." (Extracts from the Records of the Burgh of Edinburgh, (1626-1641), xlvii).
1747 Broughton lost its regality under the Act of Parliament and was eventually merged into the city (R.C., lx).

Brown Square
This very small square lay at the west end of what is now Chambers Street.

1763–4 Brown Square built by James Brown (O.E.C., XI, 7; Wilson, II, 152; Grant, II, 269). It contained the residences of Jeanie Elliot, who wrote *Flowers of the Forest* (Chambers, 5) and Henry Mackenzie, author of *Man of Feeling* (Chambers, 6; Wilson, II, 153). In the Square lived Scott's Saunders Fairford, and there Alan met Lady Greenmantle (Scott, *Redgauntlet*, note in Letter 2).
1870 Brown Square demolished for building of Chambers Street (Gilbert, 146).

Brown's Close see Webster's Close.

Brunstane House, near Newcraighall.
1639 House rebuilt by Lord Thirlestane (Grant, III, 150), and bears the date.
1875 Duke of Abercorn sold the house to a coal company (Grant, III, 150).
      The house is still occupied as two dwellings.

Bruntsfield House, Whitehouse Loan.
The name is derived from Richard Broune who owned the land, Broune's Field becoming Bruntsfield (R.C., 233). The early house was destroyed in Hertford's 1544 raid and a new house built (Smith, I, 50).
c.1550 House built (O.E.C., VIII, app. 6; Grant, III, 45). "Bruntsfield House is a composite structure consisting of the manor erected during the sixteenth century, to which extensive additions have subsequently been made." (O.E.C., X, 23).
1579 Golf was being played on Bruntsfield Links (Smeaton, (b), 364).
1695 George Warrender bought the house (O.E.C., X, 24).
1750's Quarrying in Bruntsfield Links (Smith, I, 50).
1827 Building forbidden on Bruntsfield Links (Youngson, 181).
1847 Bruntsfield Parks opened for grazing of all kinds of stock (Scotsman, 29-5-1847).
1869 Alvanley Terrace, Bruntsfield Links, built (O.E.C., X, 32).
1935 Bruntsfield House and grounds bought by Town Council (Smith, I, 53).
1966 James Gillespie's School for Girls (q.v.) sited in Bruntsfield House and grounds.

Buccleuch Place
c.1770 Buccleuch Place built.
1777 Dancing Assembly in Buccleuch Place (Grant, II, 148; 347; III, 125; Youngson, 252).
1801–3 Lord Francis Jeffrey lived at No. 18 (Smeaton, (b), 356; W. Harrison, 32).

1803 David Bryce, architect, born in Buccleuch Place.
1958-62 University of Edinburgh bought houses in Buccleuch Place and
now uses them for small units or departmental offices. Buccleuch
Place now communicates by steps with the George Square
University complex.

Buccleuch Street
Tenements on the model of Old Town lands built in the second half
of the eighteenth century.
1776 Archers' Hall (q.v.) built facing on to what was to become
Buccleuch Street but what was then London Road.
1780 Houses erected (Scott-Moncrieff, 87; Smeaton, (a), 330; (b), 356,
says 1788).
1787 Robert Burns lodged in an attic above Buccleuch Pend which led
from Buccleuch Street to St. Patrick Square (Scotsman, 3-3-1938),
but which has been demolished.

Burgh of Barony
A corporation erected by the Sovereign consisting of the
inhabitants of a certain tract of ground. Sometimes its magistrates
were chosen by the inhabitants, sometimes they were named by the
superior (Arnot, 502).

Burgh Loch see South Loch.

Burgh Muir see also Drumselch Forest.
An expanse of grazing land and woods, originally called Burrow
Muir, which extended south of the Old Town from Duddingston
to Tipperlinn (O.E.C., X, 4, f.n.).
1128 Burgh Muir gifted to town by David I (O.E.C., X, 2).
1335 Skirmish between Scots and foreign mercenaries (O.E.C., X, 61;
Arnot, 7; Grant, I, 297; Maxwell, 32; Smith, I, 2).
1384 Scots army assembled there for the first time (O.E.C., X, 61;
Smith, I, 2). "There were . . . at least six occasions on which the
Scottish army held its rendezvous for the invasion of England upon
the Burgh Muir." (O.E.C., X, 190).
1508 Burgh Muir leased to town by James IV (Grant, III, 28; Dunlop and
Dunlop, 19).
1508 Feuing of Muir permitted (O.E.C., X, 67; Maitland, 11; 177).
1510 Feuars to build kilns for making beer (O.E.C., X, 227; Grant, III,
28; Fraser, 57).
1513 James IV's standard raised on the Harestane (O.E.C., II, 61; X, 77;
Maitland, 11; Arnot, 13; Grant, III, 28; Maxwell, 85). The
Harestane or Borestone was placed on the wall of Morningside
Parish Church in 1852 (O.E.C., X, 80) but there is no historical

evidence for the statements engraved on the stone (O.E.C., XXIV, 108-125).
1586 Feuing began on the Burgh Muir (O.E.C., X, 192).

Burlaw Courts
Burlaw (or Byrlaw) Courts were local courts to decide minor quarrels among neighbours — from Dutch *baur* — husbandsman (O.E.C., XV, 165-205; Russell, 33).

Burnet's Close, High Street — south side.
Burnet's Close was the home of Lord Auchinleck, father of James Boswell (John Reid, *New Lights on Old Edinburgh*, (1894), 153).
       Here Sir William Johnston started the business which became W. & A. K. Johnston, the map publishers (Reid, loc. cit., 159).
       The close now ends blindly.

Byre's Close, 373 High Street — north side.
The Close opened to the north opposite the west end of St. Giles Church and was named after Sir John Byres of Coates who owned a house near the Luckenbooths in the reign of James VI (Chambers, 95).
       Here lived Adam Bothwell, Bishop of Orkney (q.v.) whose house was near the foot of the Close. Sir William Dick of Braid also resided in the Close (R.C., 86).
1650 Oliver Cromwell occupied Bothwell's house (Chambers, 99).
       Bothwell's house was partly removed to make way for St. Giles Street but may still be seen from Advocate's Close. Byre's Close was smothered by buildings of the City Chambers (Grant, I, 154; 219; Chambers, 96-7). Byre's Close is now only a name plate on the wall above a municipal office window, but behind the façade of the window derelict buildings in the Close are being restored.

THE JAIL GOVERNOR'S HOUSE
This castellated edifice, the residence of the governor of the jail, is finely situated on the ledge of a rocky hill, and with its embattled turrets, parapets, and other architectural features, presents to the eye an appearance at once imposing and picturesque. Part of the Trinity College Church is introduced into the foreground; one of the oldest religious edifices in Edinburgh.

Cady or Caddie

A cady was a street messenger, the name being derived from French *cadet* — junior. "The Cross was . . . the rallying-point of a species of lazzaroni called caddies or cawdies." (Chambers, 175). "The cadies are a fraternity of people who run errands. Individuals must, at their admission, find surety for their good behaviour. They are acquainted with the whole persons and places in Edinburgh: and the moment a stranger comes to town, they get notice of it." (Arnot, 503). "They are the tutelary guardians of the city: and it is entirely owing to them that there are fewer robberies and less housebreaking in Edinburgh than anywhere else." (Topham, 87). See also Maitland, 326 and Maxwell, 217.

The name was also given to water-caddies who carried water to the houses at a fee of one penny for each barrel (Cockburn, 353-5). (See Water Supply).

Callsay or Calsey

A callsay was a causeway or street paved down the middle with a drain on either side.

Calton Hill

1718 Old Calton Burying Ground opened on the south-western slope of Calton Hill (328 ft. (100 m.) high) (O.E.C., XII, app. 28; R.C., LXI).

1724 City Council bought lands of Calton from Lord Balmerino (O.E.C., XII, app. 28; Wilson, II, 181; Russell, 103).

1725 Calton erected into a Burgh of Barony (q.v.) (Maitland, 212; Grant, II, 103, says 1669).

1776 City Observatory founded on Calton Hill (Maitland, 375; Arnot, 416; Grant, II, 105; Smeaton, (a), 345). It was planned by James Craig with advice from Robert Adam.

1777 Robert Adam's monument to David Hume erected in the Burying Ground (Grant, II, 108).

EDINBURGH CASTLE FROM THE GRASS-MARKET
This point of view is the only one which can at all do justice to the towering grandeur of this ancient edifice. In one of the rooms of the Castle Queen Mary gave birth to James I of England. The Scottish Regalia are kept here, with other relics of antiquity.

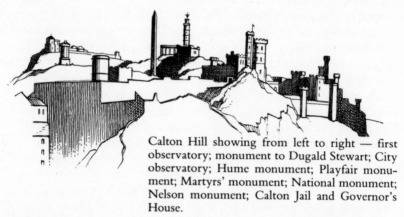

Calton Hill showing from left to right — first observatory; monument to Dugald Stewart; City observatory; Hume monument; Playfair monument; Martyrs' monument; National monument; Nelson monument; Calton Jail and Governor's House.

1792 Building of Observatory completed (Grant, II, 106; Youngson, 159).

1796 Bridewell (House of Correction) erected, architect was Robert Adam (Grant, II, 106).

1808 Calton Jail begun (Smeaton, (a), 345), designed by Archibald Elliott, to replace the Old Tolbooth (q.v.) which was due for demolition. "It was a piece of undoubted bad taste to give so glorious an eminence to a prison." (Cockburn, 240).

1812 Astronomical Institution founded (Cockburn, 270).

1814 Act for Calton Road and Regent Bridge erection (O.E.C., XII, app. 28).

1815 Waterloo Place cut through the Burying Ground (Grant, II, 104; Russell, 102).

1815-19 Regent Bridge built, architect Archibald Elliott (Grant, II, 104).

1815 Governor's House for Calton Jail built (Youngson, 159) to the design of Archibald Elliot.

1816 Nelson Monument, designed by Robert Burn, built (102 ft. (31 m.) high) Grant, II, 107; Smeaton, (a), 135; 345). A circular stair of 145 steps leads to an observation platform with an extensive view. The basement was occupied by a confectioner's shop until 1849 (Scotsman, 3-2-1849).

1816 National Monument mooted (Cockburn, 304).

1817 Calton Jail opened (O.E.C., XX, app. 7; Grant, II, 107).

1817 New Calton Burying Ground opened further east (Grant, II, 105).

1818 New observatory built, designed by William Playfair (Smeaton, (a), 345; Youngson, 159).

1819-60 Building of Regent Terrace, Carlton Terrace and finally Royal Terrace to the design of William Playfair.

1822 National Monument begun (Grant, II, 108), designed as a church by William Playfair on the lines of the Parthenon in Athens, but never completed from lack of funds, and the work stopped in 1829.

1826 Playfair's Monument to his uncle, Professor John Playfair, mathematician and natural philosopher (Grant, II, 110).

1829 Royal High School (q.v.) built, architect Thomas Hamilton (Grant, II, 110).

1830 Burns Monument, Regent Road, erected to the design of Thomas Hamilton (Grant, II, 110).

1832 Monument to Dugald Stewart, philosopher, designed by William Playfair (Grant, II, 109).

1845 Obelisk, designed by Thomas Hamilton, to the Scottish political martyrs of 1793-4 erected in the Old Burying Ground (Grant, II, 107; Scotsman, 1-10-1845).

1845 Tunnel completed through the south flank of Calton Hill for North British Railway (Scotsman, 20-12-1845).

1852 Time-ball on Nelson Monument (Grant, II, 108). The ball, 5 ft. 6 in. (1 m. 70 cm.) in diameter and made of zinc (Scotsman, 11-9-1850), is raised daily by machinery and descends at 1 p.m. (1300 hours) (Scotsman, 12-1-1848 with a footnote added on 12-1-1948). It was linked in 1861 by an electrical device to the time-gun in the Castle (Grant, II, 108; Gilbert, 132).

1893 Monument to Scottish soldiers killed in the American Civil War erected in Old Burying Ground, surmounted by a statue of Abraham Lincoln; sculptor George Bissell.

1925 Calton Jail closed.

1937 Calton Jail and Bridewell demolished for building of St. Andrew's House (O.E.C., XXIII, 53). Governor's House remains *in situ*.

Calton Village

Originally called Craigend, Calton Village was part of Restalrig and comprised houses on and against Calton Hill on land owned by Lord Balmerino.

1623 Craigend became a Burgh of Barony (q.v.).

1631 Trade Incorporation, mainly of shoemakers (O.E.C., XVII, app. 17).

1673 Barony acquired by Edinburgh, but Calton lands were not merged into the city until 1856 (R.C., lxi).

Candlemaker Row

Candlemaker Row led from the Bristo Port to the east end of the Grassmarket at its junction with the Cowgate. Society (q.v.) lay to the east and the land of the Grey Friars to the west. The Harrow Inn and the Selkirk and Peebles Inn stood at the head of the Row (Stuart, 125-6).

1559 Cunzie House (q.v.) was in Candlemaker Row opposite the junction with the Cowgate (Chambers, 260, f.n.; Smeaton, (a), 208; Minto and Armstrong, 3).

Early 1600's Tam o' the Cowgate (q.v.) lived near the junction of the Cowgate and Candlemaker Row (Chambers, 244).

1691 Merchant Company (q.v.) occupied the house which had belonged to Tam o' the Cowgate (Grant, I, 378), and left it in 1726.

1694 Merchant Maiden Hospital (q.v.) was accommodated in this house (O.E.C., XXIX, 11).

Before 1722 Henry's Land (now No. 40) built, the upper two storeys being added in 1722 (R.C., 109).

1722 Candlemakers Hall (now No. 36) built (O.E.C., XVII, 106; R.C., 109).

1730 Excise Office in Tam o' the Cowgate's house (Grant, II, 260; Chambers, 247).

1829 Tam o' the Cowgate's house demolished for the building of George IV Bridge (Chambers, 244).

Candlemakers

1488 Earliest reference to the Craft of Candlemakers (Maitland, 311). "From [1488] until the introduction of gas-lighting early in the nineteenth century candlemaking was one of the most flourishing of Edinburgh crafts." (O.E.C., XVII, 93).

1722 Candlemakers' Hall built, No. 36 Candlemaker Row (O.E.C., XVII, 106; R.C. 109).

1929 Hall restored, and is now used by the Iona Community.

Cannonball House, Castlehill — south side.

1630 Cannonball House built (O.E.C., I, 2).

1650, 1689, 1745 House underwent sieges (O.E.C., II, 117-19). The ball in the wall of the gable facing the Castle is popularly supposed to have been fired from the Castle during the 1745 siege, but Keir (50) says that the cannon ball was a "lump of lead stuck in the wall by the German engineer, Peter Brusche, in 1609, to show the Corporation the height of the Pentland wells from which he hoped to bring water." (See Water Supply; date must surely be wrong).

Blair's Close led through the house to the Duke of Gordon's mansion, replaced by Castlehill School in 1887.

1909 House unsuccessfully offered for sale (O.E.C., II, 117, f.n.).

1913 Acquired by the School Board and incorporated in North Castle (later Castlehill) School.

Later used as a theatre workshop.

Canongate

The canons' gait or road from Edinburgh (where they lodged in the Castle until 1176) to Holyrood Abbey (Steuart, 99).

The Canongate had three Crosses — (i) St. John Cross (q.v.)

near the head of St. John Street where Charles I knighted the Provost of Edinburgh in 1633, the site being marked in the roadway at St. John Street; (ii) Market (Burgh) Cross opposite the Canongate Tolbooth from where it was moved in 1888 from the centre of the street to the north side at Canongate Church where it stayed until 1953 when it was place inside the Canongate Churchyard (Catford, 82); it bears the dates 1128 and 1888; (iii) Girth Cross where executions took place and from which proclamations were made (Catford, 82), and which stood near the Abbey Strand (q.v.), the site being marked by a circle of stones in the road at the foot of the Canongate (Grant, II, 2).

1128 Burgh of Canongate founded by David I (Grant, II, 1). "The ancient burgh sprang wholly independent of the neighbouring capital, gathering as naturally around the consecrated walls of the monastery, whose dependants and vassals were its earliest builders, as did its warlike neighbour under the shelter of the overhanging battlements of the more ancient fortress." (Wilson, II, 76).

1380 Canongate burned by Richard II (Grant, II, 2).

1469 Act of Parliament allowed for a council and magistrates to be elected to the number of thirteen (R.C., liii).

1485 Building of houses begun in Canongate (R.C., liii), the houses being less crowded, and characterised by having gardens at the back, as compared with those of Edinburgh. The Canongate was never enclosed by a wall.

1535 Street paved with cobbles (R.C., liii).

1540 First Canongate Craft Incorporation (R.C., liii).

1541 St. Thomas's Hospital founded (q.v.).

1591 Canongate Tolbooth rebuilt (q.v.).

1603 Previous to the Union of 1603, owing to its proximity to Holyrood, the place was densely populated by 'persons of the first distinction'.

1636 Edinburgh acquired Canongate Burgh (O.E.C., XVI, 100; Maitland, 110; Arnot, 253; Wilson, II, 99; Grant, II, 3; Smeaton, (a), 110; (R.C., liv).

1753 The Canongate "has suffered more by the Union of the Kingdoms than all other parts of Scotland; for having, before that period, been the residence of the chief of the Scottish nobility, it was then in a flourishing condition: but being deserted by them, many of their houses are fallen down, and others in a ruinous condition: it is a piteous case!" (Maitland, 151).

1769 In spite of this comment, a list of 61 persons of note who lived in the Canongate is given by Chambers (296, f.n.) and includes two dukes, many earls, lords, judges and baronets.

1817 "The last grand blow was given to the place by the opening of the road along the Calton Hill . . . which rendered it no longer the avenue of approach to the city from the east." (Chambers, 297).

1856 Canongate incorporated into the city (O.E.C., XII, 89).

1906 "The once fashionable suburb of the Canongate is now degraded to a slum and brewers surround the ancient palace of the Scottish kings." (Williamson, 105).

1960's Considerable renovation by the Town Council maintaining, in many instances, original features, the architect being Robert Hurd. (See Chessel's Court and White Horse Close).

Canongate Church, Canongate — north side.

1688 Church built by James Smith for the congregation ousted from the Abbey Church of Holyrood when the Catholic James VII (II) converted it into a Chapel for the Knights of the Thistle (O.E.C., I, 12; XVII, 43; Maitland, 142; Arnot, 276; Grant, II, 28).

1691 Church opened for worship, the congregation having used Lady Yester's Church from 1687 (Sitwell and Bamford, 137).

1946-53 Exterior of Church cleaned and interior restored (Keir, 41) and the Market (Burgh) Cross was rebuilt in the Churchyard, having previously stood on the pavement outside the gate (Catford, 82).
In the Churchyard are buried Robert Fergusson, Adam Smith, Dugald Stewart, George Drummond and Burns' 'Clarinda' (Mrs MacLehose).

Canongate Tolbooth, Canongate — north side.

1477 Canongate Tolbooth existed before this date (R.C., liii).

1591 Tolbooth rebuilt (O.E.C., II, app. 7; IV, 103; XVII, 40; Arnot, 302; Wilson, II, 97; Grant, II, 30) as a civic centre for the burgh. The Council chamber was on the first floor reached by an outside stair (Cruft, 29).

1840 Tolbooth discontinued as a Council chamber and offered for sale (O.E.C., IV, 103).

1842 Re-opened as an overflow from Calton Jail (O.E.C., IV, 103).

1848 Again closed (O.E.C., IV, 103).

1879 Tolbooth restored (Cruft, 29).

1884 This date appears on the external clock overhanging the pavement, but the drawing in Butchart (*Prints and Drawings of Edinburgh* (1955), 80/1), dated 1829, shows a similar clock bracket, as does that of George IV's procession down the Canongate in 1822 (Sitwell and Bamford, 8/9).
The Canongate Tolbooth is now a city museum exhibiting Highland costumes, tartans etc.

Canonmills

Flour mills erected on the Water of Leith and worked by the Augustinian monks of Holyrood (Arnot, 253; Wilson, II, 210).

Canongate Tolbooth.

1761 Bridge built at Canonmills (O.E.C., XX, app. 21).

1825 Tanfield House (q.v.) built (Grant, III, 87).

1840's Canonmills Loch drained.

1865 Royal Patent Gymnasium erected (Grant, III, 87) on the site of the Loch and near the old Scotland Street Railway Station. Later the site was the football ground of St. Bernards Football Club from c.1890. Part of this area is still King George's Playing Fields, reached from Eyre Place (Cruft, 79–80).

Cap and Feathers Close, High Street — north side.

1750 Birthplace of Robert Fergusson, the poet (Grant, I, 238, who says that this may have been in the neighbouring Halkerston's Wynd (q.v.)). Fergusson died in Bedlam (q.v.), aged 24 years, and was buried in Canongate Churchyard, his tombstone being erected by Robert Burns.

1763 Close demolished for building of North Bridge.

Cardinal Bethune's (Beaton's) House, Blackfriars Wynd.

1509 Built by James Bethune, Archbishop of Glasgow, Lord Chancellor and a Lord Regent during the minority of James V (Chambers, 228). "Common report represents it as the house of Cardinal Beaton, nephew of the Archbishop of Glasgow." (Chambers, 228). It stood at the foot of the Wynd at its junction with the Cowgate where there is a plaque.

1528 House occupied by James V (Chambers, 229; R.C., 128).
1554 House rented for a year for the High School (Grant, II, 287).
1561 Mary, Queen of Scots, entertained by the Town to a banquet in the house (R.C., 128).
1867 Ruins of the building demolished with the rest of Blackfriars Wynd for building of Blackfriars Street.

Carmelite Friars (White Friars)
1526 Church and Monastery of Carmelite (White) Friars founded on Calton Hill (Arnot, 257). Grant (II, 101) says that it was at Greenside (q.v.) where land was conveyed under a Charter in 1518, and that the monastery was opened in 1525. Fraser (61) says that the Carmelites arrived in 1520 to look after a leper colony in the area.
1534 Order suppressed after a priest had been found guilty of heresy (Grant, II, 102).
1591 Building used as a hospital for lepers (Grant, II, 102; Smeaton, (b), 90).
1652-56 Leper Hospital removed (O.E.C., XV, 137).

Caroline Park, Granton.
Formerly Royston House which gave the title of Lord Royston, to George Mackenzie, Lord Justice General and Earl of Cromartie (Smeaton, (b), 386; H. Fenwick, *Scotland's Historic Buildings,* (1974), 228).
1685 Caroline Park House erected (O.E.C., VIII, app. 4; XX, app. 27) and it still exists being used as offices.

Carrubber's Close, High Street — north side.
Probably named after William of Caribris, one of three bailies in 1454 (Grant, II, 241). Contains Bishop's Land (q.v.).
1689 Retreat of faithful Jacobites who worshipped in a small chapel in a wool store at the foot of the Close before building Old St. Paul's Church (q.v.) in 1883.
1736 Allan Ramsay opened a playhouse at the foot of the Close, but this was speedily closed by the Magistrates (Grant, I, 83; Scott-Moncrieff, 55, says 1738).
1758 Fire in Carrubber's Close (Grant, I, 240).
    Carrubber's Close Mission, once in the Close, is now built at No. 65 High Street.

Carving on Houses see also Architecture and Early Houses.
"The practice of carving over the threshold the year, along with the intitials, and sometimes the arms or trade-mark, of the proprietor of the house and of his wife, accompanied by a scriptural motto or sage and pithy proverb, appears to have come to a head . . . in the reign of James VI and his successor." (O.E.C., XIV, 50).

Door ornaments of old houses — e.g. 'Get and save and ye shall have', 'If we did as we should we might have as we would' — are "of earlier date than the religious legends, none of which is earlier than 1543 when . . . the vernacular Bible was first allowed to the people." (Dunlop and Dunlop, 56).

"Dwellers in Old Edinburgh seem to have believed that mottoes, especially those containing the name of God, exercised a beneficent influence on their house." (Williamson, 218).

Castle of Edinburgh

The Britons called it *Castelh Mynedh Agnedh* which means 'The hill overlooking the plain'. The Castle is an observation point, 437 feet (134 m) high, on basalt rock created by volcanic eruption.

"The Castle Rock which was a stronghold of the tribe . . . the Votadini." (G. Donaldson *et al.*, *Edinburgh — a Symposium* (1975), 5). Eric Linklater (*Edinburgh* (1960), 69) refers to a Caledonian tribe, the Ottadeni, who defied Agricola and his army.

"There is no part of the history of Edinburgh, from St. Margaret onwards, that cannot trace some connection with the Castle." (Williamson, 86).

c.629 Edwin of Northumbria built the Castle (O.E.C., III, app. 10; Maitland, 6; Smeaton, (a), 4).

c.900 Castle in possession of Scoto-Pictish kingdom of Alba (G. Donaldson *et al.*, *Edinburgh, a Symposium* (1975), 5).

1018 Castle, as part of the Lothians, became Scottish (Smeaton, (a), 8) after Malcolm II defeated the Northumbrians at Carham.

1093 Queen Margaret, wife of Malcolm III, died in the Castle (O.E.C., V, 1-66; Arnot, 4; Maxwell, 10); she was canonised in 1250 (O.E.C., V, 35; Weirter, 18, says 1251).

1124 David I made the Castle a permanent Royal residence (Wilson, I, 6; Maxwell, 14).

1174 Castle pledged to Henry II as security for William the Lion's ransom (Arnot, 5).

1291 Edward I spent a night in the Castle (O.E.C., V. 33; Wilson, I, 7; Maxwell, 26; Smeaton, (a), 12; Sitwell and Bamford, 28, say 1292).

1296 Edward I acknowledged as Lord Paramount (Wilson, I, 7; II, 139; Smeaton, (a), 12).

1311 Castle in English hands (Wilson, I, 8).

1312 Castle retaken by Sir Thomas Randolph and William Francis

(O.E.C., V, 38; Wilson, I, 8; Maxwell, 30; Smeaton, (a), 12; Sitwell and Bamford, 29, say 1313).

1335 Edward III rebuilt the Castle (O.E.C., V, 40; Smeaton, (a), 13, and Weirter, 33, both say 1336).

1337 Buildings restored and withstood siege by Sir Andrew Moray (Maxwell, 33).

1341 Castle recaptured by Sir William Douglas (Arnot, 8; Wilson, I, 10; Maxwell, 33; Russell, 55).

1361 Well constructed at northern base of rock (Maxwell, 36).

1367-77 David II's Tower built (O.E.C., VI, 2; Wilson, I, 11; Maxwell, 36).

1371 David II died in the Castle (Maxwell, 36; Smeaton, (a), 15, says 1370).

1390 Henry IV's unsuccessful siege (Wilson, I, 18).

1400 Henry IV again unsuccessful (Maxwell, 36; Grant, I, 27; Smeaton, (a), 15).

1437 The first parliament of James II's reign held in the Parliament Hall of the Castle (Wilson, I, 163), where he was proclaimed king.

1438-40 James II confined in the Castle (Smeaton, (a), 22).

1440 'Black Dinner' held (Arnot, 11; Maxwell, 59; Grant, I. 30; Smeaton, (a), 25; Scott, *Tales of a Grandfather*, chap. XX).

c.1450 Well House Tower built (Arnot, 235; Wilson, I, 171).

1479 Duke of Albany escaped (Maxwell, 75; Scott, loc. cit., chap. XXII; Grant, I, 33, says 1482).

1481 James III held captive (Wilson, I, 26; Grant, I, 34; Russell, 143).

1517 James V brought for safety to the Castle from Stirling (O.E.C., IX, 15).

1545-6 George Wishart, reformer, imprisoned (Wilson, I, 68; Grant, I, 44; Russell, 267).

1556 Palace built in south-east angle of the Castle (O.E.C., XI, 12).

1559 Mint House (see Cunzie House) brought from Holyrood to the Castle (Wilson, II, 130).

1560 Death of Mary of Guise in the Castle (O.E.C., V, 54; Smeaton, (a), 79).

1561 Mary, Queen of Scots, entertained in Banqueting Hall (Smeaton, (b), 76).

1566 James VI born in the Castle (O.E.C., V, 58; Arnot, 291; Maitland, 161; Wilson, I, 100; 164; Maxwell, 146).

1567-73 Castle held for Mary by Sir William Kirkcaldy of Grange (Arnot, 30; Wilson, I, 108; Williamson, 58) who was later accused of coining base money in the Castle and was hanged at the Cross in 1573 (Weirter, 112).

1573 Siege lasting 33 days with enormous damage to the fortress including the demolition of St. Margaret's Chapel (O.E.C., XVI, 9-14; Arnot, 33; Maxwell, 137; Smeaton, (a), 92; Cochrane, 42).

One of Regent Morton's batteries attacking King David's Tower (with flag) the destruction of which brought about the end of the long siege of 1567-73 when Sir William Kirkcaldy held the Castle for Mary, Queen of Scots. The Half-moon battery was built on the ruins of David's Tower.

1573 Half-moon battery erected by Regent Morton (Wilson, I, 159; Smeaton, (a), 145; 150), and rebuilt in 1662.

1574 Portcullis Gate built by Regent Morton.

1639-40 Castle captured by Alexander Leslie (O.E.C., V, 64; Wilson, I, 122; Maxwell, 166). Montrose held a prisoner in 1641.

1650 Cromwell captured the Castle (Weirter, 145).

1651 Castle remodelled; Crown Room built (O.E.C., XVIII, 207).

1686 Duke of Gordon held the Castle for James VII (II) (O.E.C., XVI, 151).

1689 Siege by William III's troop (O.E.C., XVI, 171-213; Arnot, 183, Maxwell, 180). Castle surrendered (Williamson, 78; Sitwell and Bamford, 144, say 1690).

1714 Old ecclesiastical right of sanctuary discontinued (Grant, I, 67).

1715 Earl of Mar's attempt to seize the Castle failed (Sitwell and Bamford, 160).

1745 Blockade of the Castle against Jacobites (Grant, I, 329).

1753 Esplanade formed from foundation material removed during building of the Royal Exchange (Wilson, I, 160; Smeaton, (a), 144). It now contains many War Memorials (q.v.).

1818 Regalia of Scotland (q.v.) discovered in a chest in the Crown Room (O.E.C., VIII, 205-211; Wilson, I, 166; Grant, I, 71; Smeaton, (a),

136; 152; Cockburn, 348; Gilbert, 65).

1845 St. Margaret's Chapel rediscovered (O.E.C., V, 27; Wilson, I, 167; Maxwell, 12). It is the oldest structure in Edinburgh (Keir, 12).

1853 St. Margaret's Chapel restored by Queen Victoria (O.E.C., V, 25).

1861 Time gun first fired by electrical arrangement in connection with the ball on Nelson Monument, Calton Hill (q.v.) (Grant, II, 108; Gilbert, 132).

1873 Well House Tower restored (O.E.C., V, 63; Wilson, I, 111; Robertson, 49).

1888 Outer gateway erected (Cochrane, 29).

1892 Wiliam Nelson completed restoration of St. Margaret's Chapel (Smeaton, (a), 149).

1912-13 Excavation of David's Tower (Fraser, 88).

1927 National War Memorial, designed by Sir Robert Lorimer, built on site of ancient Church of St. Mary (Scott-Moncrieff, 3).

1929 Statues of Robert Bruce and William Wallace erected at the gateway to mark sexcentenary of Bruce's Charter to Edinburgh.

1930 Naval and Military Museum opened; renamed in 1948 the Scottish United Services Museum (Keir, 933).

1948 Military Tattoo on Esplanade for the first time during the Edinburgh International Festival of Music and Drama, and was a recognised part of the Festival from 1950.

Castlehill, from Esplanade to Lawnmarket at Upper Bow.
The Oratory of Mary of Guise, built after 1544, stood on the north side of Castlehill until demolition in 1845.

c.1437-1670 Castlehill was the principal place of some 2000 executions (Smeaton, (a), 144; (b), 140).

1590-91 Many witches burned on Castlehill (Smeaton, (b), 90). There is a bronze plaque marking the site of these burnings.

1659 Five burnings for witchcraft (Williamson, 102).

1674 Water reservoir constructed on Castlehill (see Water Supply).

1681 Executions on Castlehill ceased (O.E.C., III, 55).
"The road most favoured by [promenaders] led from what is now the esplanade past the Well-house Tower and along the side of the Castlehill to St. Cuthbert's Church." (Williamson, 102).
"The Castle Hill, which extends from the outward gate [of the Castle] to the upper end of the High Street, is used as a public walk for citizens, and commands a prospect, equally extensive and delightful, over the county of Fife." (Smollett, 283).

1883 Somerville's Land, a timber-fronted block of houses on the north side of Castlehill opposite the Upper Bow, removed for extensions to the Free Church College (Cruft, 4).

Castle Terrace
Erected in the 1830's (Youngson, 188; 215).

1877 Edinburgh Theatre, opened in 1875, sold to United Presbyterian Church for building of Synod Hall and Theological College (Scotsman, 20-9-1877).
1890 Methodists used Synod Hall (Keir, 184).
1900's-1960's Synod Hall used as a cinema and lecture hall until its demolition, leaving a hole the eventual use for which has long been the source of argument in the Town Council and the press, but in 1978 it was agreed that it be used for hotel development.

Cemeteries and Crematoria
These exclude small churchyards. See Keir, 431-440.
1843 Warriston Cemetery (Grant, III, 101; Russell, 174).
1845 Dean Cemetery (Grant, III, 68); extended in 1872.
1846 Newington Cemetery (Grant, III, 57).
1846 Rosebank Cemetery (Grant, III, 89; Russell, 174).
1847 Grange Cemetery (Keir, 438).
1881 New Dalry (North Merchiston) Cemetery (Keir, 439).
1883 Eastern Cemetery, Drum Terrace (Keir, 439).
1887 Piershill Cemetery (Keir, 439).
1888 Seafield Cemetery (Keir, 439).
1895 Mount Vernon Cemetery (Roman Catholic) (Keir, 439).
1898 Comely Bank Cemetery (Keir, 439).
1929 Warriston Crematorium (Keir, 441); Cloister Chapel opened in 1957.
1939 Seafield Crematorium.
1969 Mortonhall Crematorium.

Chamber
A chamber was a room in a lodging (q.v.) before the end of the 17th century.

Chambers Street, from George IV Bridge to South Bridge.
1871 Built under the Improvement Act (q.v.) at the expense of, from west to east, Society, Brown Square, Argyle Square and Adam Square (all q.v.). The street was paved with wooden bricks in 1876 (Daiches, 211). It contained on the north side the Dental Hospital (q.v.), Watt Institute, later Heriot-Watt College (University) (q.v.), Minto House (q.v.), Training Collge for Church of Scotland students, and, at the east end, Little Theatre of Varieties (demolished for shops). The buildings to the east of Heriot-Watt University are now all in the hands of the University of Edinburgh. Horse Wynd (q.v.) and College Wynd (q.v.) may still be seen. On the south the Royal Scottish Museum (q.v.), built in 1861, and the Old College of the University of Edinburgh (q.v.), built in 1789, occupy nearly the whole side. In the centre of the street is a statue,

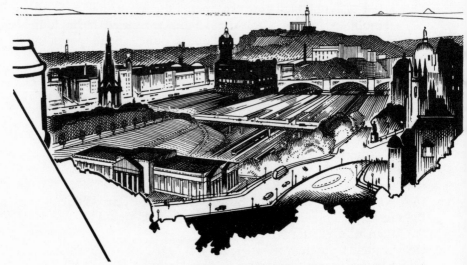

A panoramic view of Edinburgh from the Castle battlements on a summer's evening during the Edinburgh International Festival. (Smollett's "extensive and delightful prospect" would have been far removed from this!).

erected in 1891, to Lord Provost William Chambers, after whom the street is named.

Chapel House, Potterrow.
Built in the 18th century on ground owned by Sir John Nicolson (O.E.C., XXII, 85). It was owned in the 1790's by Sir Hugh Dalrymple, and in the 1830's by Andrew Melrose, the tea blender.
It is now a wholesale drysalter's premises.

Charity Workhouse see Paul's Work and Hospitals (Charity).

Charlotte Square, George Street — west end.
Named on Craig's original plan for the New Town as St. George's Square, but changed in 1786 to Charlotte Square.
1791 Houses planned by Robert Adam to create symmetrical north and south fronts, but not adhered to because Adam died in 1792 and his brother, James, died in 1794 (R.C., 207). The north side is Adam's original plan.
1794 First house completed (O.E.C., XXIII, 24; R.C., 207).
1800 Two-thirds of north side built (Youngson, 97).

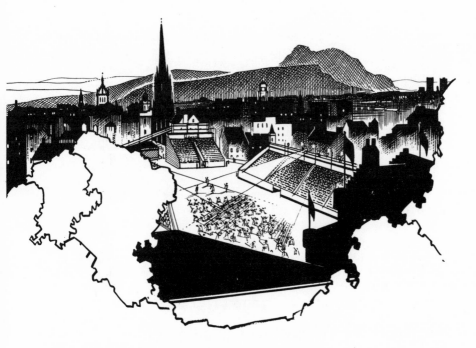

1808 About one-third of the Square built, the slow rate being due to the high cost of houses inhibiting speculation (Youngson, 223).

1812-30 Lord Cockburn lived at No. 14 (W. Harrison, 60).

1814 St. George's Church, designed by Robert Reid, opened (Grant, II, 175).

1874 Gardens laid out (Grant, II, 172).

1876 Albert Memorial, by John Steell, unveiled (Grant, II, 175).

No. 6 Charlotte Square is now the official residence in Edinburgh of the Secretary of State for Scotland, and is called Bute House, being leased by the Bute Trust to the National Trust for Scotland, which also uses Nos. 5 and 7. No. 7 is the Georgian House (opened in 1975) the lower floors being furnished in that period and on show to the public. The upper floor of No. 7 is the official residence of the Moderator of the General Assembly of the Church of Scotland during his year in office.

Among the other householders were James Syme (a professor of Surgery) in No. 9; Lord Lister in No. 8 and Sir William Fettes in No. 13 (*Edinburgh Evening Dispatch*, 30-11-1944). Alexander Graham Bell, inventor of the telephone, was born in South Charlotte Street in 1847, and Earl Haig was born in the house on the south-west corner of Charlotte Square in 1861.

At the junction of North Charlotte Street and St. Colme Street is the Sinclair Monument, erected in 1859, to Catherine Sinclair, novelist and philanthropist.

1961 St. George's Church showed evidence of being seriously infested with dry rot which the congregation could not afford to repair, and it was sold for conversion into the West Register House. This was opened in 1971 as a public record office which exhibits to the public, from time to time, historical documents etc. The Church congregation united with St. Andrew's, George Street.

Chessel's Court, 240 Canongate — south side.
c.1748 Built by Archibald Chessel (Cruft, 25), and was "the finest example of mansion flats in the Old Town." (R.C., 180).
1760's Used for a short time as an hotel (Catford, 85).
1769 Housed the Excise Office which was robbed by Deacon Brodie in 1788 (Chambers, 91; Grant, I, 114; Catford, 85).
    Later used as flats with St. Saviour's Child Garden, a charitable kindergarten for local children, on the ground level (Cruft, 25).
1963–4 Renovated by Town Council as flats, but still containing St. Saviour's Child Garden until it closed in 1977.

Church of Scotland, see Assembley Hall.

Churches, see also Religion and Assembly Hall.
Some churches are mentioned separately — Canongate, Greyfriars, St. Cuthbert's, St. Giles, St. Mary's Cathedral, Old St. Paul's, Tron — and the list given is not exhaustive as many churches are mentioned in the literature without dates, and many no longer exist.
1143 Duddingston Church (Russell, 146).
1143–7 Liberton Church referred to (Grant, III, 326).
1380 Corstorphine Church of St. John the Baptist (O.E.C., VII, app. 9); enlarged 1429 (Grant, III, 115).
1483 St. Mary's Church, later South Leith (R.C., lvii; Geddie, 169 and Keir, 437 say 1485; Russell, 30, says 1488).
1487 Parish Church of Restalrig, existing from 12th century, rebuilt (R.C., 253).

HIGH SCHOOL WYND
This steep and narrow street, leading down into Cowgate, is a spot of much interest to the antiquary and the tourist, as affording some of the best examples extant of the residence of the nobility and gentry of former-days, and of the style of buildings of the period. The fronts of the houses are mostly of wood.

1504 St. Mary's Chapel, Niddry Wynd (Wilson, II, 54).

1508 Chapel of St. Mary, Wester Portsburgh (R.C., 216), demolished in 1788.

1511 Chapel of St. Sebastian, Easter Portsburgh (R.C., 216).

1516 Episcopal Church, Queen Street, Leith (Grant, III, 230).

1637 Christ's Church, Castlehill (Grant, I, 82).

1647 Christ's Church at the Tron (Grant, I, 187), later called Tron Church (q.v.).

1647 Lady Yester's Church, High School Wynd (O.E.C., III, 25; Maitland, 181; Arnot, 275; Grant, II, 286), demolished in 1803 and rebuilt (*vide infra*).

1656 Cramond Church (Grant, III, 30).

1681 First Quaker Meeting House, West Port (Keir, 183).

1722 Episcopal Church, Blackfriars Wynd (Wilson, II, 61; Smeaton, (a), 206).

1729 Quaker Meeting House, Peebles Wynd, Cowgate, moved to Pleasance in 1791 (Keir, 183).

1741 Bristo Secession Church, West Crosscauseway.

1753 Nicolson Street Secession Church.

1756 Chapel of Ease, Chapel Street (Arnot, 278; Grant, II, 346), restored in 1866 (Grant, II, 346).

1765 Methodist Meeting House, Low Calton (Keir, 184), demolished in 1814 for Regent Bridge.

1766 Meeting House for Scottish Baptists, Argyle Square (Grant, II, 274), became Bristo Baptist Church, Queensferry Road (Keir, 185).

1769 Gaelic Church, Castle Wynd (Arnot, 283; Grant, II, 235); marked by a plaque in Johnston Terrace.

1771 Colinton Church (Grant, III, 322) rebuilt (see Colinton).

1771 Episcopal Church, Cowgate (Arnot, 283; Grant, I, 278; II, 247), became St. Patrick's R.C. Church in 1856.

HOLYROOD PALACE AND CHAPEL

This venerable seat of Scottish royalty was originally a convent, said to have been founded by David I. Holyrood Palace was the scene of all the principal transactions during the reigns of Mary and James VI. The left hand tower, next to the chapel, was the residence of Queen Mary and Darnley. Holyrood Palace twice afforded an asylum for Charles X of France.

1774 Lady Glenorchy's Chapel on land feued from the Orphan Hospital (q.v.) (Arnot, 279). The chapel was demolished during the building of the railways when the congregation moved to the Relief Chapel of 1809 (Grant, II, 338).

1784 United Secession Church, Slateford (Grant, III, 326).

1787 Baptist Church, Richmond Court (Keir, 185), the first church building for Baptists. Grant (II, 338) says "The independent congregation in Richmond Court was established in 1833; but their place of worship until 1840 was built about 1795 by the Baptists."

1787 St. Andrew's Church, George Street, designed by Andrew Fraser and William Sibbald (Grant, II, 144; Nimmo, 123, says 1784), now St. Andrew's and St. George's.

1791 St. Peter's Episcopal Church, Roxburgh Place (Grant, II, 338).

1794 St. George's Episcopal Church, York Place, designed by James Adam (O.E.C., II, 172; Grant, II, 190), now united with St. Paul's, and building is a commercial showroom.

1798 Congregational Church, Leith Walk (Keir, 186).

1801 The Tabernacle, Leith Walk, a Baptist Meeting House until 1864 when the congregation moved to the Baptist Chapel in Duncan Street (Minto and Armstrong, 40).

1802 Congregational Church, North College Street (Keir, 186), the congregation is now in the Augustine-Bristo Church, George IV Bridge.

1803 Lady Yester's Church rebuilt near previous Church in present Infirmary Street (O.E.C., V, 85; Grant, II, 287). The congregation joined Greyfriars in 1938, and the church building is a University store.

1804 Seceders' Land, Bristo Street (O.E.C., XXIII, 75; Grant, II, 326, says 1802; Cruft, 41, says premises occupied from 1741). Became the Pollock Hall, now demolished.

1808 Charlotte Baptist Chapel.

1809 Lady Glenorchy's Church built as a Relief Chapel "east of Nicolson Street" (Grant, II, 338). The congregation from the original church came in 1859 and the church in Roxburgh Place was rebuilt in 1909. Now Edinburgh University property.

1810 Established Church, Portobello, began as a Chapel of Ease (Grant, III, 147).

1811 St. George's Church, Charlotte Square, designed by Robert Reid (O.E.C., XIV, 151), became West Register House in 1971, the congregation having joined St. Andrew's, George Street some years earlier.

1813 Original Seceders moved to Richmond Street (Grant, II, 333).

1813 St. Mary's R.C. Chapel, Broughton Street, designed by
Gillespie Graham (Wilson, II, 61; Grant, II, 179). The first
Roman Catholic Church in the city; it had a major restoration
in 1977.

1814 North Leith Parish Church built, designed by William Burn
(*Edinburgh — An Architectural Guide*; Russell, 464, says
1816).

1814 Wesleyan Methodist Church, Nicolson Square (Grant, II, 335;
Keir, 184).

1815 New Church built at Liberton (Grant, III, 327; Geddie, 125,
says 1825).

1816 Independent Church, Albany Street (Grant, II, 184), restored
in 1867. Now industrial premises.

1816 First Jewish Synagogue in city, possibly in temporary
buildings near the Pleasance (Keir, 190).

1817 St. John's Episcopal Church, Lothian Road, designed by
William Burn (Grant, II, 125; Smeaton, (a), 262).

1818 St. Paul's Episcopal Church, York Place, designed by
Archibald Elliott (Grant, II, 188) for the use of the Cowgate
Episcopal congregation, now St. Paul's and St. George's
Episcopal Church.

1819-20 Nicolson Street Church, designed by Gillespie Graham,
(Grant, II, 338), now a saleroom.

1821 Broughton U.P. Church (Grant, II, 184), designed by
Archibald Elliott, now Broughton-McDonald Church in
Broughton Place.

1823 Unitarian Chapel, Young Street (Lindsay, *Georgian
Edinburgh*, (1973), 48).

1823 Hope Park Chapel, South Clerk Street, (Grant, III, 51), built
as a Chapel of Ease for St. Cuthbert's, became St. Leonard's,
Newington, and has been converted into a hall for concerts by
the Scottish Philharmonic Orchestra, and is renamed The
Queen's Hall.

1823 St. Bernard's Church, Saxe Coburg Street, formerly
Claremont Street Chapel of Ease (Grant, III, 75), designed by
James Mylne; now St. Bernard's-Davidson Church.
Davidson Church, Eyre Place, is now a sweet store.

1824 Newington Parish Church (O.E.C., XIV, app. 9).

1824-6 St. Mary's Church, Bellevue Crescent (Grant, II, 191),
architect, Thomas Brown.

1826-8 St. Stephen's Church, designed by William Playfair, St.
Vincent Street (Grant, III, 83).

1827 Chapel in Gardner's Crescent, bought in 1831 from the
United Secession congregation for the Free Church of St.
Cuthbert's (Grant, II, 215). This may have been renamed St.

David's, Morrison Street, now in Broomhouse.

1829 St. James's Episcopal Church, Broughton Street (Grant, II, 184), now a schools research centre.

1830 Lothian Road Church, designed by William Burn, united with Palmerston Place Church in 1976. The building is now the Film House for the Edinburgh International Festival.

1832 Greenside Church, Royal Terrace, built, opened in 1836 (Grant, II, 103; Gilbert, 95).

1834 Martyrs' or Reformed Presbyterian Church, Lady Lawson Street, later moved to George IV Bridge (Grant, I, 294), now the City Temple of the Elim Pentecostal Church.

1835 Brighton Chapel, Lothian Street (Grant, II, 326).

1835 St. Margaret's Convent, Whitehouse Loan (O.E.C., X, 31; Grant, III, 45; Smeaton, (a), 338).

1835 St. Mark's Unitarian Chapel, Castle Terrace (Grant, II, 214) having moved from the 1823 Chapel in Young Street.

1836 St. Paul's Church, St Leonard's Street (Gilbert, 95) now bricked up.

1836 St. Luke's Church, Young Street, designed by William Burn (Lindsay, *Georgian Edinburgh*, (1973), 48), demolished in 1970.

1836 Established Church, Grange Loan (Grant, III, 38), now demolished.

1836 Dean Church, Dean Path (Grant, III, 67; Gilbert, 95).

1838 St. John's Established Church, Victoria Street (Grant, I, 291), now a licenced betting office.

1838 Morningside Parish Church, Morningside Road; united with Morningside High (Free) Church.

1838 Holy Trinity Episcopal Church, Dean Bridge (Grant, III, 70), became an electricity sub-station in 1957.

1839 St. Mary's R.C. Church, Bristo (Grant, II, 326), became a Roman Catholic School.

1839 Buccleuch Parish Church (Gilbert, 103).

1840 Mariners' Church, Leith (Grant, III, 259).

1843 St. Thomas's Episcopal Church, Rutland Street (Grant, II, 209), now in Glasgow Road.

1843 Newington Free Church (Grant, III, 51), became St. Paul's.

1843 Lady Glenorchy North, united in 1956 with St. James and Barony Churches as Hillside Church, Greenside Place; building now under Kirk Care.

1843 St. John's Free Church, Charlotte Street, Leith (Grant, III, 244), became Established Church in 1867.

1844 Chalmers Territorial Church, West Port (Grant, II, 224), now Chalmers-Lauriston Church, and Chalmers Church.

1845 Free St. George's Church, Rutland Street, designed by David Cousin (Grant, II, 138); site sold to Caledonian Railway and a new church built in Shandwick Place in 1869. The old church was taken down and reconstructed in Deanhaugh Street in 1868 (Grant, II, 138).

1845 St. Columba's Episcopal Church, Johnston Terrace (Grant, I, 295).

1846 New North Church, Bristo (Grant, II, 326), later University of Edinburgh Chaplaincy Centre in the 1960's and the congregation joined Greyfriars in 1941.

1847 St. John's Free Church, Johnston Terrace (Grant, I, 295), renamed Free St. Columba's Church.

1850 Buccleuch Free Church, Crosscauseway (Grant, II, 346), now Free Buccleuch and Greyfriars Church.

1850 Moray Free (Knox) Church, High Street (Grant, I, 213), became Church of Scotland Netherbow Centre in 1972.

1853 R.C. Church, Constitution Street, Leith (Grant, III, 244).

1856 St. Patrick's R.C. Church, Cowgate, in building of Episcopal Church of 1771 (Grant, I, 278).

1857 St. Augustine Congregational Church, George IV Bridge (Grant, I, 294; Keir, 186, says 1861), became Augustine-Bristo Congregational Church, and now shares the building with the Scottish Churches Council.

1858 North Leith Free Church (Grant, III, 255).

1859 Convent of St. Catherine of Sienna, Lauriston Gardens (Grant, II, 363).

1859 St. Mary's Free Church, Broughton Street (Grant, II, 184).

1859 Lauriston U.P. Church (Grant, II, 363), now Chalmers-Lauriston Church.

1860 Church of the Sacred Heart, Lauriston (Grant, II, 223).

1861 Free Church, Cowgate, later Halls for Greyfriars Church, now a Skin Clinic.

1861-2 Pilrig Free Church (Grant, III, 163).

1862 St. James's Episcopal Church, Leith (Grant, III, 243).

1862-3 Barclay Free Church, Bruntsfield Place (Grant, III, 30; Smeaton, (a), 337), architect, F. T. Pilkington, now Barclay-Bruntsfield Church.

1863 Morningside U.P. Church (Grant, III, 38), Chamberlain Road; rebuilt in 1881 on opposite side of the road; became U.F. Church in 1900 and North Morningside Parish Church in 1929 (Smith, I, 88). Linked with Morningside Congregational Church in 1974.

1866 Chalmers Memorial Free Church, Grange Road (Grant, III, 50), later Grange U.F. church, renamed St. Catherine's-in-the-Grange and united with Argyle Place Church to form St. Catherine's-Argyle (Smith, I, 44).

1866 Building of Roseburn Free Church begun, opened for worship in 1868, became Wester Coates Church.

1867 Hope Park U.P. Church (Grant, III, 51), demolished for building

Veterinary College extension.

1867 All Saints Episcopal Church, Tollcross (Keir, 181).

1868 St. Andrews Church, Drumsheugh Gardens, building demolished and became St. Andrews-Clermiston.

1869 West Coates Church, Haymarket Terrace (Grant, II, 214), united in 1962 with Roseburn U.F. Church to become Wester Coates Church, which dissolved in 1973; the building has been adapted for use by the National Bible Society of Scotland since 1976.

1869 Free St. George's Church, Shandwick Place (Gilbert, 146), the Free St. George's Church in Rutland Street of 1845; now St. George's West Church. Designed by David Bryce.

1871 Robertson Memorial Church, Kilgraston Road (Grant, III, 50), renamed Grange Church and united with West St. Giles and Warrender Churches to become Marchmont-St. Giles Church. West St. Giles has been demolished and Warrender is a chemist's store.

1871-2 Viewforth Free Church (Grant, III, 30) united with Barclay Church as Barclay-Bruntsfield Church, and the building is Bruntsfield Evangelical Church.

1873 Palmerston Place U.P. Church (Gilbert, 150), later Parish Church.

1874 Morningside Free Church, Morningside Road (Grant, III, 38), moved to Churchhill as Morningside High Church which united with Morningside Parish Church and Churchhill building became Churchhill Theatre in 1965 (Smith, I, 108). The original building became a Baptist Church.

1875 Gaelic Church, Albany Street, formerly old Catholic and Apostolic Church (Grant, II, 184), now industrial premises.

1876 New Catholic and Apostolic Church, East London Street (Grant, II, 185), now Bellevue Reformed Baptist Church.

1876 Mayfield Free Church (Grant, III, 51).

1876 Baptist Church, Marshall Street (Grant, II, 333).

1876 Free Tron Church, Chambers Street.

1876 Hope Park Congregational Church (Grant, III, 51).

1876 Granton and Wardie Free Church (Grant, III, 307).

1876-7 Christ's Church (Episcopal), Morningside (Grant, III, 38).

1877 Mayfield Established Church (Grant, III, 51) superseding previous temporary building.

1878 Dalry U.P. Church, united with Haymarket, then with St. Brides to form St. Colms.

1879 German Church, Bellevue Crescent (Gilbert, 155), now situated in Chalmers Crescent.

1879 Argyle Place Church, united with St. Catherines-in-the-Grange to form St. Catherine's-Argyle. The building was damaged by fire in 1974, and was recently demolished.

1880 United Presbyterian Church, Canonmills (Grant, III, 88).

1880 New North (West St. Giles) Church (from St. Giles Church), Meadow Place, now demolished and united with Grange Church (1871) to form Marchmont-St. Giles.

1881 Gilmore Place U.P. Church (Grant, III, 30), united with St. Oswald's, Montpelier Park, to form Viewforth-St. Davids and St. Oswald's.

1887 St. Michael's Church, Slateford Road.

1887 St. Martin's Episcopal Church, Gorgie (Keir, 181).

1889 Belford Church, Douglas Gardens, united with Palmerston Place Church and building closed, now a school.

1890 St. Matthew's Church, Cluny Gardens (Smith, I, 142, says 1884), united with South Morningside to form Cluny Parish Church.

1890 Morningside Congregational Church established in the building of 1863 Morningside U.P. Church, having bought it from Morningside Athenaeum Club; rebuilt in 1929; linked with North Morningside in 1974 (Smith, I, 88).

1892 John Ker Memorial Church, Polwarth Gardens (Gilbert, 173).

1892 South Morningside Church, united with St. Matthew's Church to form Cluny Parish Church a few years ago.

1893 St. Cuthbert's Episcopal Church, Colinton (Keir, 181).

1894 Baptists occupied Morningside Free Church; damaged by fire in 1972 and rebuilt in 1976 (Smith, I, 90).

1894 Episcopal Church of the Good Shepherd, Murrayfield Avenue.

Cinemas

Fifty years ago there were three cinemas in Princes Street, the Palace, the New and the Princes. The Palace Cinema (1913) disappeared with the enlargement of Woolworth's store; the New Picture House (1913) also became a multiple store; the Princes Cinema was renamed the Monseigneur News Theatre which closed, but was re-opened in 1965 as the Jacey Cinema to show exotic Continental films (Keir, 948). It has now been demolished.

In the central area the Rutland Cinema in Canning Street, renamed the Gaumont, was destroyed by fire and the site is an office block. The Caley Cinema in Lothian Road still exists, but the city's largest cinema, the Playhouse in Leith Walk, closed some ten years ago and the site has still not been redeveloped.

Further from the centre the Regal in Lothian Road, now the ABC, has been successfully divided into three smaller cinemas. The Dominion, Newbattle Terrace, has been converted into three and continues to entertain. The New Victoria in Clerk Street, renamed the Odeon, is also still in business.

Many of the smaller cinemas, and there were 23 in 1963 (Keir, 948), have found the increasing competition of television beyond their financial resources. Some, notably the Capitol in Leith, have become Bingo Halls, while many others, such as the Astoria in Corstorphine, have closed.

In 1929 the Edinburgh Film Guild was formed and it established an unofficial Festival of Documentary Films at the first (1947) Edinburgh International Festival. This was formally integrated with the Festival in 1962 (Keir, 949) based originally on the Cameo Theatre in Home Street, which continues to show films throughout the year. In 1978 the building of Lothian Road Church became the Festival Film House.

City Chambers see Royal Exchange.

City Debt
The old City Debt (Robertson and Wood, 221-256) was James VI's demand that the Town Council should pay for a ship to bring his bride, Anne, from Denmark in 1589 and provide £40,000 Scots (£3333 stg.) as part of her dowry. Redemption was not complete until 1926, the debt having grown to £792,921 Scots (£66,077 stg.) by 1660, and again to £400,000 sterling by 1883 owing to the system of the Town Council borrowing money for capital expenditure. This resulted in the town's financial affairs being put into the hands of trustees after investigations.

City Guard see Town Guard.

'City of Queens'
So Lord Rosebery called Leith on account of its association with:
1424 Jane Beaufort, landed at Leith with her husband, James I (Sitwell and Bamford, 32; Geddie, 162, says 1423, which is incorrect).
1449 Mary of Gueldres, James II's bride, arrived at Leith (O.E.C., III, 46; Wilson, II, 166; Grant, II, 54; Maxwell, 64; Russell, 137).
1469 Margaret of Denmark, James III's bride, arrived at Leith (Grant, II, 55; Smeaton, (a), 40).
1537 Madeleine (Magdalene) de Valois and her husband, James V, arrived at Leith (O.E.C., X, 158; Grant, II, 63; Maxwell, 102; Geddie, 162).
1561 Mary, Queen of Scots, arrived at Leith (Wilson, I, 89; II, 138; Grant, III, 179; Maxwell, 116; Smeaton, (a), 81).
1590 Anne of Denmark and her husband, James VI, arrived at Leith (Wilson, I, 113; Smeaton, (a), 95).

City Walls see Town Walls.

'Cleanse the Causeway'
A brawling fight between parties under the Earl of Arran (grandson

of James II) and the Earl of Angus (husband of James IV's widow, Margaret Tudor) which took place in the High Street and Blackfriars Wynd in 1520. Angus's adherents, the Douglases, dispersed with many casualties the Hamiltons under Arran (O.E.C., III, 53; IX, 29; Chambers, 241; Wilson, I, 50; Grant, I, 258; Maxwell, 95; Smeaton, (a), 207).

Clermiston House
1792 House built (R.C., 229). Bought by Lord Francis Jeffrey about 1840. The grounds are now engulfed by a housing scheme, and the house no longer exists, having been demolished for building of Queen Margaret College.

Clermiston Tower
1871 Tower built on summit of Corstorphine Hill by William Macfie of Clermiston on the centenary of the birth of Sir Walter Scott, whose father had feued ground in North Clermiston.

1932 Tower presented to the city by W. G. Walker on the centenary of Scott's death.

Clockmaking
Early clocks in Scotland were public clocks on churches etc., and there were few local clockmakers in the 16th century. Thereafter numbers increased and in Edinburgh they became members of the Incorporation of Hammermen in 1646. Parliament Close was the centre of clockmaking in the 18th century when long case clocks, which were most frequently manufactured, had ingenious and accurate astronomical devices incorporated. The trade grew rapidly in the 19th century. Watchmakers were much less numerous, the first in Edinburgh being a Frenchman, Paul Roumieu, who lived in Clockmakers' Land in the West Bow from 1677 to 1694. The building is long since demolished. His work led to a high standard of excellence in watchmaking from 1700. (John Smith, *Old Scottish Clockmakers from 1453 to 1850*, (2nd edition, 1921), Introduction).

Close
A private passage, open only at one end and closed at night; c.f. wynd (q.v.); from French *clos*—a narrow enclosed space.
1775 "From . . . the High Street you pass down by a number of different alleys, or as they call them here, wynds and closes, to the different parts of the old town. There are many of them so very steep that it requires great attention to the feet to prevent falling, but so well accustomed are the Scotch to that position of the body required in descending these declivities that I have seen a Scotch girl run down them with great swiftness in pattens." (Topham, 14).

1790 Town Council ordered naming of Closes in the Old Town
(O.E.C., XII, 2).
1849 Superintendent of Streets renewed names on Closes and Wynds in
the High Street (Scotsman, 15-9-1849).
    Notes on the origin of the names of Closes and Wynds will be
found in O.E.C., XII, 1-156.

Clubs see also Inns and Societies.
Notes on various old Clubs will be found in O.E.C., III, 105-178;
Chambers, 149-157; Grant, III, 122-126; and Stuart, *Old Edinburgh
Taverns*.
c.1733 Cape Club (*vide infra*) met in James Mann's Tavern, Craig's
Close (Stuart, 48).
c.1758 Ante Manum Club — disbanded in 1818 (Cockburn, 224).
1758 The Luggy Club (O.E.C., XXXI, 43-51); ceased in 1782.
1762 Poker Club (Carlyle, 439) met in Thomas Nicholson's Inn, West
Bow (Stuart, 67).
1763 Cape Club a regular institution, but Wilson (II, 22) and Smeaton
((a), 196) state that it was formally founded in 1764.
1773 Aesculapian Club, a medical dining club (Keir, 329).
1773 Pantheon Literary Club (O.E.C., I, 47-76) met in Carrubber's
Close (Steuart, 62).
1775 Wagering Club (O.E.C., II, 149-166); still in existence.
1775 Wig Club (Youngson, 247) met in Fortune's Tavern and Royal
Exchange Coffee House (Youngson, 248).
1778 Mirror Club met in Stewart's Oyster House, Old Fishmarket Close
(Stuart, 60).
1778 Crochallan Fencibles (from *Crodh Chailein* — Colin's Cattle) met
in Dawnay Douglas's Tavern, Anchor Close (Stuart, 53).
1787 New Club founded (Keir, 561), opened buildings in Princes Street
in 1834 (Cruft, 65), designed by William Burn, later extended by
David Bryce (*Edinburgh — An Architectural Guide*).
1803 Friday Club (Cockburn, *Life of Lord Jeffrey*, 290, f.n.; Youngson,
247) met in Boyle's Tavern, then Fortune's Tavern (Youngson,
247), and later in Barry's Tavern (Stuart, 83).
1814 Right and Wrong Club (James Hogg, *Memoir of the Author's Life*,
(1807), (1972 edition), 46).
1823 Bannatyne Club (Walter Scott the first President) (O.E.C., XVI,
ix), ceased in 1861.
1825 Gowk's Club met in Barry's Tavern (Stuart, 83).
1825 Caledonian United Services Club, merged in 1960's with the
Northern Club (Keir, 562).
1833 Oyster Club met in Barry's Tavern (Stuart, 83).
1842 Bonaly Friday Club.
1845 Young Edinburgh Club.

1851 Marrow Bone Club met in Paterson's Tavern, Fleshmarket Close (Stuart, 63).
1852 Monks of St. Giles, formed from the Young Edinburgh Club; still in existence (Keir, 562); now meets in Candlemaker Row.
1866 University Club (Grant, II, 125), merged in late 1950's with New Club (Keir, 561).
1874 Scottish Artists' Club, became Scottish Arts Club in 1894 (Keir, 561), in Rutland Square.
1877 Conservative Club, Princes Street, merged in 1970's with Caledonian United Services Club and moved to Abercromby Place as the Caledonian Club.
1879 Liberal Club, Princes Street, closed in 1977.
1919 Royal Scots Club, Abercromby Place (Keir, 562).
1929 Royal Overseas League Club, Princes Street (Keir, 559).

Cockburn Street
1859 Street laid as a means of access between High Street and Waverley Station, and named after Lord Cockburn (Grant, I, 282). Its building resulted in the partial demolition of a number of closes. At present Advocate's Close, Writers' Court, Warriston Close, Anchor Close, Jackson's Close and Fleshmarket Close open into it from the High Street, while Craig's Close, Fleshmarket Close and unnamed steps descend from Cockburn Street to Market Street.

Cock-fighting
1702 Cock-pit in Leith Links (Arnot, 195; Grant, III, 262; Marshall, 9).
1704 Cock-fighting banned in the streets of Leith (Marshall, 9).
1763 No cock-fighting in Edinburgh (Grant, II, 236).
1783 Much cock-fighting in the Grassmarket (Grant, II, 236).
1869 Last cock-fight in Leith (Marshall, 9) when it was officially banned.

Coinage see also Cunzie House.
There was no coinage until the twelfth century (Smout, 19).
1574 Lyon pieces, unicorns, angel pieces, bonnet pieces, nobles, nonsunts, ryders, ryals, merks, half-merks, crown groats, groats of flower-de-luce, pennies, placks, bodles and bawbees were all current coins (Dunlop and Dunlop, 50). 2 bawbees = 1 penny, 2 pennies = 1 bodle, 2 bodles = 1 plack, 40 placks = 1 merk, 1 merk = 13 shillings and 4 pence (Scots).
   In the 16th century trade tokens made of lead, pewter, tin or even leather could be cashed or exchanged for commodities in the shops issuing them (Edinburgh Evening Dispatch, 13-5-1950).
1790 T. & A. Hutchison issued half-pennies bearing on the obverse the Arms of the City and on the reverse St. Andrew with his cross, flanked by thistles and surmounted *'Nemo me impune lacessit'*.

(Edinburgh Evening Dispatch, 13-5-1950).

Colinton
Colinton was known as Hailes until 1697 (Grant, III, 322).

1234 Ancient Church of Hailes (c. 1095) founded by Malcolm III, was granted to Dunfermline Abbey by Ethelred, confirmed by a Royal Charter of David I and by a Bull of Pope Gregory (Grant, III, 322). It was dedicated in 1248.

c. 1560 Church had disappeared, perhaps destroyed in Hertford's raid of 1544.

1636 New Church built.

1650 Colinton occupied by General Monk's troops (Grant, III, 322).

1666 Covenanters rested in Colinton before Rullion Green.

1771 Colinton Church rebuilt (Grant, III, 322); again in 1908.

1875 Railway to Colinton (Keir, 78).

1920 Colinton became a ward of Edinburgh (Keir, 79).

College of Art
1729 Academy of St. Luke for copying sculpture, accommodated in the University in 1731.

1735 Richard Cooper's Academy for engravings.

1754 Select Society founded by Allan Ramsay (Maxwell, 234; Carlyle, 311).

1760 Trustees Drawing Academy arose from Select Society to encourage craftsmanship.

1780's Alexander Nasmyth's Academy.

1808 First exhibition by Scottish artists (Grant, II, 90; Cockburn, 242).

1819 Institution for the Encouragement of Fine Arts founded, and was united with the Royal Scottish Academy (q.v.) in 1829.

1907 College of Art built in Lady Lawson Street on the site of the old cattle market (Minto and Armstrong, 44).

1960 Constitution altered by Royal Assent to make a single body responsible for government of the College which contained five schools — architecture; town and country planning; drawing and painting; design and crafts; and sculpture (Keir, 877).

1977 New building facing on to Lauriston Place completed.

College of Physicians
1681 College of Physicians incorporated (O.E.C., XV, 139; Arnot, 322; Maxwell, 81; 141; Maitland, 376), having been decreed by James VI in 1617.

1704 Library (founded in 1681) of College of Physicians in Fountain Close (q.v.) (Grant, I, 278). The building was sold in 1720 and new premises built (Grant, I, 278).

1722-70 College of Physicians Hall in Fountain Close (Grant, II, 147).

1775-7 Physicians Hall, designed by James Craig, built in George Street (Arnot, 323; Grant, II, 147; Youngson, 95).

1843 Hall demolished for Commercial Bank building (O.E.C., XXIII, 9).

1843-6 Physicians' Hall, designed by Thomas Hamilton, built at Nos. 9 and 10 Queen Street (Grant, II, 153; Youngson, 275).

1955 No. 8 Queen Street, designed by Robert Adam, added for new College Library (Keir, 325).

College of Surgeons

1505 Seal of Cause for Surgeons and Barbers; ratified by James IV's Charter in 1506 (Grant, I, 382; Maxwell, 81).

1656 Town Council sold Curriehill House to the Surgeons (O.E.C., IV, 148). This stood just within the Flodden Wall on land formerly owned by the Black Friars (Grant, I. 383; II, 302) and the Surgeons moved there from rented premises in Dickson's Close, Cowgate (Grant, II, 302).

1657 Surgeons and Apothecaries united (Grant, I, 382).

1697 Surgeons built an anatomy room required to enable them to license surgeons and apothecaries (Turner, 34).

1722 Barbers came out of the Corporation of Surgeons (O.E.C., IV, 13; Maitland, 296; Arnot, 525; Grant, I, 383; Maxwell, 141).

1775 Foundation Stone of new Surgeons' Hall in Surgeons' Square (Grant, II, 302). This building still stands in Infirmary Street behind the University of Edinburgh's Department of Geography.

1778 Royal College of Surgeons re-incorporated (Arnot, 525; Grant, I, 383).

1828-32 Surgeons' Hall, designed by William Playfair, built in Nicolson Street (O.E.C., V, 87; Grant, II, 335; Youngson, 279). It was built on the site of a riding-school, the Royal Menage (Scotsman, 24-5-1828), and contains a museum founded in the 16th century (Keir, 927) and a library dating from 1696 (Keir, 919).

College Wynd, Chambers Street — north side.
Originally the Wynd of the Blessed Virgin Mary-in-the-Fields (the Kirk o' Field of the Darnley murder). College Wynd led up from the Cowgate and was the main access to the buildings of the College (University) of Edinburgh.

1736 Surgeons opened a hospital in College Wynd in opposition to the Infirmary (O.E.C., XV, 148; Turner, 66).

1752 Oliver Goldsmith reputed to have lived in the Wynd as a medical student (Pennycook, 44).

1771 Walter Scott born in College Wynd (Chambers, 242), the approximate site being marked by a tablet high up on the wall of Guthrie Street (q.v.), which now represents the site of the old Wynd.

Colonies

A series of eleven short rows of houses running from Glenogle Road north to the Water of Leith. Built in 1861 by the Edinburgh Co-operative Building Society (Daiches, 220) as artisans' houses, each gable end is ornamented by a plaque displaying tools of their trades.

Comely Gardens

The eighteenth century gardens lay in a delta between London Road and the Regent Road area.

"A wretched attempt to imitate Vauxhall, for which neither the climate nor the gardens are adapted." (Arnot, 383).

"They are open twice a week, from the beginning of June till the latter end of August, and the admission is only a shilling . . . But the greatest objection is, that it has been thought unfashionable [as a resort]; and when that is the case it is effectually condemned for ever." (Topham, 134).

"Comely Gardens . . . would seem to have been a lively species of Tivoli Gardens for the lower classes of Edinburgh." (Grant, III, 128).

Comiston, see also Water Supply.

1610 Comiston House built (Geddie, 102).

1674 Water supplies for the city brought from Comiston (see Water Supply); among the three oldest gravitation supplies in the United Kingdom.

1815 Comiston House rebuilt by Sir James Forrest (Grant, III, 326); R.C., 235), and is presently an hotel.

Common Good

The Common Good has been defined as the corporate property and estate of a Burgh as distinct from monies available to it by the levying of taxes and assessments for particular purposes. The original Common Good of the town has been increased from time to time by purchases of land from the Crown and other proprietors, e.g. the village of Newhaven in 1510, the town and links of Leith in 1567 and the Canongate in 1636.

From the Common Good came the income of the burgh consisting of feu-duties and rents; customs of trades and markets; harbour dues and fines of court (Robertson and Wood, 188). The expenditure of the Common Good Account may be divided into two sections, compulsory and optional. Compulsory expenditure includes such as is necessary to earn the income of the Common Good; any expenditure imposed on the Common Good under Charters by which it was created; and a contribution towards the

Corporation's general expenses of management. Optional
expenditure includes donations to public institutions and charities;
Freedom of the City ceremonies, receptions, lunches etc.; the Lord
Provost's honorarium; lunches to Town Councillors while
engaged on civic work; advertising the city; music in the public
parks etc.
1950's The Corporation obtained power to meet expenses of public
    entertainment from the city rates (Keir, 303).
1963 Common Good held funds amounting to £450,000 (Keir, 303).

Cordiners
Cordiners were bootmakers (Wilson, II, 97). See Incorporations.
1768 Strike of cordiners for better pay and shorter hours (Grant, II, 264;
    Sitwell and Bamford, 183).
    (See Bible Land and Shoemakers' Land).

Correction House, see Paul's Work.

Corstorphine, see also Lampacre.
Suggested derivations of the name include French *croix d'or fin*;
Latin *crura Storphinium* or *crus Torphinium* — the Cross of
Torphin (Grant, III, 112). In 1143 David I granted lands in
Crostorfin to the monks of Holyrood.
    Excavations in 1958 (Scotsman, 20-6-1959) for building at
nearby Broomhall showed clear evidence of a Roman stone
embankment at the western end of what had been Corstorphine
Loch. Here there was a Roman fort and Corstorphine is on or near
the intersection of two Roman roads, the one leading from the
Roman port at Cramond towards the Pentland Hills and the other
thought to connect Dere Street with the Antonine Wall.
    Corstorphine Loch extended from Coltbridge and was partly
reclaimed in the 1650's and finally drained in 1837 (R.C., xxxvi).
(See Lampacre). Corstorphine Hill stands 520 feet (160m) above sea
level.
1376 Sir Adam Forrester acquired Corstorphine lands (O.E.C., III, 180).
1380 Church of St. John the Baptist built by Forrester (O.E.C., VII, app.
    9). Geddie (60) says Church founded in 1386.
1429 Church enlarged (O.E.C., VII, app. 9; Grant, III, 115).
1589 Sir Henry Forrester succeeded to land of Corstorphine (Geddie,
    57).
1644 Old Parish Church demolished (Grant, III, 118).
1650 General David Leslie marched troops through Corstorphine to
    deceive Cromwell (Grant, III, 113).
1746 Duke of Cumberland at Beechwood House (q.v.) (Grant, III, 104).
1749 Coach service to Corstorphine which was a place of great gaiety

during summer when balls and other amusements were common (Grant, III, 114).

1827 Church restored by William Burn (O.E.C., III, 183).

1831 Last vestige of a mineral well removed (Grant, III, 114).

1837 Loch completely drained (Keir, 70; R.C., xxxvi).

1867 Corstorphine Hospital built (Turner, 175), now a convalescent home.

1902 Branch railway to Corstorphine.

1910 Zoological Park laid out (q.v.) (Keir, 1008), opened in 1913.

1920 Corstorphine annexed by Edinburgh (Geddie, 57).

County Hall, junction of George IV Bridge and Lawnmarket.

1817 Midlothian County Hall built on site of Liberton's Wynd (q.v.), east side of George IV Bridge (Grant, I, 123).

1907 County Hall rebuilt opening into Parliament Square (Keir, 1008, says 1905).

It is now renamed Lothian Region Hall.

Courts of Law

See Robertson and Wood, 202–220 and Keir, 193–218.

1483 Charter of James III appointed Provost and Bailies as Sheriff and Sheriffs-Depute, thus creating Burgh Court (Robertson and Wood, 203).

1532 College of Justice formed in Holyroodhouse (Williamson, 40).

1532 Court of Session established (O.E.C., IV, 83; XIII, 6; Arnot, 468; Wilson, I, 246; Smeaton, (a), 183). It is the supreme court in civil matters and was divided in 1808 into an Inner and an Outer Court (Cockburn, 244).

1537 Court of Justice established (Wilson, I, 54).

1563 Commissary Court, dealing with consistorial matters, such as divorce; incorporated in Court of Session in 1836 (Keir, 194).

1672 High Court of Justiciary (O.E.C., IV, 83) to hear criminal trials.

1708 Court of Exchequer (O.E.C., XXIII, 39); abolished 1856-7.

1805 Police Court in Riddle's Court (q.v.); replaced by Burgh Court in 1812 (see Police).

1816 First Jury Court (Cockburn, 295); merged with Court of Session in 1830.

1856-8 Sheriff Court, designed by David Bryce, built (Grant, I, 295; Smeaton, (a), 311) in George IV Bridge.

1926 Court of Criminal Appeal (Keir, 196).

1937-8 Sheriff Court building demolished for National Library (q.v.) (Minto and Armstrong, 46) and a new court built on the site cleared between Bank Street and St. Giles Street, facing on to the Lawnmarket.

Covenant Close, 164 High Street — south side.

c. 1600 Houses built.

Tradition says that the National Covenant was renewed in an inn in the Close (Stuart, 61); (see Inns — Covenant House).

The Close was the home of Lord Braxfield, the prototype of R. L. Stevenson's *Weir of Hermiston* (Williamson, 230).

The Close now ends blindly.

Cowgate

Cowgate or Cow-gait was the road taken by cows from St. Cuthbert's meadows to the pastures of St. Leonards (Geddie, *Romantic Edinburgh*, (1900), 144); or Sou' Gate, i.e. South Street (Grant, II, 239); or Well-gate because public and private water wells were here (Fraser, 30). The part east of the Cowgate Port was formerly called South Back of the Canongate, now Holyrood Road.

1460 Cowgate became a fashionable suburb (Chambers, 240). "The date of erection of the first house in the ancient thoroughfare of the Cowgate may be referred, without hesitation, to the reign of James III [1460-88]." (Wilson, II, 124), but Fraser (30) says that houses were being built here in 1438.

1513 Cowgate Port built (Maitland, 140; Grant, I, 298).

16th century The home of Thomas Hamilton, 1st Earl of Haddington, 'Tam o' the Cowgate' (q.v.) in the latter years of the 16th century.

1616 House of Sir Thomas Hope, Lord Advocate to Charles I, was close to the present bridge over the Cowgate at the Central Library into the doorway of which two lintels from Hope's house have been built (Minto and Armstrong, 4).

1621 Tailors' Hall (q.v.) built for the Incorporation of Tailors (O.E.C., XI, 125-171; Wilson, II, 144; Grant, II, 258).

1730 Excise Office (q.v.) moved to the Cowgate from Parliament Close.

1763 Serious riots in the Cowgate (Grant, II, 246).

1775 "Tradition says, the Cowgate two hundred years ago was the polite part of the town, and in it were the houses of the nobility and the senators of the Court of Justice; but, at present, the buildings are much inferior to those on top of the hill." (Topham, 26).

1865 "The Cowgate is the Irish portion of the city. Edinburgh leaps over it with bridges: the inhabitants are morally and geographically the lower orders. They keep to their own quarters, and seldom come up to the light of day. Many an Edinburgh man has never set his foot in the street: the condition of the inhabitants is as little known to respectable Edinburgh as are the habits of moles, earth worms and the mining population. The people of the Cowgate seldom visit the upper streets." (Alexander Smith, *A Summer in Skye*, (1865), 20). There is an illustration in R. L. Stevenson's *Edinburgh* —

Picturesque Notes, p. 49, which is, unintentionally, most apposite to this quotation.

Cowlies
An Edinburgh term applied to a class of rogues (Chambers, 117, f.n.). It is thought to be a corruption of the English word *cully*— to fool, to cheat. It may be an antecedent of the modern 'keelie'.

Craft Industries
"The state of a community's traditional crafts is a sure touchstone of the state of its culture." (Keir, 706). The Scottish Craft Centre developed from Acheson House (q.v.) in 1949, and Keir (706-726) outlines the city's contribution to silversmithing; enamelling and jewellery; glass engraving; pottery; bookbinding; caligraphy; tapestry-weaving; wrought-iron; wood-carving; furnishing; embroidery and mosaics.

Craigcrook Castle, north side of Corstorphine Hill.
The property of Craigcrook can be traced back to 1376 when lands were feued for support of a chapel. Taken over by Edinburgh in 1540, the lands were subsequently owned by William Adamson who was killed at the Battle of Pinkie (1547). (*Murrayfield Golf Course*, ed. J. Robb, (1947), 20). Geddie (48) says that Adamson took over in 1542.

The home of the Grahams of Kinpunt and Dundaff, the castle was modernised by Archibald Constable, the publisher, (Smeaton, (a), 308; Geddie, 48) and was sold to become the summer house of Lord Francis Jeffrey from 1815 until his death in 1850 (Cockburn, 294).

The castle is now used as offices by a firm of architects.

Craig End or Craigengalt
The high Calton (Wilson, II, 183) — see Calton Village.

Craigentinny
From Gaelic meaning 'rock of fire' (O.E.C., XXII, 201).
1604 Barony of Craigentinny erected (O.E.C., XXII, 201-262).
c.1700 Craigentinny House built (R.C., 262). Now used as a Social Work centre in Loaning Road.
1856 The Craigentinny Marbles are panels on the mausoleum of William Henry Miller whose body is buried sixty feet below (O.E.C., XXII, 236; Wilson, II, 122). The mausoleum was designed by David Rhind, and is in Craigentinny Crescent.

Craigleith, near Blackhall.
The stone for building the New Town came from Craigleith quarry

Craiglockhart Hills
1565 Craig House built on Easter Hill (Grant, III, 42); now part of the Royal Edinburgh Hospital.
1870 Craiglockhart Poorhouse built on Wester Hill (O.E.C., XXII, 55); now Greenlea Old People's Home.
1904 City Fever Hospital built at the base of Wester Hill (Keir, 1008); now incorporates a general Hospital.

Craigmillar Castle
"A chiefless castle breathing fond farewells
From stern but leafy walls, where ruin greenly dwells."
1212 First reference to the Castle.
1374 Simon Preston bought Craigmillar (O.E.C., VII, app. 8; Grant, III, 58; Geddie, 132).
1427 Rampart built around the Castle (Geddie, 133).
1517 James V lived in the Castle (O.E.C., IX, 23).
1544 Castle burned during Hertford's invasion.
1566 Mary, Queen of Scots, retreated here after Rizzio's murder (Grant, III, 59).
1661 Sir John Gilmour acquired the Castle (Grant, III, 62; Geddie, 132).
1951 Restoration by Ministry of Public Buildings and Works (now Department of the Environment) (Keir, 246).

Craig's Close, High Street — north side.
1610 Andro Hart, printer, displayed his Bible here (Grant, I, 229). The Close was the home of William Creech and Archibald Constable (Grant, I, 229), both famous booksellers of their time. It housed James Mann's 'Isle of Man Tavern' and its Cape Club patronised by Robert Fergusson, Deacon William Brodie, Henry Raeburn and others (Grant, I, 230).
1932 The Close was sacrificed during the enlargement of the City Chambers (O.E.C., XXIII, 149, f.n.). The High Street site is marked by a plaque on the wall of the City Collector's Office. In Cockburn Street there is a short opening for the Close, closed by a gate and marked 'Private', and the lower end continues to Market Street.

Cramond
The name is perhaps derived from the Gaelic *caer avon* — a river fort. It was the Roman Alaterva. Roman remains have been found

(Grant, III, 314) and are still being dug up between the grounds of Cramond Church and the shore.

208 Severus landed at Cramond (Russell, 19).

1574 Douglas family acquired 15th century Cramond Tower, the former palace of the Bishops of Dunkeld.

1656 Cramond Church built (Grant, III, 316).

1680 Cramond House built.

1791 Iron works at Cramond (Grant, III, 315) worked by water power of the River Almond.

Cramond Brig
The old bridge dates back to the 15th century and it became a ruin in 1607 (Smeaton, (b), 387).

1823 John Rennie built Cramond Bridge (Geddie, 38).
The present bridge taking the road to the Forth Road Bridge is of modern construction.

Cranston Street, Canongate — north side.
1867 Built during city improvements at the expense of some old closes (Grant, II, 17). It leads to Market Street. Williamson (135) considered that Cranston Street is on the line of the old Leith Wynd.

Croft-an-Righ
A former mansion near Holyrood Abbey said to have been occupied by the Regent Moray (R.C., 153). The name means 'Field of the King' (Grant, II, 41) but in Gaelic is *Croit-an-Righ* — King's croft. It is associated (Williamson, 105) with Scott's Mr Croftangry (Introduction to *Chronicles of the Canongate*). The house was repaired in 1859 (Grant, II, 41) and is now the home of the Palace gardeners (R.C., 153).

Cross or Mercat Cross
"Among the many relics of the past it [the Mercat Cross] is surpassed in interest by none and equalled by few." (Williamson, 162).

1365 First mention of the Cross on the south side of the High Street, east of St. Giles Church (R.C., 121).

1503 Basin at the foot of the Cross flowed with wine when James IV and his Queen entered the town (Steuart, 45).

1513 Citizens mustered under the Blue Blanket (q.v.) at the Cross to march to Flodden (Steuart, 45).

1555 Cross taken down and re-erected on the same site (R.C., 121).

1563 James Tarbat, a Roman Catholic priest, tied to the Cross and stoned for saying Mass at Holyrood on Easter Day (Steuart, 45).

1565 Darnley proclaimed King from the Cross (Wilson, I, 96).

1566 Darnley professed his innocence of Rizzio's murder at the foot of the Cross (Steuart, 45).

1567 Bothwell accused at the Cross of murder of Darnley (Steuart, 45).

1567 James VI proclaimed King (Steuart, 45).

1573 Kirkcaldy of Grange hanged at the Cross (Steuart, 46).

1581 Regent Morton executed by the Maiden (q.v.) at the Cross (Steuart, 46).

1603 Death of Queen Elizabeth proclaimed (Williamson, 167).

1617 Cross rebuilt on a new site (Maxwell, 294; David Calderwood, *Historie of the Kirk of Scotland* (1845 edition) vol. 7, 243) preparatory to the widening of the High Street (R.C., 121). The site is marked by an octagonal design on the road.

1649 Charles II proclaimed King (Maxwell, 170).

1650 Marquis of Montrose executed at the Cross (Williamson, 169; Sitwell and Bamford, 120).

1654 Cromwell proclaimed Protector (R.C. l.).

1660 Centre of rejoicing at the Restoration of the Monarchy (Williamson, 171) when the Cross fountain ran with claret (Steuart, 46).

1661 Marquis of Argyle executed at the Cross (Sitwell and Bamford, 125).

A proclamation by the Lord Lyon from the Mercat Cross.

1682 Solemn League and Covenant burned at the Cross (O.E.C., XVI, 112).

1685 Earl of Argyle executed (Sitwell and Bamford, 136).

1688 William and Mary proclaimed (Wilson, I, 139; Sitwell and Bamford, 143, say 1689).

1702 Anne proclaimed Queen at the Cross (Grant, I, 203).

1756 Cross removed to Drum House (q.v.) (Chambers, 175; Arnot, 303; Wilson, I, 151; II, 6, f.n.; Smeaton, (a), 198; Williamson, 174). It seems that it was broken during this operation and that it was only a collection of stones that was removed to Drum where they were dressed square so as to bed one on top of the other (O.E.C., XXXIII, 151).

1869 Truncated shaft taken from Drum to St. Giles (O.E.C., XX, app. 32).

1885 W. Ewart Gladstone restored the Cross (O.E.C., XX, app. 19; Williamson, 175; Chambers, 175, f.n., who adds that "a little to the south of its former site between St. Giles Church and the Police Office, the original pillar was replaced in its old position.").

1970 Town Council replaced the shaft and the capital (O.E.C., XXXIII, 150).

Cunzie House, see also Coinage.
Cunzie or Cunye — coin.
    The Cunzie House was the Scottish Mint. It was originally in the outer court of Holyroodhouse, somewhere in the region of the Horse Wynd (Grant, I, 267) in the days of Mary, Queen of Scots (Chambers, 260; Smeaton, (a), 208).
    Later dates are confusing, as there appear to have been two Cunzie Houses.

c.1550 Cunzie House in Candlemaker Row during the Regency of Mary of Guise (Chambers, 260, f.n.; Minto and Armstrong, 3). Grant (II, 269) illustrates this house, and Smeaton ((a), 208) says that the Cunzie House was removed from Holyrood to Candlemaker Row in 1559 where it was in a timber-fronted house near the junction with the Cowgate.

1559 Mint removed from Holyrood to the Castle (Wilson, II, 130; Grant, I, 267). Malcolm ((a), 48) says that the Cunzie House was removed from Holyrood to the Cowgate in 1581 and was built at the foot of South Gray's Close (q.v.) (i.e. the Mint Close of Edgar's map of 1765).

1572 Cunzie House in the Castle destroyed during the siege (Wilson, II, 131; Grant, I, 267; Dunlop and Dunlop, 49). In 1573 William Kirkcaldy, then Governor of the Castle and defending it for Mary, Queen of Scots, was hanged for coining base money in the Castle (Weirter, 112).

1574 Cunzie House built in South Gray's Close near the Cowgate with the inscription and date 1574, in the Regency of Morton (Chambers, 260; Maitland, 182; Wilson, II, 131; Grant, I, 267; Smeaton, (a), 208; Dunlop and Dunlop, 50; R.C., 128). Chambers in *Traditions of Edinburgh*, (1868), said that the house may still be seen, but in the notes for the 1912 edition it is stated (260, f.n.) that the house has been removed and the site built over. St. Ann's School was built on the site and although the primary department remains on the Cowgate as St. Ann's Community Centre, the main school, where the Cunzie House stood has been demolished. There is unfortunately no plaque erected.

c.1650 Other buildings added to this Cunzie House in the reign of Charles II to form a rectangle (Chambers, 260).

1687 Mint House established and opened (O.E.C., XVI, 160), but the record does not say where.

1707 Coining ceased in Scotland (Chambers, 260; Dunlop and Dunlop, 50).

1870 Coinage Act prohibited making or issue, except by the Royal Mint, of coin or token for money.

1877 Scottish Mint in South Gray's Close demolished (O.E.C., XII, 84; Grant, I, 268; R.C., 128).

Currie

The name may have come from the Roman *coria*, but is more probably derived from the Celtic *corrie*—a hollow or glen (Grant, III, 330).

Among the relics dating from at least the 16th century are Lennox Tower, reported to have been the residence of Mary, Queen of Scots, and Darnley (Grant, III, 333), and Curriehill Castle (Grant, III, 334).

1785 Currie Church built on the site of a mediaeval church, possibly a Chapel of the Knights Templar.

Currie Bridge was "said to be above five hundred years old" (Grant, III, 332), which would make it now six hundred years old.

Currie became part of the City of Edinburgh in the local government reorganisation of 1975.

Curriehill House, see College of Surgeons.

Customs and Excise, see also Excise Office.

c.1790 Two separate boards, Board of Customs and Board of Excise (Keir, 237).

1823 Amalgamation of these two boards (Keir, 238).

1849 Office of Assessed Taxes and Stamp Office amalgamated with Excise to become Inland Revenue (Keir, 238).

1909 Excise separated from Inland Revenue and amalgamated with
H.M. Customs to become H.M. Customs and Excise (Keir, 238).
Present head office is in York Place.

Dalry
Dalry means the King's Farm (O.E.C., XIV, 102).
1661 Dalry House built by Walter Chieslie (O.E.C., II, 143; XX, 26-60);
it is now facing on to Orwell Place, off Dalry Road.
1675-9 First paper Mills built on Water of Leith at Dalry (O.E.C., III,
184; XXV, 46-70 says earliest mills were c.1591).
Dalry House was the Episcopal Church Training College
(Chambers, 75) and is now under the auspices of the Edinburgh and
Leith Old People's Welfare Council as a Day Centre.

Dalrymple House, Bristo Street.
c.1760 House built (O.E.C., XXII, 79) by Sir Hugh Dalrymple at the
junction of Potterrow and Bristo Street. It was a three-storey
building.
1813 Ground floor converted into shops (O.E.C., XXII, 79). The house
has vanished with the demolition of Bristo Street (q.v.).

Dancing Assemblies
1602 Old Assembly Rooms, West Bow (q.v.), built (Wilson, II, 162;
R.C., 196).
1710 First Dancing Assembly in West Bow (O.E.C., IX, 191; Maitland,
187; Arnot, 381; Chambers, 43; Graham, 97).
1720 Dancing Academy in Old Assembly Close (q.v.) (O.E.C., IX, 192;
Wilson, II, 32; Grant, I, 243; Graham, 98; Youngson, 250, says
1723).
"When the Assembly was over, footmen hastened to get their
ladies into their chairs, after which the chairmen trotted off with
their burdens, preceded by link-bearers and accompanied by
gallants with hat in hand and sword at side." (O.E.C., IX, 193).
1753 Oliver Goldsmith's account of a Dancing Assembly in a letter while
he was a medical student at Edinburgh University (Chambers, 45;
Wilson, II, 32; Graham, 99).
1756 Assembly Rooms opened in Bell's Wynd (q.v.) (Chambers, 46,
f.n.; Wilson, II, 32; Grant, I, 245, says 1758). These Assemblies
were under the direction and virtual dictatorship of Hon. Miss
Nicky Murray (Chambers, 265; Graham, 99; Williamson, 310).
"These Assemblies began about five and stopped at eleven. As
the bells of St. Giles rung out the hour, Miss Nicky waved her fan,
the fiddlers stopped playing, and the dancing was at an end."
(Williamson, 311).
1776 Assembly in New Assembly Close (q.v.).

1777 Assembly in Buccleuch Place (q.v.) (Grant, II, 148; 347; III, 125; Youngson, 252).
1784 Assembly Rooms in George Street (Grant, II, 149; Cockburn, 30; Youngson, 95).
1836 Old Assembly Rooms in West Bow demolished (Chambers, 44, f.n.).

Darien Scheme
1695 Scheme formulated in Darien House, east of Bristo Port, by William Paterson, founder of the Bank of England, for the Scottish Parliament to speed trade with the East by forming a trading company to use the unoccupied isthmus of Darien (Panama) for landward passage of goods from east to west between ships. Practically all the liquid funds were invested in it.
1698 First fleet sailed from Leith (Grant, II, 323; Russell, 376; Arnot, 184, says 1696).
1700 Darien riots in the city when the Company failed (Chambers, 52).
1719 Capital lost by company repaid (Russell, 384) out of Scottish revenue (P. H. Scott, Scotsman, 10-9-1977).
1871 Darien House demolished, having been used as a lunatic asylum (Grant, II, 324).

Davidson's Mains
Formerly called Mutton Hole (Grant, III, 110) Davidson's Mains was named after Rev. R. T. Davidson, Archbishop of Canterbury (1903-28).

Deacon Brodie, see Brodie's Close.

Dean of Guild's Court
At least as early as the Burgh Court (1483) it was composed of all members of the Guild. In Edinburgh this Court was practically synonymous with the Town Council, yet it retained a separate identity (Robertson and Wood, 213).
1529 Court included Provost, Dean of Guild, two bailies, Treasurer, two to five councillors and occasionally other burgesses (Roberston and Wood, 214).
1584 The Edinburgh constitution provided that "the commanding offices of provost, the four bailies, dean of guild and treasurer were all reserved for merchants, while of the other eighteen seats on the council ten were always to be reserved for merchants and only eight for craftsmen." (Smout, 149).
   The powers included admission and booking of apprentices, burgesses and guild brethren; collection of their dues; of rents of booths round St. Giles; repair of St. Giles and Trinity College Kirk;

provision of elements etc. for sacraments; registration of all cargoes and collection of their dues; also inspection of 'neighbourhoods' and supervision of weights and measures (Robertson and Wood, 216).

1833 Burgh Reform Act abolished the Dean of Guild as an *ex officio* member of Town Council (Wood *et al.*, 313). The recent (1960's) Dean of Guild Court consisted of 15 members, seven Town Councillors and seven qualified laymen (e.g. architects, builders, surveyors etc.) presided over by the Dean of Guild, who was a qualified laymen. The Court had the legal advice of an advocate as required. It regulated and controlled any building construction or alteration within the city (Keir, 200).

Under the local government reorganisation of 1975 the Dean of Guild and his Court were abolished, and have been replaced by a Director of Building Control.

Dean House

1614 Dean House built and owned by the Nisbets of Dean. It was "covered with dates, inscriptions and armorial bearings." (Grant, III, 65).

1845 House demolished and the stone used for building the walls of Dean Cemetery which was laid out in the grounds (Wilson, II, 210; Grant, III, 67).

Dean Lands

The Lands of Dean, or Deanhaugh, lie to the south of the Dean Valley through which runs the Water of Leith (q.v.). Apart from Dean House, John Watson's Hospital and the Dean Orphanage were built on the lands of Dean.

1825 John Watson's Hospital built to the design of William Burn (O.E.C., XXIX, 164; Grant, III, 68). The school closed in 1975 and the building is to house the Scottish National Gallery of Modern Art, which is to be moved from Inverleith House.

1832 Dean Bridge built, designed by Thomas Telford (Grant, III, 70), the cost of which was met by Lord Provost Learmonth who owned the land across the Water of Leith and hoped to feu it.

Dean Orphanage, see also Orphan Hospital.

1831 Erected to replace the Orphan Hospital (q.v.), it was designed by Thomas Hamilton, the clock from the Netherbow being transferred (Grant, III, 67; Steuart, 75).

1947 Orphanage sold owing to insufficient income for its upkeep (Scotsman, 20-8-1947). The children were moved to a house in Ravelston Park.

The building was used for a time as a pre-nursing school, is now renamed Dean Centre, and is an Education Advisory College under Lothian Region.

Dean Village

Dean Village was originally called Water of Leith Village, its ancient bridge over the river being for centuries the only crossing for traffic from Edinburgh bound for Queensferry and the north. It grew around a number of mills and contained a tolbooth and granary dated 1675 although the original granary was built in 1582. There were eleven mills where baxters (bakers) ground flour to supply the town (the earliest being West Mill of 1463 which was rebuilt in 1805 and is now modern flats). The village contained a tannery which had been moved from the Nor' Loch area, and a colony of linen and damask weavers whose Seal of Cause was granted in 1728 (Catford, 222; 225). The baxters built a Cathedral Mission in Bell's Brae in 1675. A toll-house stood at the head of this brae and was enlarged in 1887, and stands next to the Baxters' House of Call, an inn dating from 1640, and now a private house.

The separate existence of Dean Village disappeared by 1881 (Grant, III, 67) but the erection of Well Court in 1884 to replace old cottages and create community flat life (Catford, 225) and recent development of flats has restored new life to the old village. The mills have ceased, Lindsey's (1643) in 1931 and the Jericho Mill

Dean Village, with the Baxters' "peels"
which appear on the bridge/inset.

(1619) in a fire in 1956 being the last survivors; and the tannery is now derelict.

Dearenough, see Pleasance.

Death Rate, see Mortality Rate.

Defence Services

Edinburgh's principal association with the Royal Navy lies in the proximity of Rosyth, Scotland's premier naval base. The Forth Division of the Royal Naval Reserve, H.M.S Claverhouse, is centred at Granton, and a branch of the Woman's Royal Navy Volunteer Reserve was added in 1952 (Keir, 263). There are a number of Sea Cadet Units in the city.

The Army's association with Edinburgh dates from the Town Guard (q.v.). The King's Own Scottish Borderers, raised in 1689, was known as the Edinburgh Regiment until 1782. The Royal Scots have been connected with the city since 1881 when their depot was sited at Glencorse. The Redford Barracks at Colinton house the Garrison Battalion for Edinburgh (Keir, 265). The Headquarters of the Army in Scotland have found their home at Craigiehall, west of Barnton.

The Royal Air Force 603 (City of Edinburgh) Squadron, stationed at Turnhouse, was one of the first to be equipped with Spitfires in World War II. Flying began at Turnhouse in 1915 and continued there until the Squadron was disbanded in 1957. A solitary Spitfire stands opposite the Squadron's headquarters (Keir, 270).

'Deid Chack'

The name given to the dinner eaten by Magistrates after attending an execution (Chambers, 114). It was abolished (c.1812) by William Creech when Provost (Chambers, 114, f.n.).

Dental Hospital and School

1764 Classes on Diseases of the Teeth held by James Rae in the Surgeons' Hall.
1860 Dental Dispensary in Drummond Street (Keir, 331).
1880 Dental Hospital and School in Lauriston Lane (Keir, 331).
1892 Dental Hospital and School moved to the west end of Chambers Street (Grant, II, 276; Turner, 282).
1953 Modern Hospital and School opened on the same site (Keir, 331).

Directories, see Maps.

Donaldson's Hospital, West Coates.

1842-51 Erected to the design of William Playfair in the style of the late 16th and early 17th century (Grant, II, 214; O.E.C., II, app. 6; Smeaton, (a), 206), from a legacy from James Donaldson for poor children some of whom were deaf and dumb.

1938 Amalgamated with Royal Institution for the Education of the Deaf and Dumb, founded in 1810 in Henderson Row, and became Donaldson's School for the Deaf (Keir, 795). The profoundly deaf are taught in these two schools which have united since the Henderson Row property was sold to the Edinburgh Academy in 1977. The school for the partly hearing children is St. Giles School in Broomhouse Crescent.

Dow Craig

The most southern spur of the Calton Hill on which the Calton Jail was built, and, since 1937, the site of St. Andrew's House (O.E.C., XXIII, 53).

'Dozen'

'The Dozen' was the name given to the twelve members of the 16th century Town Council summoned in rotation for the discharge of ordinary civic business (Maxwell, 98, f.n.) although there were eventually more than twelve so summoned.

Drum House, Gilmerton.

c.1320 Drum House built at the southern end of Drumselch Forest (*vide infra*).

1585 Drum House rebuilt by John Mylne for Lord Somerville (O.E.C., XX, app. 31; Grant, III, 346; Geddie, 138).

1629 House burned; restored in 1730.

1756 Mercat Cross removed to Drum House (Chambers, 175; Wilson, I, 151; II, 6, f.n.; Arnot, 303; Smeaton, (a), 198; Williamson, 174), and remained there until 1869. In the grounds of the mansion there is a monument, erected in 1892, recording the event.

Presently the house and grounds are privately owned.

Drumselch Forest

"The country immediately adjoining the Castle was his [David I's] favourite hunting ground, being clothed with 'ane great forest full of hartis, hyndis, toddis [i.e. foxes] and siclike maner of beastis.' Hence it was called Drumselch from the Gaelic *druim seileach* meaning the willow ridge, a name still preserved in the form of Drumsheuch" (Maxwell, 14). The modern spelling is Drumsheugh.

In this forest David I is said to have encountered the stag, been

miraculously preserved, and to have founded the Abbey of
Holyrood. For this reason the heraldic device of the Burgh of
Canongate shows a cross within the stag's antlers, although the
cross was not added until 1453 (Fraser, 16).

The forest seems to have extended as far as Gilmerton and
covered the Burgh Muir. It is now extensively built upon. In
Hertford's raid on Edinburgh in 1544 "the house-fronts of timber,
cut in the Forest of Drumsheugh, blazed furiously."
(Scott-Moncrieff, 34).

Drylaw House, south of Ferry Road.
The original Drylaw House was destroyed by Hertford in 1544
(R.C., 222).
1648 House rebuilt on same site, and again in 1718 (R.C., 222).

It is still in existence and opens from Groathill Road North.

Duddingston
1143 Duddingston Church built (Russell, 146) on the shore of
Duddingston Loch.
1631 Prestonfield Aisle in Duddingston Church (Grant, II, 314).
1670 Sheep Heid Inn built (Keir, 91).
1743 Prince Charles camped in the park, south-east of the Church,
before the Battle of Prestonpans. It is said that he slept in a house in
the village (Grant, II, 316) and there is still a house in Duddingston
bearing his name.
1768 Duddingston House, designed by William Chambers, completed
for the Duke of Abercorn (Grant, II, 317; R.C., 237). It is now a
hotel.
1901 Duddingston incorporated into Edinburgh.
1923 Duddingston Loch became a bird sanctuary.

Duke's Walk
"A walk in the vicinity of Holyrood House so called because often
frequented by the Duke of York, afterwards James VII [II], during
his residence in Scotland. It was for a long time the usual place of
rendezvous for settling affairs of honour." (Scott, *The Bride of
Lammermoor,* note in Chapter 34). It leads from St. Margaret's
Loch to the Willowbrae entrance to Holyrood Park.

Dumbiedikes or **Dumbiedykes**
"A house bordering on the King's Park, so called because the late
Mr Braidwood, an instructor of the deaf and dumb, resided there
with his pupils." (Scott, *The Heart of Midlothian,* Chap. 8). It is
thought that Scott drew his picture of the Laird of Dumbiedykes
from Peffermill House (q.v.) (Geddie, 135). Braidwood's school

pioneered the education of the deaf in Edinburgh.

Dumbiedykes Road opens south from Holyrood Road.

Dunbar's Close, Lawnmarket — north side.
This Close was formerly Ireland's Close and lay west of Byre's
Close (q.v.). It should not be confused with Dunbar's Close which
still exists in the north side of the Canongate.
1650 Cromwell, who was reputed to have lived in Adam Bothwell's
House (q.v.) (Chambers, 99), garrisoned his guard in Dunbar's
Close after the Battle of Dunbar. This, according to Chambers (99,
f.n.), was not the origin of the name of the Close which was called
after a family who lived in it (O.E.C., XII, 19).
1798 Demolished during the construction of Bank Street.

Dyvours
Dyvours were bankrupts (Wilson, II, 5). The Dyvours' Stone was a
pillory for bankrupts erected near the Mercat Cross.

Early Houses see also Architecture, Carving and Lands.
Early houses were built of wood and covered with thatch, and
cannot have been more than two storeys high. 'Timmer-lands'
were wood-faced houses, the wood being readily obtainable from
the Drumselch Forest (q.v.). Fires were common. Glass-making
was then unknown locally and windows were cut in the wooden
facings (Fraser, 57).
16th century "From the abbey to the castle there is a continued street,
which, on both sides, contains a range of excellent houses, and the
better sort are built of hewn stone." (Braun Agrippinensis, writing
at that time and quoted by Williamson, 210).
1510 There was a felling of large trees to clear spaces for the erection of
malt kilns on feued sites (Fraser, 57).
1511 The Town Council got rid of the glut of timber by allowing
burgesses who bought it to extend their houses seven feet (2 m) into
the street, thus narrowing the High Street by fourteen feet (4 m)
(Fraser, 57).
1514 The building of the Flodden Wall (see Town Walls) meant that few
houses were erected outside it, and thus the houses built inside the
Wall had to grow in height to accommodate the increasing
population seeking safety. This state of affairs continued for nearly
250 years (Williamson, 37). Most buildings before this time
contained a shop or booth on the ground floor while the house
above might consist of only one chamber, often reached by an
outside stair.
1544 Practically the only buildings of this period of Hertford's raids
which survived until the middle of the 18th century were parts of

the Castle, the north-west wing of Holyrood Palace and the churches. After Hertford's destructive raids of 1544 and 1547 "a great stimulus was given to building, the style being mostly an imitation of the French baronial." (Smeaton, (b), 67).

1598 "The houses . . . are built of unpolished stone . . . the outsides of them are faced with wooden galleries built upon the second storey of the houses." (Quoted from *Fynes Moryson, Itinerary*, (1617) by Smeaton, (b), 95 and Hume Brown, 84). The houses of the 16th century were very sparsely furnished (R.C., xvii).

17th century The destruction by raids, by fires, and by natural wear of the building materials used, added to the increased population and the desire to live within the town walls, led to old houses being bought, pulled down and rebuilt in stone. The motivations for this were financial on the part of the builder who could erect high buildings with many separate houses on each floor, while the Town Council approved on account of the reduced risk of fire and the enhanced appearance of the town. The ceiling and walls were painted, while rich people might hang tapestries. Plaster ceilings appeared about the end of the century.

1621 Act against thatched roofs which were to be made of slate (Arnot, 240).

1670 Windows began to replace the holes cut in wooden facings (Fraser, 121).

1674 Stone to be used exclusively in all new private buildings (G. Stell, Scotsman, 24-9-1977). Forestairs were forbidden on account of the narrowness of the street (Smith, I, 5).

1677 Wooden houses condemned, as were thatched roofs (Maitland, 100).

1698 Local Act of Parliament that no houses were to be built more than five storeys above street level (Stell, loc. cit.).

18th century In the early 18th century flats of six or seven apartments were not uncommon in tenements which were usually five storeys high (R.C., lxix).

1862 Landlords were compelled to install water into the houses (Grierson, 17; Wood *et al.*, 27).

Easter Coates House, Palmerston Place.

c.1611 Easter Coates House built (Grant, II, 116; Scott-Moncrieff, 87, says 1600; Cruft, 71, says 1615; Wilson, II, 7, refers to "the picturesque rural mansion of the sixteenth century."). It stands now in the Cathedral Close of St. Mary's Cathedral (Wilson, II, 7) and is "destined long to serve as a deanery" (Grant, II, 116).

It is now used as St. Mary's Music School (Cruft, 72).

Edinburgh see also Miscellaneous Dates and Royal Occasions.

The derivation of the name is uncertain. The popular theory that it derived from Edwinesburgh after Edwin, the Northumbrian king of the 7th century, "may be disregarded" (R.C., xxxv). The currently accepted view is that Edinburgh is referred to as Dineidin in Aneirin's Welsh poem, the *Gododdin,* written in the 6th century (Fraser, 11). The Gaelic-speaking population called Edinburgh Dunedin (fort of Eden, or fort of Edwin), while other Gaelic names such as Brae of the Hill or High Slope derive from the Gaelic prefix *Edin* meaning a slope (Scott-Moncrieff, 29).

The name Edina was due to George Buchanan (1506–82), and the city has been called 'Mine own romantic town' (Scott, *Marmion,* Canto IV), and 'Scotia's darling seat' (Burns, *Address to Edinburgh*). Edinburgh was first compared with Athens in 1762 by James Stuart in the preface of *Antiquities of Athens* (Daiches, 195). The title 'Modern Athens' was bestowed by the painter 'Grecian' Williams (H.W. Williams, *Travels in Italy and Greece,* (1820), II, 384) because Edinburgh is built on hills near the sea, and had an 18th century pre-eminence in the literary life. Cockburn (288) considered this a foolish phrase. Other names are 'Auld Reekie' (q.v.), 'Queen of Cities', and 'Queen of the North' (Cockburn, 291).

The question of when Edinburgh became capital of Scotland is also in doubt. Catford (15) suggests that David I's Charter to the Canons of Holyrood Abbey in 1128, which mentioned 'my burgh of Edinburgh', implied that it was a Royal Burgh before that date. Edinburgh was constituted a Royal Burgh about the middle of the 12th century (O.E.C., X, 4), but others date this from the Charter of Robert the Bruce in 1329. 1437 has been suggested as the date

Easter Coates House, before
St. Mary's Cathedral
was built.

when Edinburgh could offer security for royalty. Maitland (137) says "After the year 1456 . . . when the States of the Nation continued to hold their Convention therein, I think we may . . . date its first being reckoned the chief Town of the Kingdom." The Royal Commission on Ancient and Historic Monuments says that Edinburgh was the chief Burgh in 1452 (R.C., 144).

"Edinburgh is the capital of the Stuarts: it rose with them, and when they deserted it [i.e. in 1603] it sank — not into insignificance (its memories averted that fate) but into a mere shadow of its former self . . . it is pre-eminently the capital of the Jameses." (Williamson, 21). "The City was further attenuated by the Union of the Parliaments in 1707." (Williamson, 58).

Edinburgh was made a City by Charles I in 1633 (Wilson, I. 163; Grant, II, 2).

638 Edinburgh was captured by the Northumbrians (Daiches, 12).
854 Edinburgh was still under the Sea of Durham (Wilson, II, 217), but was recaptured by Indulf (954-62) (Daiches, 13).
12th century Edinburgh was "systematically planned and laid out" (O.E.C., XXII, 167).
1650-1700 "The citizens were beginning to lose their zest for religious controversy and became keenly alive to commercial and economic interests." (O.E.C., XVI, xxxiii).
1752 Publication of 'Proposals' for extending the city (Youngson, 3).
1767 Craig's plan for the New Town (q.v.) accepted (O.E.C., I, 146; XXIII, 1-37; Arnot, 316; Wilson, II, 204; Grant, II, 117; Smeaton, (a), 133; Catford, 111; Youngson, 70) after the passing of the Act for extending the Royalty of the City (Chambers, 6; Maxwell, 238).
1820-30 'Improvements' in the Old Town (O.E.C., XII, 249).
1867 Improvement Act (q.v.) (Wood et al., 33).
1951 Report of the Royal Commission on Ancient and Historic Monuments (see Monuments).

Edinburgh Chamber of Commerce and Manufacturers
1785 Edinburgh Chamber of Commerce founded (Keir, 643).
1786 Charter issued (Keir, 644).

It was an off-shoot of the Merchant Company (q.v.) (Grant, I, 379), and at one time it occupied a building in Melbourne Place (q.v.); moved in 1920 to Charlotte Square (Keir, 646); and it shared a building in Hanover Street with the Merchant Company before moving to Randolph Crescent.

Edinburgh International Festival
1947 Edinburgh International Festival of Music and Drama inaugurated (Keir, 833).

"The Fringe" at the Edinburgh International Festival. A student "circus" on Calton Hill.

1948 Military Tattoo on the Castle Esplanade for the first time, and became an official part of the Festival in 1950.
1949 Special Exhibition of paintings in the Royal Scottish Academy to coincide with the Festival for the first time.
1962 International Film Festival became a part (Keir, 949), and in 1978 the Film House was established in the empty Lothian Road Church.

The 'Fringe' has been a recognised, if separate, part of the Festival for thirty years, but has its own booking office.

Edinburgh Musical Society
1727 Edinburgh Musical Society formed, and organised concerts in St. Mary's Chapel, Niddry's Wynd (R.C., 101), the Reformation and the removal of the Court to London having bereft Edinburgh of light music.
1762 Society moved to St. Cecilia's Hall (q.v.) where concerts were augmented by Italian and German performers living in the city.
1978 Edinburgh Musical Society closed.
1798, 1819, 1824 Edinburgh Musical Festivals held for charitable causes (O.E.C., XXIX, 157, f.n.).

Engraving
1681 Engravers began work in the city, but the real start of the Edinburgh School was not until the 1720's (O.E.C., IX, 82).

"No other city of the Empire outside of London can present a record in the art of engraving at all approaching that of Edinburgh." (O.E.C., IX, 113).

Excise Office see also Customs and Excise.

The Excise Office has been housed in a number of sites — a floor in a land in the Netherbow (Grant, I, 217); Parliament Square from which it moved in 1730 to the house once owned by Tam o' the Cowgate (q.v.) (Grant, II, 260; Chambers, 247); in 1769 it was in Chessel's Court (q.v.) where it was robbed in 1788 by Deacon Brodie (Chambers, 91; Catford, 85); thence it moved in 1794 to Dundas House, 36 St. Andrew Square, which was sold to the Royal Bank in 1825 (O.E.C., XXIX, 159) and the Excise Office moved to Bellevue House (q.v.) in Drummond Place (Grant, I, 217). This building was demolished in 1846, and three years later the Excise, Assessed Taxes and Stamp Offices amalgamated to become the Inland Revenue (Keir, 238).

The Excise Office now occupies the Post Office building in Waterloo Place (C. McWilliam, *New Town Guide*, (1978), 16).

Extramural Medical School

1838 There was an extramural school in Argyle Square (q.v.) and some lectures were given in Brown Square (q.v.). These continued until 1870 (Guthrie, 16).

1877 The Medical Schol in Teviot Place (Bristo Street) was founded (Smeaton, (a), 142). Other schools were at Minto House (q.v.) and Nicolson Square, but details of these are "scanty or absent" (Guthrie, 23).

1895 School of Medicine of the two Royal Colleges in Edinburgh was incorporated by Charter with classes being held within the precincts of the Royal College of Surgeons (Guthrie, 7). This School, jointly with the Glasgow School, granted the Triple Qualification to practise medicine.

1948 Extramural School closed (Guthrie, 7).

Eyre Place

1827 Eyre Place built and named after James Eyre, a brewer in Canonmills (O.E.C., XII, 140).

1865 Royal Patent Gymnasium erected, now King George's Playing Fields (see Canonmills).

Faculty of Actuaries of Scotland

1856 Faculty established (Keir, 590).

1868 Charter of Incorporation (Keir, 590).

Fellows use the initials F.F.A. The Faculty premises are in St. Andrew Square.

Faculty of Advocates, Parliament Hall.

1532 Established by Act of Parliament but did not function until 1652.

"The Faculty of Advocates — who are privileged to plead in any Court in Scotland, and in all Scottish appeals before the House of Lords — is a body . . . inseparably connected with the old Parliament House." (Grant, I, 166).

From the advocates the judges of the Supreme Courts and the sheriffs of various counties are selected (Grant, I, 166). "The rules for elevation to the Bench go . . . back to the 1707 Treaty of Union . . . which provided that the qualifications for appointment to the Bench of the Court of Session should be either service as an Advocate for five years or as a Writer to the Signet for ten years." (Keir, 210).

The Faculty is presided over by a Dean. The Scottish advocate is equivalent in status to an English barrister.

Famines
1571 Scarcity of food in the town (O.E.C., XVI, xviii).
1784 Riots in city on account of food shortage (O.E.C., IX, 219; Grant, III, 87).
1795 Great dearth of food — 11,000 fed by charity (Grant, II, 283; Cockburn, 72).

Famous Visitors see also Royal Occasions.
This list includes some visitors to Edinburgh until 1832, after which such notables were less of a novelty.
1495 Perkin Warbeck (Wilson, I, 34; O.E.C., III, 48, says that James IV entertained him in 1499).
1619 Ben Jonson (O.E.C., I, 106) who had walked all the way from London, having to buy new shoes in Darlington.
1657 George Fox, founder of the Society of Friends (Sitwell and Bamford, 123).
1682 Samuel Pepys, in attendance on the Duke of York, left no account of his visit.
1706-8 Daniel Defoe, first editor of the *Edinburgh Courant* (Grant, I, 216; 242), wrote his *Tour through Great Britain* in 1727.
1751-90 John Wesley on 22 occasions (O.E.C., VII, 159-203) when he used the visits to preach on Calton Hill.
1753 Oliver Goldsmith stayed in College Wynd while a medical student at the University (Grant, II, 254).
1759 Benjamin Franklin (Carlyle, 413).
1766 Tobias Smollett (Wilson, II, 92; Grant, II, 26), lived in St. John Street.
1773 Dr Samuel Johnson (O.E.C., VIII, 163; XIV, 129; Boswell, 11; Chambers, 172; Grant, I, 299; Smeaton, (a), 172).
1774-5 Captain Elias Topham (Wilson, I. 254; Chambers, 49; 176; 267, who calls him Major Topham).

1779 John Paul Jones off Leith (Grant, III, 197; Russell, 410; Geddie, 167).

1785 Edmund Burke (Gray, 61).

1786 Robert Burns (Wilson, I, 214; Maxwell, 260; Smeaton, (a), 134) stayed in different lodgings during his seven visits (Scotsman, 3-3-1948).

1811 Percy Bysshe Shelley (O.E.C., XI, 75-85), and again in 1813 when he lived in North Frederick Street (W. Harrison, 53).

1825-7 Charles Darwin while taking medical classes.

1828 Thomas de Quincey lived in Edinburgh, at times in Sanctuary, until he died in 1859 (Catford, 102).

1832 Earl Grey (Grant, II, 104).

Feu
A feu is a perpetual lease at a fixed rent; a piece of land so held (O.E.D.). Hence to feu, feuar etc.

Figgate Whins
Waste lands between Leith and Musselburgh (Russell, 34; 380). Infested with robbers and smugglers until 1762 (Grant, III, 144). The name possibly derives from the Saxon meaning a cow's ditch. The Figgate Burn runs from Duddingston, where it is a continuation of the Braid Burn, reaching the sea at Portobello.

1296 William Wallace mustered 200 patriots on Figgate lands (Grant, III, 143).

1742 Portobello Hut built; demolished in 1851 (Grant, III, 144).
     Portobello was built on Figgate lands (Smeaton, (a), 361; Russell, 380). See Portobello.

Fires
1544 Fire in town following Hertford's raid (Grant, I. 276).

1676 Town Council required inhabitants to sweep chimneys twice in the year. In 1677 this was increased to once in each quarter (Robertson, 135).

1676 Fire in Parliament Close (Wilson, I, 266).

1700 Fire in Parliament Close (O.E.C., III, 228; Maitland, 112; Arnot, 185, f.n.; Chambers, III; Wilson, I, 266; Grant, I, 161; II, 246; Smeaton, (b), 117).

1703 Attempt to make a fire-fighting organisation in the city (Keir, 442).

1725 Big fire in the Lawnmarket (Arnot, 205).

1824 Great fire from Police Office, Parliament Square to Hunter Square (O.E.C., I, 6; III, 228; XXIX, 151; Wilson, I, 266; Grant, I, 182; Cockburn, 420). Description of the fire (Wilson, I, chap. XX; Grant, I, 188-91; Cockburn, 420). It apparently began in Old Assembly Close.

1824 Fire Brigade formed (Robertson, 231).

1892 Fire in Jenners, Princes Street (Grierson, 27).

1900 Fire Station, Lauriston Place, at the head of Lady Lawson Street, at the south-west corner of the old cattle market the remainder of which was replaced, in 1907, by the College of Art (q.v.) (Smeaton, (a), 355; (b), 361). Fire engines were then horse drawn (Keir, 443).

1913 First motor fire engine (Robertson, 236).

1961 Six fire stations in the city (Keir, 443).

1977 Lothian Region budgets over £3m. per annum for fire services.

Fisher's Close, Lawnmarket — south side.

1699 Built by Thomas Fisher, first Chamberlain of the city. Later the town house of Buccleuch family.

1953 Reconstructed during the building of the Scottish Central Library, it now contains the administrative offices of the National Library.

    The Close now leads to Victoria Terrace, but before this was built it led south to the Cowgate (Grant, II, 242).

Fleshmarket Close, 197-207 High Street — north side.

This opened off the High Street almost opposite, but to the west of, where the Tron Church now stands, and it led down to the valley of the Nor' Loch.

    William Creech started his bookselling business here (Keir, 54) and Henry Dundas (Lord Melville) began his legal practice near the Close (Grant, I, 236; Keir, 54).

1859 Part demolished during the building of Cockburn Street into which it still opens and from which it continues to Market Street.

Flodden Wall see Town Walls.

Fore-Stairs

Outside stairs ascending to the first floor of buildings, as seen in John Knox's House and Canongate Tolbooth (Chambers, 271).

Fountain Close, High Street — south side.

Opposite stone conduit near John Knox's House, named after Endmylie's Well (Grant, I, 276) which stood at the head of the Close (O.E.C., XII, 85).

1722-70 Physicians' Hall in the Close (Grant, II, 147). Now a locked gate.

Free Church of Scotland see Assembly Hall.

Freedom of the City

The ceremony of creating Honorary Burgesses of the City. The following selection until 1900 is taken from Robertson and Wood, 52-87.

1513 Gavin Douglas (c. 1474-1522), poet and bishop.

1618 Ben Jonson (1573-1637), dramatist and poet.

1719 John Law of Lauriston (1671-1729), economist.

1759 Benjamin Franklin (1706-1790), American statesman (Sitwell and Bamford, 183, say 1768).

1760 Tobias Smollett (1721-1771), novelist.

1770 Adam Smith (1730-1790), political economist.

1813 Sir Walter Scott (1771-1832), novelist and poet.

1839 Thomas Babington Macaulay (1800-1895), historian.

1841 Charles Dickens (1812-1870), novelist.

1853 William Ewart Gladstone (1809-1895), statesman.

1856 Henry John Temple, Viscount Palmerston (1784-1865), statesman.

1857 David Livingstone (1813-1873), missionary.

1863 Giuseppe Garibaldi (1807-1882), Italian patriot.

1867 Benjamin Disraeli (1804-1881), statesman.

1877 Ulysses Simpson Grant (1822-1885), American statesman.

1890 Henry Morton Stanley (1840-1906), explorer.

1898 General Horatio Herbert Kitchener (1850-1916), soldier.

Freemasonry

1736 Grand Lodge of Scotland formed and met in Hyndford's Close (q.v.).

1737-63 Meetings of Grand Lodge held in Mary's Chapel (? Niddry's Wynd (q.v.) or ? Burnet's Close (q.v.), High Street which has 'Mary's Chapel' carved over the entrance).

1763-1809 Grand Lodge met in various halls.

1809 St. Cecilia's Hall (q.v.) bought by Grand Lodge as the Freemasons' Hall (Harris, 34).

1812 Additional Hall added to St. Cecilia's Hall by the Freemasons with the date carved above the door in the Cowgate.

1844 St. Cecilia's Hall sold to the Town Council for school purposes (Harris, 36).

1845-58 Grand Lodge met in various halls.

1858 Freemasons' hall founded in No. 98 George Street (O.E.C., XIV, 166; Grant, II, 151; Gilbert, 130).

1911 Present Freemasons' Hall built at No. 96 George Street, to the design of A. Hunter Crawford.

In Edinburgh there meet some of the oldest and most famous Masonic Lodges in Scotland, in particular the Lodge of Edinburgh, Mary's Chapel, No. 1, (dating from before 1598) which now meets in Hill Street, and Lodge Canongate Kilwinning, No. 2, (1677), which meets in the very old Lodge Room in St. John Street (q.v.).

"Gardy Loo."

Gabriel's Road

This road led from Multrie's Hill (q.v.), the site of the Register House in Princes Street, north-west across what is now the New Town to Canonmills on the Water of Leith (O.E.C., XVII, 79; XXIII, 3; Chambers, 366). It was the eastern boundary of the original New Town (Wilson, II, 204). The road led via Broughton and Silvermills, and the last vestiges are the steps at Glenogle Road which are still called Gabriel's Road (*Edinburgh Weekly*, 21-10-1966).

Gait

A gait was a street. The word for a gate was yett (Wilson, II, 57, f.n.).

Gallow-Lee

The place of public execution on a hillock half-way between Edinburgh and Leith, on Leith Walk at the present Shrubhill (Wilson, II, 184; Chambers, 361).

'Gardy Loo'

Derived from the 18th century French *gare de l'eau* — look out for water.

A warning in old Edinburgh that slops and refuse were about to be thrown from a window into the street (Chambers, 148, f.n.; Maxwell, 207, f.n.). "By ten o'clock each night the filth collected in each household was poured from the high windows, and fell in malodorous plash upon the pavement, and not seldom on the unwary passers by . . .

89

....The passengers passing beneath would agonisingly cry out 'Haud yer hand', but too often the shout was unheard or was too late." (Graham, 83; 106, f.n.). "The maid calls *Gardy loo* to the passengers which signifies *Lord have mercy upon you.*" (Smollett, 269).

1730 The habit of throwing slops and rubbish from windows was repressed by the Town Council (Grant, I, 203).

Gayfield House, East London Street.

1763 Gayfield House built (R.C., 219).

1767 Earl of Leven occupied the house (Grant, III, 161).

c.1790 Gayfield Square built.

c.1880 House was a veterinary college (Grant, III, 161).

George IV Bridge

"If we except the Old Mint and the venerable Chapel of St. Magdalen, no other site could have been chosen for the new bridge where their proceedings [i.e. of the Improvements Commission] would have been so destructive." (Wilson, II, 147).

1827 George IV Bridge founded (O.E.C., XVIII, 79-99), designed by Thomas Hamilton.

1828 Liberton's Wynd (q.v.) pulled down for the building (Scotsman, 21-6-1828).

1835-40 Victoria Street built (Chambers, 54, f.n.).

1836 George IV Bridge completed (Grant, I, 292).

1836 Highland Institution, one of the first buildings on the Bridge, later became the Music and Arts department of the Central Library (Cruft, 13).

1867 India Buildings erected near the top of Victoria Street (Grant, I, 291), and is now an additional Sheriff Court.

1868 Sheriff Court built on the east side of the Bridge (Grant, I. 295; Smeaton, (a), 311).

1890 Free Library founded (Smeaton, (a), 311), now the Central Public Library.

1905 County Buildings (built in 1818) were rebuilt (Minto and Armstrong, 45; Keir, 1008; Cruft, 2) at the corner of the east side of the Bridge and the Lawnmarket.

1938 Sheriff Court demolished for the National Library, and moved to its present site on the north side of the Lawnmarket (Minto and Armstrong, 46).

1956 National Library opened (Keir, 912).

1974 Office block for Lothian Region opened in Melbourne Place (q.v.), the north-west end of George IV Bridge.

George Heriot's Hospital (School)

1623 Death of George Heriot ('Jingling Geordie') in London. He was

90

goldsmith to James VI (Maxwell, 156), and had a tiny shop, traditionally seven feet square, amongst the krames (q.v.) (Catford, 45).

1628 Governors of Heriot's Trust bought 8½ acres (3.5 hectares) in Lauriston on the High Riggs, and building of the Hospital started (O.E.C., II, 76; 83; IV, app. 5; XVIII, 154; Maitland, 439; Grant, II, 366; Smeaton, (a), 109).

1636 Heriot's Governors obtained the lands of Broughton (q.v.) (O.E.C., XVIII, app. 16; Grant, II, 181).

1636 Telfer's Wall (see Town Walls) built round the Lauriston ground (O.E.C., XVIII, 155).

1650 Heriot's Hospital completed (O.E.C., IV, app. 5; Arnot 566; Wilson, II, 168, f.n.) the designers being William Wallace and William Ayton.

1650-58 Cromwell's sick and injured troops occupied the Hospital (O.E.C., XV, 138; Grant, II, 367; Maxwell, 156). In 1658 they were moved to the Canongate.

1659 Heriot's Hospital opened for 30 boys (Grant, II, 367; Smeaton, (a), 344), later increased to 150 resident boys.

1692 Cupolas removed from the Hospital (Grant, II, 367).

1693 Clock tower and statue of George Heriot (by Robert Mylne) added.

1828 Lauriston gateway erected, the previous entrance being from the Grassmarket.

1837 Heriot's Free School built on the site of the Cowgate Port at the junction of the Cowgate and Pleasance (Grant, I, 298; III, 250). This still stands.

George Heriot's School, the frontage as seen from the West Bow.

1884 Under the Heriot Trust there were 13 Free Heriot's Schools in Edinburgh, in addition to 5 infant schools and 9 other free schools for instruction in writing, arithmetic, grammar, German, French and drawing (Grant, II, 371). All were structurally similar to the original George Heriot's School, and a number still exist.
1886 Heriot's Hospital renamed George Heriot's School (Keir, 773).

George Square
Named after George Brown who planned the Square and whose brother, James, built it (Grant, II, 339).

O.E.C., XXVI deals in detail with the Square. Walter Scott lived in No. 25, and among others who stayed here were Duchess of Gordon, Countess of Sutherland, Lord Melville, Viscount Duncan, Lord Braxfield and Henry Erskine, later the Lord Advocate (Youngson, 69; R.T. Skinner, Edinburgh Evening Dispatch, 20-2-1945; Steuart, 145).
1761 James Brown bought land in the policies of Ross House (O.E.C., XII, app. 18).
1766 George Square laid out (O.E.C., XXVI, 4) as George's Square (Arnot, 324).
1792 Dundas riots in the Square (Grant, II, 343).
1871 George Watson's Ladies' College built at Melville's house in the north side (Grant, II, 363; Keir, 778; Catford, 77 and Stewart, 22 say 1876).
1914 Edinburgh University Department of Agriculture built (Stewart, 22).
1920 Edinburgh University Women's Union built (Stewart, 22).
1929 Cowan House, Edinburgh University Hall of Residence, built (Stewart, 22).
1949 Edinburgh University School of Medicine spread into the Square (Stewart, 22)
1963 Further demolition of George Square for erection of University of Edinburgh buildings so that only the west side and a small part of the east side remain in the original form, and even these contain small departments and units. (See University of Edinburgh). The Square is now a College quadrangle (Catford, 77).

George Street
Laid out by James Craig in his 1767 plan as a mainly residential street to lie between two symmetrical squares.
1776-7 Physicians' Hall, designed by James Craig (Youngson, 95).
1787 St. Andrew's Church, designed by Andrew Fraser and William Sibbald (Grant, II, 144).
1787 Assembly Rooms (q.v.) built by public subscription (Youngson, 95), designed by John Henderson (*Edinburgh — An Architectural Guide*).

1831 George IV statue, by Francis Chantrey, at intersection of Hanover Street (Grant, II, 151).

1833 William Pitt statue, by Francis Chantrey, at intersection of Frederick Street (Grant, II, 151).

1841 Physicians' Hall demolished for Commercial Bank, designed by David Rhind (O.E.C., XXIII, 9). This building is now owned by the Royal Bank.

1843 Music Hall added to Assembly Rooms (Grant, II, 150; *Edinburgh — An Architectural Guide* gives 1834 and says designed by William Burn).

1855 George Hotel opened (Keir, 679).

1859 Freemasons' Hall (O.E.C., XIV, 166; Gilbert, 130; Grant, II, 151 says at No. 98 in 1858).

1878 Dr Thomas Chalmers statue, by John Steell, at intersection of Castle Street (Grant, II, 151).

1911 Freemasons' Hall rebuilt at No. 96, designed by A. Hunter Crawford.

1911 Church of Scotland Offices built at No. 121 (Keir, 1009).

George Watson's Hospital (College)

1723 George Watson, a merchant in Rotterdam and an accountant to the Bank of Scotland, died and left money to the Company of Merchants for the erection of a Hospital (Maitland, 482; Grant, I, 378) which was to be accommodated in Thomson's Yards near Lady Yester's Church, but this arrangement fell through (J. Harrison, 17).

1738 George Watson's Hospital built (O.E.C., II, 8; Arnot, 568; Grant, II, 358) on the site of the present Royal Infirmary. It was designed by William Adam.

1870 The site having been sold to the Royal Infirmary, Watson's Merchant Academy, as it was then called (Grant, II, 359), took over the building used by the Merchant Maiden Hospital (q.v.) at the foot of Archibald Place, off Lauriston Place, and became George Watson's Boys' College.

1871 George Watson's Ladies' College opened in Melville House on the north side of George Square (Grant, II, 363; Keir, 778; Catford, 77 and Stewart, 22 both give the incorrect date of 1876).

1931 The site of George Watson's Boys' College was sold to the expanding Royal Infirmary and a new College built in Merchiston Castle School's playing fields, Colinton Road.

1974 George Watson's Ladies' College site having been sold to Edinburgh University, the boys' and girls' schools gradually merged into a co-educational college in Colinton Road.

'Giants' Causeway'
The name formerly given locally to the pavement of No. 133
George Street where lived Sir John Sinclair and his sixteen children,
each of whom exceeded six feet in height (*Edinburgh Weekly*,
7-10-1966).

Gibbet

1586 New gibbet on Burgh Muir (O.E.C., X, 86; Maitland, 176) on the
west side of Dalkeith Road near the site of the present Preston Street
School.
1675 Gibbet at Dalkeith Road removed (O.E.C., X, 96). This 'Tyburn
of Edinburgh' had been a permanent structure under which the
remains of the Marquis of Montrose had been buried in 1650
(O.E.C., X, 93), and were removed to St. Giles Church in 1661.

There was also a gibbet, called the Gallow-Lee (q.v.) midway
between Edinburgh and Leith (Chambers, 361; Wilson, II,
184). In the 17th and 18th centuries the town gibbet, called the
Widdy-tree, stood near Pilrig.
1815 Two Irishmen were hanged on a thorn tree overhanging what is
now Braid Road (Grant, III, 40).

Gillespie's School see James Gillespie's School.

Gilmerton
1550 Gilmerton House built (Geddie, 142, who said in 1926 that it was an
"abomination of desolation"). It was known as the Place of
Gilmerton and was the home of the Kinlochs.
1720-4 Paterson's Cave constructed by the local blacksmith as a house
dug into the soft sandstone (Grant, III, 345; Geddie, 142).
1735 Paterson died having lived for eleven years in his cave (Grant, III,
345; Geddie, 142, says in 1755 after thirty years of cave dwelling).
1837 Gilmerton Church built (Grant, III, 343).
1920 Gilmerton included within Edinburgh.

Girth Cross, foot of Canongate.
The position of the Girth Cross, marking the ancient boundary of
the Abbey Sanctuary (q.v.) is denoted by radiated stones on the
road (Arnot, 304; Maitland, 154; Wilson, II, 116; Maxwell, 251;
Smeaton, (b), 240).

Gladstone's Land, 483-9 Lawnmarket — north side.
1617 A six-storey tenement (dating from c.1550), it was "a very old
house when bought by Thomas Gledstanes." (Nimmo, 66). It is the
last building left in Edinburgh with an arcaded front (R.C., 74).

94

Gladstone's Land
in late 18th Century.

1631 Gladstone's Land built (O.E.C., XIV, 10; Smeaton, (a), 173). It
was acquired by Thomas Gledstane, ancestor of W. E. Gladstone
(O.E.C., XII, 12).
1935 Restored by the Office of Works (O.E.C., XXIII, app. 10)
uncovering the pillars of a stair leading to the first floor. The
building had been acquired by the National Trust for Scotland in
the previous year. It was leased to the Saltire Society until 1977, and
is now to be renovated and the first floor furnished in the style of the
17th century.

Gogar
1625 Gogar House built (Geddie, 66) by John Couper. It is still occupied
but is called Castle Gogar now.
1650 A skirmish between Cromwell's and General David Leslie's troops
(Arnot, 131; Grant, III, 318; Geddie, 62), the 'Gogar Flashes'.

Golden Charter
1482 The Golden Charter (Wilson, I, 27; Grant, I, 34; II, 278) under

which provosts and bailies were made sheriffs within the bounds of their territories; magistrates to make laws for government of the town; citizens to levy custom on certain imported goods and on certain exports from Leith. Under the Charter the Lord Provost is Lord Lieutenant of the County of the City of Edinburgh (Smeaton, (b), 46).

Golden Penny
A levy on ships built or sold in Leith (Robertson, 130).

Goldsmiths
1586 Goldsmiths, previously included in the Incorporation of the Hammermen (established in 1483), formed a separate company (Grant, I, 376). A Charter of James VI established this and a Charter of James VII (II) empowered the Company to stamp gold and silver (Grant, I, 376).

    The Goldsmiths' Hall was in the west side of Parliament Close (Grant, I, 174). The goldsmiths were deemed superior tradesmen, and they wore cocked hats and scarlet cloaks and carried gold-topped canes (Grant, I, 174). Until 1780 goldsmiths were craftsmen in Parliament Square (Chambers, 112) and were manual craftsmen (Grant, I, 174). They moved to their Hall in Bridge Street, South Bridge, which was also the Assay Office, in 1780 (Grant, I, 376).

    Goldsmiths' Hall is now in Queen Street.

Golf
"The diversion which is peculiar to Scotland, and in which all ages find great pleasure, is golf. They play at it with a small leathern ball . . . and a piece of wood, flat on one side, in the shape of a small bat, which is fastened at the end of a stick of three or four feet long, at right angles to it. The art consists of striking the ball with this instrument into a hole in the ground in a smaller number of strokes than your adversary. The game has the superiority of cricket and tennis in being less violent and dangerous, but in point of dexterity and amusement by no means to be compared with them." (Topham, 96).

1457 Statute by James II against golf lest it interfere with archery (Arnot, 360; Grant, III, 31; Wilson, II, 110). "Fute-ball and Golfe to be utterly cryed down, and not to be used . . ."

1503 James IV played golf (Grant, III, 31).

1579 Golf played on Bruntsfield Links (Smeaton, (b), 364).

1593 Golf course on Leith Links, said to be second only to St. Andrews in seniority.

1627 Earl of Montrose golfed on Leith Links (Grant, III, 260).

Duke of York (later James VII(II))and John Paterson playing
golf on Leith Links, which traditionally gave rise to Golfers' Land.

1642 Charles I golfed on Leith Links (Grant, III, 260; Marshall, 38, says
1640).
1717 Golfhall built, the earliest tavern on Bruntsfield Links (O.E.C., X,
244). (See Wright's Houses.)
1724 Captain Porteous (of Riots fame) golfed on Leith Links (Grant, III,
262). During the 17th and 18th centuries many Edinburgh
aristocrats played golf on Leith Links (Grant, III, 260).
1735 (Royal) Burgess Golfing Society formed.
1744 Honourable Company of Edinburgh Golfers founded (O.E.C., II,
15; Arnot, 361). Silver Club presented by the city (Grant, III, 31;
262).
1761 Bruntsfield Links Golfing Society formed.
1768 Club House built on Leith Links (Arnot, 361; Marshall, 13).
1889 Braid Hills municipal golf course laid out.
1892-7 Seven private golf courses opened — Mortonhall (1892);
Baberton (1893); Lothianburn (1893); Torphin (1895); Craigmillar
Park (1896); Murrayfield (1896); Duddingston (1897).
    There are presently some 25 private and public courses in
Edinburgh.

Golfers' Land, 81 Canongate — north side.
Traditionally built with John Paterson's share of the stakes in a golf
match on Leith Links when the Duke of York (later James VII (II))
and Paterson beat two English nobles (O.E.C., XII, 103; Grant, II,
10; Wilson, II, 110; Chambers, 320). John Paterson was a

shoemaker who made the leather golf balls used in those days.
1609 Golfers' Land acquired by John's father, Nicol Paterson (Grant, II, 11).

The site is now a public house on the wall of which is a plaque and the Paterson coat-of-arms.

'Goose-Pie', see also Ramsay Garden.
'Goose-pie' or 'Guse-pie' was the name given to Allan Ramsay's house on the Castlehill because of the roundness of its shape (Chambers, 14). The rooms were all octagonal.
1751 House built (O.E.C., XI, 13; Wilson, I, 185; Grant, I, 82; Steuart, 22, says 1743). Later called Ramsay Lodge.

Government Departments, see also Scottish Assembly.
As the capital city Edinburgh is the Scottish seat of two main classes of Government; (i) the departments of the Secretary of State for Scotland, Agriculture and Fisheries, Education, Home and Health, and Development which are accommodated in St. Andrew's House and New St. Andrew's House and partly in Government offices in Saughton and Sighthill; and (ii) other United Kingdom departments, Inland Revenue, H.M. Customs and Excise, Employment (formerly Labour), Health and Social Security (formerly Pensions), Environment (formerly Public Buildings and Works), Post Office and Telephones, Stationery Office (Keir, 219-260).
1937 St. Andrew's House opened, Calton Hill.
1971 New St. Andrew's House, St. James's Centre.

Grange House, Grange Loan.
The old Grange or Granary of the clergy of St. Giles (Smeaton, (b), 370).
1592 Original House built (R.C., 241) and greatly enlarged over the years.
1631 William Dick of Braid bought Grange Estate (see Adam Bothwell's House for notes on Dick) (O.E.C., VIII, app. 8).
1792 Principal William Robertson (of Edinburgh University) died in the house which had been occupied by the Dick Lauders of Grange and Fountainhall (Grant, III, 49; Smeaton, (b), 370).
1827 House extensively reconstructed to the design of William Playfair (Smith, I, 40).
1936 House demolished (R.C., 240).

Granton
1544 Granton (Royston) Castle built (O.E.C., VIII, app. 4) and was occupied until 1794.

1544 Hertford landed a force at Granton which advanced to capture Leith (R.C., lvi).

1834 Docks proposed (Smeaton, (a), 139).

1835 Harbour built (Grant, III, 312; Smeaton, (a), 356).

1842 Queen Victoria landed at Granton for her first official visit to Edinburgh during which she stayed at Dalkeith Palace.

1845 Steamers between Granton and Stirling (Scotsman, 27-9-1845).

1846 Branch railway to Granton (Scotsman, 28-1-1846).

1850-52 Patent slip for repair of vessels of up to 1200 tons (Grant, III, 312; Scotsman, 10-8-1850).

1873 Granton Gas Works built (Keir, 69).

1920 Granton incorporated into the city.

1920 Granton Castle demolished (see Royston Castle).

1936 West Harbour improved as an extension for trawler fleet.

Granton Castle, see Royston Castle.

Grassmarket, from the West Port to the West Bow.
In the south-west corner of the Grasmarket stood the Franciscan Monastery or Monastery of the Greyfriars (q.v.) (Williamson, 256).

Scene of hanging of common people, especially the Covenanters 'to glorify God in the Grassmarket'; the site of the gallows was marked by a St. Andrew's Cross in rose-coloured

The Grassmarket in its heyday as a fair, with the Castle.

cobblestones in the roadway centrally at the east end of the Grassmarket (Chambers, 51). The site was later enclosed within a railing.

1477 James III chartered markets to be held in the Grassmarket (Maitland, 8; Grant, II, 230). (See Markets).

1560 Corn market at east end of Grassmarket (Grant, II, 231; Steuart, 129, says west end).

1661-88 100 martyrs of Covenant executed (Grant, II, 231; 378).

1736 Andrew Wilson and Captain John Porteous hanged (Grant, I, 128-131; Williamson, 258).

1758 Alexander Nasmyth, the artist, born in a house in the Grassmarket (Pennycook, 40).

1784 Executions in Grassmarket ceased (Chambers, 51; Grant, II, 231; Wilson, I, 244, says 1785).

1791 Robert Burns stayed at the White Hart Inn (see Inns).

1849 New corn exchange erected to the design of David Cousin (Grant, II, 234; Smeaton, (a), 259); since 1968 an exension of Heriot-Watt University stands on the site (Minto and Armstrong, 1).

1977 Commemorative plaque to celebrate 500th anniversary of the Charter of James III unveiled in the west end of the Grassmarket.

The Grassmarket is the principal area of the Common Lodging Houses in Edinburgh, the main two being Castle Trades Hotel and Greyfriars Hotel, which is just inside the Cowgate.

Greenside
The gully between the north side of Calton Hill and the New Town.

1456 Place for tournaments (O.E.C., XVIII, 43; Maitland, 214; Wilson, II, 214; Smeaton, (a), 34).

1518 White Friars (Carmelites, q.v.) settled here (Wilson, II, 266; Grant, II, 101; Maitland, 214, says 1520; Fraser, 61, says that they came in 1520 to look after a leper colony).

1534 Two heretics burned at Greenside (Grant, II, 102).

1539-44 Lyndsay's play *The Pleasant Satyre of the Three Estaits* produced at Greenside (Grant, II, 102).

1554 *The Pleasant Satyre* staged in the presence of the Queen Regent (Mary of Guise) and lasted for nine hours (O.E.C., XVII, app. 14; Grant, II, 102). This play was not produced again until 1948 at the Edinburgh Festival.

1594 Leper Colony at Greenside (O.E.C., XVII, app. 16; XV, 136 and Maitland, 214, say 1591).

1652-56 Leper Hospital removed (O.E.C., XV, 137).

Greenside is now a large car and bus park, but there are plans to build the British Broadcasting Corporation centre here.

'Greping Office', see John's Coffee House, Edinburgh.

Grey Friars (Franciscans)

1429 Grey Friars came to town (Smeaton, (a), 313; R.C., 125, says that the Friary was colonised in 1447).

1449 Mary of Gueldres lodged here before her wedding to James II (Steuart, 134).

1558 City mob despoiled the monastery, which was in the angle between the Grassmarket and Candlemaker Row (Smeaton, (b), 336; R.C., 44, says 1559; Scott-Moncrieff, 80, also gives 1559 and ascribes the despoliation to Argyle and his Reformers).

1562 Queen Mary granted the grounds of Greyfriars to the Town Council for a graveyard (O.E.C., II, 76; III, 219; Maitland, 23; Arnot, 239; Grant, II, 379; Maxwell, 125; Wilson, I, 263, says 1566).

1566 Friary buildings removed.

Greyfriars Bobby, junction of Candlemaker Row and George IV Bridge.

1873 Bronze statue of Skye terrier, by William Brodie, unveiled (Gilbert, 148). The dog had evoked public sympathy by lingering over a period of 14 years near his master's grave in Greyfriars Churchyard until 1872 when he died.

Greyfriars Church

1612 Old Church built (O.E.C., XI, 9; Maitland, 188; Arnot, 272; Maxwell, 121; Smeaton, (a), 105; Wilson, II, 167, says 1613; 266, says 1613 or 1614). Opened for worship in 1620 (R.C., 46).

1638 National Covenant signed in Church (Grant, II, 375; R.C., 46).

1650 Church desecrated by Cromwell's troops (Grant, II, 375) who used it as barracks.

1679 Some 1200 prisoners from Bothwell Brig brought to the Churchyard (O.E.C., II, 81-115; Arnot, 159; Chambers, 289; Grant, II, 375; Maxwell, 177; R.C., 46) and were confined there for nearly five months.

1681 Tron Church bell hung in Church (Grant, II, 378).

1718 Old Tower, used as a gunpowder store, blew up (Grant, II, 378; R.C., 46).

1721 New Church built as a separate Church attached to the west end of the Old Church (Maitland, 188; 203; Arnot, 272; Grant, II, 378; Maxwell, 121) and each Church had a minister presiding over it.

1728 Martyrs' Monument, erected in 1706 in the north-east corner of the Graveyard, repaired (Grant, II, 378) and the inscribed panel was renewed in 1771 (R.C., 55).

1845 Old Church burned (Wilson, II, 265; Grant, II, 379; Maxwell, 121) and restored by David Bryce in 1857 (Maxwell, 121).

1928 Old and New Churches united and dividing wall removed in 1938.

1979 Linked with Highland Church, Tolbooth St. Johns.

Greyfriars Churchyard
Many famous men have been buried in Greyfriars Churchyard, among them the Regent Morton, George Buchanan the historian, Allan Ramsay and his son Allan, John Mylne the Royal Master Mason, John Watson the founder of John Watson's Hospital, George Watson the founder of George Watson's Hospital, George Heriot the father of the founder of Heriot's Hospital, James Craig the architect of the New Town, John Kay the caricaturist, George Foulis of Ravelston, Captain John Porteous, Henry Mackenzie author of *Man of Feeling*, William Creech publisher and Lord Provost, Dr Thomas McCrie the church historian, Principal Robertson of Edinburgh University, William Adam the architect, James Gillespie Graham the architect, Sir George Mackenzie of Rosehaugh founder of the Advocates' Library, Clement Little founder of the University Library, and some of the Boswells of Auchinleck, ancestors of James Boswell.

Guthrie Street, Chambers Street.
1870's Built under the Improvement Act (q.v.) and includes the upper part of College Wynd (q.v.), then turns at a right angle, and forms the lower part of Horse Wynd (q.v.) to join the Cowgate.

'Gutted Haddie', see Arthur's Seat.

Haddo's Hole see also St. Giles Church.
North transept of the Old St. Giles Church, used as a prison in 1644 for Sir John Gordon of Haddo, an ancestor of the Earls of Aberdeen, before his trial and execution at the Cross (Maitland (Haddow's Hold), 179; Arnot (Haddow's Hole), 270; Wilson, II, 228; Grant, I, 146; Wood *et al.*, 79).

Halkerston's Wynd, High Street — north side.
Halkerston's Wynd led down to New Port of the Town Wall at the site of the dam for the Nor' Loch (Chambers, 117, f.n.).
1747 British Linen Company in Halkerston's Wynd (C. A. Malcolm, *The British Linen Bank, 1746-1946*, 25).
1750 Robert Fergusson, the poet, was born in a house either in the Wynd or between it and the neighbouring Cap and Feathers Close (q.v.) (Grant, I, 238).
1763 Demolished for building the North Bridge.

Hammermen's Close see Bakehouse Close and Huntly House.

Hangman's Crag, Arthur's Seat.
The rock over which the Edinburgh hangman threw himself on

being chased by a mob (Chambers, 52).

Harestane see Burgh Muir.

Hart's Close, High Street — north side.
This Close stood east of Mylne Square (q.v.), and was demolished in 1763 for the building of the North Bridge.

'Heart of Midlothian'
The Old Tolbooth (q.v.) was so termed by Walter Scott in his novel of that name.

'Heave Awa' Land', High Street — north side.
1861 A tenement fell. The entrance to Paisley Close is marked by the sculptured head of a boy and the inscription 'Heave awa', chaps, I'm no' dead yet!' (Catford, 191; Livingstone (b), 72; Grierson, 17, who says this was in Chalmer's Close). Grant (I, 240) says that the tenement, built by the Trotters in 1612, was at the head of Bailie Fyfe's Close (which is next to Paisley Close) and buried 35 persons on its collapse. Bailie Fyfe's Close and Paisley Close now both lead into the same small courtyard.

Heriot Row
1802 Building started to the design of William Sibbald and Robert Reid.
R. L. Stevenson lived in No. 17 as a boy; Henry Mackenzie, author of *Man of Feeling*, lived in No. 6; and James Ballantyne, Scott's publisher, in No. 3.

Heriot-Watt University
1821 School of Arts inaugurated in Adam Square (q.v.) (Cockburn, 384). Grant (I, 380) says it met in Niddry Street before Adam Square.
1824 It was resolved to build an edifice in memory of James Watt and to include the School of Arts (Gilbert, 78).
1841 Building in Adam Square renamed the Watt Institution and School of Arts (Grant, I, 380).
1854 Statue of Watt erected outside (Grant, I, 380; Gilbert, 125).
1871 Building demolished for construction of Chambers Street, and in 1873-4 a new larger building was erected in that street (Grant, I, 380), designed by David Rhind (Grant, II, 275).
1879 Building handed over to the Heriot Trust and became the Heriot-Watt College (Grant, I, 382), and the enlarged building was opened in 1887.
1934 and 1958-9 Buildings enlarged.
1964 Accorded University status (Keir, 817).

1974 The main part of the Heriot-Watt University moved to Riccarton, the site having been gifted in 1969, but the original building in Chambers Street is still used, and James Watt's statue still stands outside.

Hermitage of Braid, off Comiston Road.

1785 House, designed by Adam brothers, built in the valley of the Braid Burn west of Blackford Hill, and was occupied by Gordon of Cluny (O.E.C., XXVII, 25; Grant, III, 41).

1888 The old Morningside Toll-house was demolished and rebuilt as the gatehouse (Smith, I, 170).

1938 House and grounds gifted to the city.

High Constables of Holyrood

Originally the Doorward Guard of Partizans (the historic equivalent of the English Yeoman of the Guard). A partizan was a weapon like a halberd. The Doorward Guard is the oldest martial body in Scotland, and dates from the 13th century. By an arrangement made after World War II between the Lord High Constable and the Lord Chamberlain the Doorward Guard is represented on ceremonial occasions by the Holyrood High Constables who wear the Lord High Constable's badge (Keir, 144). Presided over by the Bailie of Holyrood, the High Constables form a Guard of Honour on state occasions in Holyroodhouse.

High Riggs

The elevated ridge of ground lying south of the West Port and Grassmarket on a part of which George Heriot's Hospital (q.v.) was built (Grant, II, 222).

High Street

The High Street, or Hie Gait, extended from the Lawnmarket at the level of the present St. Giles Street to the Netherbow Port where the Canongate begins.

Contemporary writings quoted in Hume Brown's *Early Travellers in Scotland* describe the various authors' impressions of the High Street, mostly, but not invariably, favourable.

Holyrood Abbey

1128 Monastery of Holy Rood founded by David I (O.E.C., V, 41; X, 2; XIV, 102; Maitland, 6; 144; Arnot, 4; 252; Maxwell, 15; Smeaton, (a), 11). The name is said to derive from the Holy Rood, a remnant of the True Cross, which David found in his hand on his escape from the stag in Drumselch Forest (q.v.) (Fraser, 17).

1141 Augustinian Abbey completed and Augustinian Canons brought from St. Andrews (Steuart, 99).

1143 Text of David I's Charter to the Church (Grant, II, 42).

1296 Edward I stayed in the Abbey during his siege of the Castle (Fraser, 22).

1309 Trial of the Knights of the Temple (Grant, II, 50).

1322 Abbey burned by Edward II (Sitwell and Bamford, 29).

1327 Robert Bruce's parliament held (Wilson, I, 8).

1371 David II interred (Grant, II, 53; Fraser, 25).

1381 John of Gaunt entertained (Grant, II, 47; Steuart, 100).

1387 Church rebuilt (Smeaton, (a), 40).

1428 Alexander of the Isles submitted to James I (Grant, II, 54; Wilson, I, 19 and Smeaton, (a), 18, both give 1430; Steuart, 101, says 1429).

1430 James II born (Smeaton, (a), 22).

1435 Visit of Æneas Sylvius Piccolomini (later Pope Pius II) to James I (Steuart, 101).

1437 James II crowned (O.E.C., XVIII, 12; Arnot, 10; Maxwell, 54).

1460 James II killed at Roxburgh and buried in the Abbey (Grant, II, 55).

1464 Restoration of Holyrood Church.

1469 James III married Margaret of Denmark (Wilson, I, 25; Maxwell, 73; Russell, 141).

1490 Royal Porch Built (Dunlop and Dunlop, 74).

1502 Vaulted gateway erected by Merlioun (O.E.C., I, 13; Wilson, I, 35).

1503 James IV married Margaret Tudor (Maxwell, 84).

1524 James V crowned (Grant, II, 62).

1537 Queen Madeleine (Magdalene) died (O.E.C., X, 166; Wilson, I, 55; Grant, II, 64). This was the first time that mournings were worn in Scotland.

1542 James V buried (Wilson, I, 58; Grant, II, 65).

1544 and 1547 Abbey severely damaged in Hertford's raids.

1559 Abbey used as Parish Church of the Canongate.

1565 Marriage of Mary, Queen of Scots, and Henry, Lord Darnley (Maxwell, 127; Smeaton, (a), 85; Grant, II, 68, says that this took place in Stirling).

1567 Nobles laid waste to the Abbey (Grant, II, 58).

1590 Queen Anne, James VI's wife, crowned (Wilson, I, 113).

1596 Princess Elizabeth, future Queen of Bohemia, baptised (Grant, II, 72).

1600 Prince Charles baptised (Grant, II, 72).

1633 Charles I crowned (Grant, II, 58).

c.1686 James VII (II) converted Abbey into a Roman Catholic Chapel Royal (Maitland, 142).

1687 Chapel Royal given to the Knights of the Thistle (O.E.C., XVIII, 31; Wilson, I, 138; Grant, II, 58; Maxwell, 247).

1688 Presbyterian mob violated the Royal Vault (Arnot, 181; Grant, II, 59).

1753 Royal Porch destroyed (Wilson, I, 35; Dunlop and Dunlop, 74).

1755 Abbey Gate "having outlived the Stewart sovereigns as well as the Canons by whom and for whom it was built, was razed, why we know not, to the ground." (Malcolm, (a), 63; O.E.C., I, 13, says 1753).

1758 New roof placed on (unsafe) Abbey (Maxwell, 247).

1768 That roof collapsed (O.E.C., IV, 192; Arnot, 254; Grant, II, 59; Maxwell, 248).

1848 Remains of Mary of Gueldres brought from Trinity College Church (q.v.) and buried in the Abbey (Grant, II, 58; Scotsman, 15-5-1948).

Holyroodhouse

"A virtuous place where no monarch dwells." (Hamilton of Bangour, quoted by Boswell, 26). "The palace of Holyrood-house is an elegant piece of architecture, but sunk in an obscure . . . unwholesome bottom, where one imagines it had been place on purpose to be concealed." (Smollett, 273). "The Palace of Holyrood has been left aside in the growth of Edinburgh, and stands grey and silent in a workman's quarter among breweries and gas works." (R. L. Stevenson, *Edinburgh — Picturesque Notes,* (1896), 5).

1490 Abbey Sanctuary and Court House built (Malcolm, (a), 49; 64).

1498 Holyrood Palace founded by James IV (O.E.C., II, app 8; Wilson, II, 260).

1502 Holyroodhouse built by James IV (Arnot, 305; Wilson, I, 35; Maxwell, 117).

1512 James V born in Holyrood.

1515–16 Palace enlarged (Wilson, I, 48).

c.1528 James V extended the Palace (Maitland, 152; Malcolm, (a), 78, says 1530–40).

Palace of Holyroodhouse.

1538 Mary of Guise, who had married James V at St. Andrews, arrived at the Palace (Wilson, I, 57; Grant, II, 64; 222; Maxwell, 106).

1544 and 1547 Palace damaged during Hertford's raids.

1561 Palace repaired for Mary, Queen of Scots.

1566 David Rizzio murdered (Arnot, 28; Wilson, I, 97; Grant, I, 317; II, 70; Maxwell, 131; Smeaton, (a), 86).

1567 Mary married James Bothwell (Wilson, II, 8; Grant, II, 71; Maxwell, 134; Smeaton, (a), 89) in the Parish Church of the Canongate, formerly the nave of the Abbey (Steuart, 111).

1591 Bothwell's attempted seizure of James VI (O.E.C., XVI, app. 14; Wilson, II, 3; Grant, II, 72).

1646 The Dukes of Hamilton have been Hereditary Keepers of the Palace of Holyroodhouse since this date (Keir, 143).

1650 Accidental fire during occupation of Palace by Oliver Cromwell's troops (O.E.C., XVI, 52; Wilson, I, 125; Grant, II, 73; Maxwell, 117).

1658 Cromwell partly rebuilt Palace (Grant, II, 73).

1671 Palace reconstructed by Robert Mylne to the design of William Bruce for Charles II (Grant, II, 74; Maxwell, 117; Maitland, 152 says 1674).

1679-82 James, Duke of York, in the Palace (Steuart, 114).

1684-5 James de Witt's (Jacob de Wet's) portraits for the Palace (Maxwell, 71; Smeaton, (a), 235).

1688 Mob purged Palace of its Roman Catholic ornaments (Fraser, 122).

1745 Prince Charles held his Court (Maxwell, 196). "The first three Hanoverian kings never saw Holyroodhouse and took no interest in it." (O.E.C., XXIII, 40).

1746 Duke of Cumberland spent a night in the Palace after Culloden (Williamson, 83).

1796-1802 Comte d'Artois, later Charles X of France, in Palace whilst in Sanctuary (q.v.) (Malcolm, (a), 153).

1822 George IV held Court in Palace, the first monarch to visit Scotland since Charles II.

1831 Charles X of France returned to Palace, in Sanctuary again (O.E.C., XV, 96; Grant, II, 78; Maxwell, 251).

1834 The Palace of Holyroodhouse has been the official residence of the Lord High Commissioner to the General Assembly of the Church of Scotland since this date (Keir, 142). (See Assembly Hall).

1851 Statue of Queen Victoria erected in the forecourt (Malcolm, (a), 49).

1857 Northern approach planned by Prince Albert.

1857-8 Abbey Sanctuary and Court House rebuilt (Malcolm, (a), 49; 64).

1861 Prince Consort erected a fountain, a copy of that in Linlithgow Palace (Fraser, 81) in place of Queen Victoria's statue (Malcolm, (a), 49; *Edinburgh — An Architectural Guide* says 1859).

1911 Extensive alterations to fit Holyroodhouse as a royal residence for George V.
1922 Scottish National Memorial to Edward VII unveiled by George V.

Holyrood Park, formerly King's (Queen's) Park.
The park belongs to the Crown and includes Arthur's Seat (q.v.). It was named King's or Queen's Park because it was "formerly dedicated to the preservation of the royal game." (Scott, *Heart of Midlothian,* chap. 9).
1540 Park enclosed by James V (O.E.C., XVIII, 184).
1849 Portion set aside for the public to bleach and dry clothes (Scotsman, 18-7-1849).
1857 St. Margaret's (artificial) Loch formed (Malcolm, (a), 96).
1860 Royal Volunteer Review on parade ground east of Holyrood Palace (Grant, II, 284).
1862 St. Margaret's Well (q.v.) brought from Restalrig and erected (Grant, II, 312).
1881 'Wet Review' on parade ground.

Honours of Scotland see Regalia.

Horse Racing
1504 James IV said to have had horses raced for him on Leith Sands.
1665 Horse racing on Leith Sands an annual event (Marshall, 46). (These sands are now reclaimed and built over, the original line being just north of Bernard Street.)
1665 His Majesty's Gold Plate established as the principal trophy (Marshall, 48).
1753 Management in the hands of the Company of Scots Hunters (Marshall, 49).
1816 Racing transferred from Leith to Musselburgh (Grant, III, 270).

Horse Wynd, Canongate — south side, at the Abbey Strand.
1560's Scottish Mint was in the region of the Horse Wynd (Grant, I, 267; Chambers, 260; Smeaton, (a), 208).
c.1775 Buildings erected into better-class flats (R.C., 183).

Horse Wynd, Chambers Street — north side.
This was the only possible descent for horses and carriages from the southern suburbs to the Royal Mews and the Cowgate (O.E.C., XII, 143; Wilson, II, 143; Grant, II, 256; Chambers, 244).
    The Wynd is now represented by steps from Chambers Street to join Guthrie Street (q.v.) and so to the Cowgate.

Hospitals
This list includes asylums, workhouses, poorhouses and

dispensaries. It excludes the Royal Infirmary and the Royal Colleges of Physicians and Surgeons which are recorded separately. Some schools and colleges were originally called hospitals, and are recorded elsewhere.

Charity Hospitals, Poorhouses, Workhouses, Orphanages

1733 Orphan Hospital (q.v.) built north-west of Trinity College Church (q.v.) (Maitland, 464; Arnot, 561; Grant, I, 359).

1743 Charity Workhouse built west of Bristo Street (Maitland, 430; Arnot, 559; Grant, II, 325; Robertson, 285) near the site of Bedlam (q.v.).

1761 Canongate Charity Workhouse (Arnot, 559).

1810 Deaf and Dumb Institution, Henderson Row, founded (Grant, III, 84). This was rebuilt in 1823 (Grant, III, 85) and the building was sold to the neighbouring Edinburgh Academy in 1977, the pupils being transferred to Donaldson's School for the Deaf (q.v.).

1831 Dean Orphanage (q.v.) built (Grant, III, 67).

1842-51 Donaldson's Hospital, West Coates, built (q.v.), originally for poor children (O.E.C., II, app. 6; Grant, II, 214; Smeaton, (a), 306, says 1851).

1868 Craigleith Poorhouse erected (Robertson, 304), now Western General Hospital.

1870 Craiglockhart Poorhouse opened (O.E.C., XXII, 55), now Greenlea Old People's Home, Glenlockhart Road.

Asylums

1793 Royal Blind Asylum, Shakespeare Square (Grant, II, 336).

1797 Magdalene Asylum for females near Canongate Tolbooth (Grant, II, 31).

1806 Blind Asylum moved to Nicolson Street (Grant, II, 336).

1809 Royal Edinburgh Asylum for the Insane, Morningside (O.E.C., X, 209; Grant, III, 39), became in 1965 the Royal Edinburgh Hospital. West House was built in 1837 and Craighouse was opened in 1894.

1822 Asylum for females, Nicolson Street (Grant, II, 336).

1876 Royal Blind Asylum and School, West Craigmillar (Gilbert, 152; Grant, III, 51, says 1877).

1923 Royal Blind Asylum workshops, Gillespie Crescent (Keir, 1008), moved in 1977 to Craigmillar.

Dispensaries

1776 First dispensary, West Richmond Street (Arnot, 552; Grant, I. 384).

1815 New Town Dispensary (Cockburn, 283).

Hospitals

1729 First Infirmary, Robertson's Close (see Royal Infirmary).

1793 Edinburgh General Lying-in Hospital, Park House (site of present University Union) (Turner, 100).
1835 Royal Maternity Hospital, St. John Street (Grant, II, 27).
1850 Leith Hospital (Grant, III, 248). New wing added after World War I as a War Memorial, subscribed by the people of Leith.
1860 Children's Hospital, Lauriston Lane (Grant, II, 362).
1864 Royal Infirmary Convalescent Home, Corstorphine (Turner, 175).
1864 Chalmers Hospital, Lauriston Place (O.E.C., XVIII, 164; Grant, II, 363).
c.1870 Eye and Ear Infirmary, Cambridge Street (R. Scott Stevenson and Douglas Guthrie, *A History of Otolaryngology*, (1949), 108). Discontinued after World War II.
1878 Simpson Memorial Hospital, Lauriston Place (Grant, II, 362), opened in the following year.
1879 Dental Hospital and School (q.v.), Chambers Street (Grant, II, 276).
1880 Longmore Hospital for Incurables (founded, 1874) (Grant, III, 55; Smith, I, 29, says opened in 1875). It was built in Salisbury Place (Grant, III, 50). Now a general hospital.
1886 Bruntsfield Hospital for Women, Whitehouse Loan (Keir, 322). The early hospital was in Grove Street and moved to Whitehouse Loan in 1898 and was rebuilt in 1911 (Smith, I, 55).
1894 Royal Victoria Hospital, Comely Bank, opened for treatment of tuberculosis, now a geriatric assessment centre.
1895 Royal Hospital for Sick Children (1860) moved to Sciennes Road after five years at Plewlands House, Morningside.
1896 Deaconess Hospital, Pleasance.
1896 Leith Public Health Home, Ferry Road, became Northern General Hospital in 1955.
1903 City Fever Hospital, Greenbank Drive (Keir, 1008), now a general hospital.
1925 Elsie Inglis Memorial Hospital, Spring Gardens (Keir, 322).
1932 Princes Margaret Rose Orthopaedic Hospital, Fairmilehead.

Hunter Square, near Tron Church.
1788 Square built on site of Peebles Wynd (q.v.), named after Lord Provost Hunter Blair (Grant, I, 245).
1788 Merchants' Hall (q.v.), later a branch of the Royal Bank of Scotland, in Hunter Square (Grant, I, 376; 376; R.C., 101).

Hunter's Bog see Salisbury Crags.

Huntly House, 146 Canongate — south side.
Tradition ascribes it, erroneously, to the first Marquess of Huntly (R.C., 168). See Bakehouse Close.

1517 House built (*Edinburgh Official Guide,* 1971).

1570 House reconstructed (O.E.C., XVII, 30; Chambers, 312).

1591 House rebuilt (O.E.C., XI, 10; Wilson, II, 102).

1647 Hammermen bought Huntly House (O.E.C., XX, 79).

1924 House bought by city (O.E.C., XIV, 1-5) and restored in 1932 as a City Museum containing relics of local history, charters, maps, prints, pictures etc.

1968 Museum extended to adjoining house on the east.

Hyndford's Close, 34 High Street — south side.

17th century House built in Close late in 17th century (R.C., 99).

1742 Home of the Earl of Selkirk (Grant, I, 274). It was next owned by Daniel Rutherford, Professor of Botany and inventor of the gas lamp (Grant, I, 274) and uncle of Walter Scott (Chambers, 264).

1868 Described as "inaccessible, literally, from filth" (Chambers, 275).

1959 Reconstructed as Museum of Childhood, the entry to which is immediately west of the Close which leads to a small open courtyard.

Ice Age

(Condensed from an article by J. B. Sissons, Scotsman, 27-1-1973).

Building activity in central Edinburgh necessitated the investigation of the ground by boreholes, and the results of some 1400 in the area of two square miles around the Castle were studied. The underlying foundation is provided by ancient solid rocks, such as sandstone, shales and lava. Beneath the Castle, at Calton Hill, and in Holyrood Park the solid rock rises up boldly because it is peculiarly resistant and has remained while the surrounding weaker rocks have been eroded by glacier ice.

One or two million years ago Scotland was covered by a vast, slow-moving ice-sheet which attained a depth of at least 2000 feet (616m) over Edinburgh. The ice-sheet was deflected by the upthrust of the Castle Rock, Salisbury Crags, the Calton Hill, and, to a lesser extent, George Street and Lauriston on ridges parallel with the Royal Mile, and each shows around it the broad sweep of movement of the glazier. In a few places this was followed by melt-water rivers that existed when the ice finally disappeared, probably between 13,000 and 14,000 years ago. One such river course may be marked by a shallow valley, noted on some old plans of Edinburgh, beneath the former Princes Street Station, leading towards Castle Terrace where boreholes showed a belt of river-deposited sand and gravel up to 30 feet (9m) thick and several hundred yards long. This glacial river then flowed eastward through the Grassmarket-Cowgate depression.

Numerous small lakes were left by the melting ice, the largest being at Corstorphine and the deepest being that which preceded the later (artificial) Nor' Loch where a borehole showed 80 feet (25m) of peat. Peat, silt and clay gradually filled in the lakes in the Meadows (South Loch) and near Holyrood until all these lakes were eventually drained or filled in by man.

Ice Rinks
There were two, the older being at Haymarket, near the Station, built in 1912 (Keir, 1008), and which was the centre for curling; and the more recent one at Murrayfield, near the rugby ground, built in 1939 (Keir, 1008), which was involved for a short time with ice hockey until the interest died (Keir, 540) and is now predominantly used for skating.

Curling and skating were always popular when Blackford and Duddingston Lochs and the Nor' Loch froze over.

1740's Duddingston Curling Club formed.

1778 Edinburgh Skating Club formed (O.E.C., XXXIII, 96-136). This existed until World War II after which it did not re-open, and it was wound up in 1966.

1838 The international legislative body for curlers was formed in Edinburgh, and became the Royal Caledonian Curling Club in 1842 (Keir, 539).

1978 Haymarket Ice Rink sold, and curlers use the Murrayfield one or a new rink at Gogar Park House.

Improvement Act
1867 An Act for improving the City of Edinburgh and constructing new, and widening, altering, improving and diverting existing streets in the city (Wood *et al.,* 33). This led to the construction of Market Street, Cranston Street, Jeffrey Street, Blackfriars Street, St. Mary's Street, Chambers Street, Guthrie Street, Lady Lawson Street, Marshall Street and Howden Street (Wood *et al.,* 34).

The first tenement erected under the Act was at the corner of St. Mary's Street and the Canongate (Peacock, 39) and this bears a plaque.

Inch House, Liberton.
1617 House built on lands belonging to the monks of Holyrood (Grant, III, 338; Geddie, 128).

1892 House enlarged (Geddie, 128).

Presently the house and grounds form the Inch Community Centre.

Incorporations and Guilds
1449 Corporation of Cordiners (Shoemakers) (Maitland, 305; Grant, II, 263; R.C., xliii).

1473 Seal of Cause★ to Hatmakers† (Wood *et al.*, 272; Grant, II, 265).

1474 Seal of Cause★ to Weavers (Websters) (Wood *et al.*, 272).

1475 Incorporation of Masons and Wrights (cabinet makers) (Maitland, 301; Arnot, 527; Grant, II, 264; Smeaton, (a), 41).

1475 Incorporation of Weavers (Maitland, 307; Arnot, 529; Grant, II, 264, says 1476).

1483 Seal of Cause★ to Hammermen (O.E.C., XIX, 1-30; Maitland, 299; Arnot, 527; Grant, II, 263; Smeaton, (a), 52).

1483 Seal of Cause★ to Fleshers (Wood *et al.*, 272; Grant, II, 265, says 1488; Maitland, 303, says date unknown).

1488 Earliest reference to Candlemakers (O.E.C., XVII, 93; Maitland, 311).

1489 Seal of Cause★ to Coopers† (Wood *et al.*, 272; Grant, II, 265).

1500 Incorporation of Tailors (O.E.C., XXII, 91-131; Maitland, 301; Wilson, II, 288; Grant, II, 266).

1500 Seal of Cause★ to Waulkers (Cloth-fullers) (Wood *et al.*, 272; Grant, II, 265).

1505 Corporation of Surgeons and Barbers (O.E.C., IV, 13; Maitland, 294; Arnot, 524; Grant, I, 382; Maxwell, 81).

1517 Incorporation of Candlemakers† (O.E.C., XVII, 91-146; Chambers, 312; Wilson, II, 287; Grant, II, 266).

1518 Merchant Guild (Wood *et al.*, 272).

1522 Incorporation of Baxters (Bakers) (Arnot, 528; Grant, II, 266).

1530 Incorporation of Bonnetmakers (Maitland, 309; Arnot, 529; Grant, II, 265).

1533 Seal of Cause★ to Furriers.

1538 Incorporation of Cordiners (Shoemakers) (O.E.C., XVIII, 100-150; Wilson, II, 96).

1546 Tailors of Canongate incorporated (O.E.C., XXII, 91).

1556 Self-government of Craft Guilds recognised (O.E.C., XIV, 26).

1564 Constitution to be observed by Litsters (Dyers) (O.E.C., XII, 50, f.n.; Maitland, 317).

1586 Goldsmiths separated from Hammermen (Maitland, 296; Grant, I, 376).

1610 Hammermen, Tailors, Baxters and Cordiners combined (O.E.C., XIV, 25-48).

1631 Incorporated Trades of Calton (O.E.C., XVII, app. 17).

1672 Hatters united with Waulkers (Clothiers) (Arnot, 529).

1684 Litsters (Dyers) united with Bonnetmakers (Roberston, 127; Grant, II, 265, says 1685).

†Means that the Incorporation was among those having no Deacon on the Town Council.

★A seal of cause meant a Charter (Dunlop and Dunlop, 149) the purpose of which was to ensure the efficiency of new applicants, to raise money to fund altars (usually in St. Giles Church), and to look after widows and retired members.

1722 Barbers came out of Corporation of Surgeons (O.E.C., IV, 13; Maitland, 296, Arnot, 525, Grant, I, 383, Maxwell, 141).

1727 Board of Fisheries and Manufacturers established (Grant, II, 83); separated in 1828.

1852 Cordiners Incorporation disbanded (O.E.C., XVIII, 150).

1877 End of Incorporation of Tailors of Canongate (O.E.C., XXII, 91).

1884 End of Incorporation of Candlemakers (O.E.C., XVII, 137).

The Guilds played a part in the Town Council until the Reform Bill of 1832, each of fourteen Incorporations being entitled to one representative or Deacon. However, only six Deacons attended every meeting, the remaining eight being present at certain meetings. Thus the Guilds played only a minor role, the control being in the hands of the Merchants. (See Dean of Guild's Court and Town Council).

Ingliston, see Royal Highland and Agricultural Society.

Inns and Taverns
(See Stuart, *Old Edinburgh Taverns* and Chambers, 158-175).

Some Inns have been mentioned individually, and only a selection is noted here. Information about many of the Closes will be found under their names.

An Inn about the early 18th century.

Inns and taverns abounded in the Old Town and, unlike their modern counterparts, many formed the focal point of learned and witty discussion, and were the meeting place of clubs and societies.

The common drinks were claret and ale; the increase in whisky drinking came after 1707. Port wine was first imported into the city in 1743 (O.E.C., II, 5, f.n.) and champagne was not imported until 1815 (Cockburn, 35).

1424 First inns in the town (Smeaton, (a), 20).

1425 A statute encouraged hostelries by decreeing that travellers were liable to a penalty of forty shillings Scots (16p) if they took up an abode with friends when there was an inn available (Stuart, 10).

Many old inns were below street level "to be removed from profane eyes" (Stuart, 12). The guid-wife who welcomed the customers was called the 'Lucky' (Stuart, 12). Old inns contained one or more cell-like rooms, lit by tallow candles, and some having no window-spaces.

"The public inns of Edinburgh are still worse than those of London." (Smollett, 267). "Before the eighteenth century closed the old-fashioned and unwholesome inn of which we read in the pages of Smollett's *Humphry Clinker* [1771] had to a large extent been transformed into the modern hotel." (O.E.C., XIV, 121).

Arnot (352) deplored the fact that formerly strangers were put into accommodation more suited to a waggoner or carrier, but noted the improvement resulting in several hotels "in which strangers of any rank may find accommodation suited to their wishes."

As tavern life played such a large part in the social habits of the old town, and as Inn names are to be found widely in literature, brief notes are given of some.

(i) Laigh coffee houses and taverns clustered near Parliament House and the Royal Exchange. The first coffee house was opened in Parliament Close c.1673 (Grant, I, 178) and was closed in 1677. John's Coffee House is dealt with elsewhere.

Peter Williamson's coffee house was at the narrow entrance leading to the court rooms (Stuart, 35). Peter Williamson published the first *Directory of Edinburgh* (1773-4) and introduced the first penny post (1774-5).

Robert Clark's Tavern, Parliament Close (Stuart, 36).

John Dowie's, Liberton's Wynd, was in this narrow lane west of St. Giles sloping down to the Cowgate. It contained a number of rooms, the largest holding fourteen people and the smallest, 'The Coffin', only six at a squeeze. It was famed for the excellence of its dishes, much appreciated by David Hume among others. The Coffin was the haunt of Robert Burns when staying in Baxter's Close in 1786. When Dowie died in 1817 the new owner erected a sign 'Burns Tavern, late John Dowie' (Stuart, 41-6; Grant, I, 3).

Cleriheugh's Tavern, 'Star and Garter' in Writers' Court, near the Royal Exchange (Stuart, 46; Chambers, 162; Wilson, II, 17; Grant, I, 120) was described by Scott in *Guy Mannering*, chap. 36.

James Mann's Tavern, Craig's Close, near Royal Exchange, where the Cape Club met (Stuart, 48).

Dawnay Douglas's Tavern, Anchor Close, was a superior tavern with a separate doorway for important patrons which led into the Crown Room (Grant, I, 235). It was used by the Crochallan Fencibles (see Clubs) (Stuart, 52). William Smellie, the printer, had a business in the same Close where Robert Burns corrected the proofs of his poems for the Edinburgh Edition (Stuart, 54).

Fortune's Tavern, Old Stamp Close (Grant, I, 231; Wilson, II, 29; Chambers, 161) was also a superior tavern with a handsome pillared doorway leading to what had been the Earl of Eglintoun's town mansion. It was popular with those attending concerts in St. Cecilia's Hall (Stuart, 55).

Patrick Steel's (Steil's) Tavern, Steel's Close which was later named the Old Assembly Close (q.v.) (Stuart, 58).

Stewart's Oyster House, Old Fishmarket Close, where the Mirror Club met (Stuart, 60).

Covenant House (Tavern), Covenant Close (Grant, I, 245), contained a long room with panelled walls and a secret door. The National Covenant was said to have been renewed here (Stuart, 61).

James Clark's Tavern, Fleshmarket Close (Stuart, 63) was patronised by Deacon Brodie.

Paterson's Tavern, Fleshmarket Close, where the Marrow Bone Club met (Stuart, 63).

(ii) Further from the centre, in the Lawnmarket and Cowgate were—

Thomas Nicholson's Carriers' Inn, West Bow, where the Poker Club met in 1762. This club was to 'poke up' resentment against England's treatment of Scotland (Stuart, 67).

Ball Tavern, opposite Lady Stair's House (Stuart, 71).

Rose and Thistle Tap, Dunbar's Close, Lawnmarket, was said to have been the guardroom of Cromwell's troops after the Battle of Dunbar (1650). Over the doorway was carved 'Faith in Crist onlie savit, 1567'. The Orange Lodge is reputed to have met here (Stuart, 73).

Lockhart's House, Cowgate, later housed the museum of the Society of Antiquaries (Stuart, 74).

Lord Duncan's Tavern, Cowgate, where the High Constables of Holyrood dined (Stuart, 75).

(iii) The stablers' inns were grouped around the Ports in the

Town Walls because the streets were too crowded for stage coaches to penetrate into the town.

White Horse Inn (q.v.) at the foot of the Canongate in White Horse Close, is believed to date from 1603 (Stuart, 108).

Jenny Ha's Change House, Callender's Entry, near Whitefoord House, Canongate (q.v.), was a resort of the poets Gay, Allan Ramsay and others (Stuart, 93).

White Hart Inn, Grassmarket, near the Cowgate Port, where Robert Burns lodged in 1791 (Scotsman, 3-3-1938) and William Wordsworth in 1803 (Chambers, 171; Stuart, 118). This inn is still in business, but, inevitably, 'Ye Olde' has been added to the name.

Boyd's Inn (q.v.), St. Mary's Wynd, near the Netherbow Port, was also known as the White Horse Inn.

Red Lion Inn, at the foot of St. Mary's Wynd, near the Cowgate Port, had exensive stabling, and was taken over in 1760 by Peter Ramsay (Stuart, 115).

George Inn, Bristo Port (Stuart, 122).

Selkirk and Peebles Inn, Candlemaker Row, opposite Bristo Port (Stuart, 125).

Harrow Inn, near Candlemakers' Hall (Stuart, 126).

Black Bull Inn, Grassmarket, on the site of the present Beehive Restaurant (Stuart, 130).

King's Head Inn (or Palfrey's), at Cowgatehead, the east end of the Grassmarket (Stuart, 133) from where stage coaches left for various parts of Scotland or England.

(iv) With the building of the North Bridge in 1763 inns were opened at its northern end—

Daniel Hogg's, Shakespeare Square (Stuart, 81).

Boyle's Tavern (1793), Shakespeare Square. This was taken over by Charles Oman in 1803 and two years later moved to West Register Street (Stuart, 81). The Friday Club met here (Youngson, 247).

Barry's Tavern, near the present Waverley steps in 1822, moved to Queen Street in 1832 where it housed the Gowks Club, the Friday Club and the Oyster Club (Stuart, 83).

Rainbow Tavern at the north end of the North Briidege (Stuart, 85).

Ambrose's Tavern "up the crooked alley which still marks the site of Gabriel's Road" (Stuart, 86); in West Register Street (Grant, II, 171). It was the locus of 'Noctes Ambrosianae' where met James Hogg (the Ettrick Shepherd), Professor John Wilson (Christopher North), Robert Sym (Timothy Tickler) and others in 1825-35 for debating and feasting (Stuart, 86). The three-storey building was demolished in 1864, but it is regarded as the original site of the present Cafe Royal, built in 1862 (*Edinburgh Weekly*, 21-10-1966).

Institute of Chartered Accountants of Scotland
Late in the 17th century there were "at least two accountants who acted for clients" (Keir, 588). About the same time Robert Colinson taught book-keeping and published in the city a treatise on accountancy (Keir, 588).
1705 John Dickson was created Master and Professor of Book-holding by the Town Council (Keir, 589).
1854 Incorporation of the Society of Accountants in Edinburgh (Keir, 588).
1951 Name changed to the Institute of Chartered Accountants of Scotland (Keir, 588) and the present office is in Queen Street.

Insurance Companies
1720 Edinburgh Friendly Insurance against Losses by Fire (Gray, 93), absorbed by Sun Life in 1847 (Keir, 579).
1727 Edinburgh Insurance Company (Maitland, 329; Gray, 94).
1733 Sun Life Office established an Edinburgh branch (Youngson, 24; Gray, 95).
1805 Caledonian Fire Insurance Company (Grant, II, 139; Gray, 97).
1809 North British Insurance Company (Grant, II, 123; Gray, 97) became the North British and Mercantile in 1862 and in the 1960's the shares were acquired by the Commercial Union (Keir, 581).
1814 Scottish Widows' Fund (Grant, II, 167; Gray, 97; Keir, 582, says 1815).
1821 Insurance Company of Scotland (Gray, 98).
1823 Edinburgh Life Assurance Company (Gray, 98), absorbed by an English company in the early 1900's (Keir, 579).
1824 Scottish Union Insurance Company (Gray, 103).
1825 Standard Life Assurance Company (Keir, 582).
1826 Scottish Amicable Insurance Company.
1831 Scottish Equitable Insurance Company (Grant, II, 170).
1838 Life Association of Scotland (Keir, 580); new building, designed by David Rhind, in Princes Street completed in 1858 (Grant, II, 123).
1838 Scottish Provident Institution (Grant, II, 168; Keir, 581, says 1837).
1841 Scottish National Insurance Company (Gray, 142).
1877 Scottish Insurance Corporation (Keir, 581); shares acquired by the Yorkshire Insurance Company.
1878 Scottish Union and Scottish National amalgamated to form Scottish Union and National Insurance Company (Gray, 178); absorbed by the Norwich Union.
1881 Scottish Life Assurance Company (Keir, 581).
1885 Century Insurance Company (Keir, 580).

Invasions and Raids, see also Castle.
1385 Town laid in ruins by Richard II's army (Wilson, I, 17; II, 225;

Smeaton, (a), 16; 40).
1482 Invasion by Gloucester (Arnot, 12).
1544 Hertford landed troops at Granton on orders from Henry VIII who was incensed because of the refusal that the infant Mary (later Queen of Scots) be surrendered to his custody for future marriage to his son, Prince Edward (O.E.C., XVI, app. 13; Grant, III, 169) and sacked the town (O.E.C., II, 66; III, 59; Maitland, 13; Arnot, 18; 253; Wilson, I, 66; Grant, II, 57; Maxwell, 111; Russell, 258).
1547 Hertford's second raid following the Battle of Pinkie (O.E.C., XIV, 51; Maitland, 13; Wilson, I, 68; Grant, II, 57; 65; III, 170) when he held the title of Protector Somerset.
   "That Hertford's two invasions were unnecessarily savage — truly Turkish in their atrocities as dictated, in the first instance, by the order of Henry VIII — is perfectly well known." (Grant, III, 218).
1650 Cromwell occupied city after the Battle of Dunbar and placed it under martial law (Grant, I, 55).
1689 Castle surrendered to William III (O.E.C., XVI, 171-213; Arnot, 183; Maxwell, 180; Williamson, 78; Sitwell and Bamford, 144, say 1690).

Inverleith, see Botanic Garden.

Jack's Land, see Little Jack's Close.

Jacobite Rebellions
1715 The city took no share in the rising (Wilson, I, 143) although there were plots to seize the Castle and city for the Old Pretender (Maitland, 118; Arnot, 191; Maxwell, 186).
1745 Prince Charles in Edinburgh for six weeks (O.E.C., II, 1-60; IV, 38; Arnot, 211; Maitland, 128; Wilson, I, 146; Grant, I, chaps. 40-1; Maxwell, 197; Williamson, 82).
   "Edinburgh had not much cause to be pround of her conduct in 1745. If she did little for King George [II], she did less for Prince Charles." (O.E.C., II, 55). "Of the ladies, two-thirds proclaimed themselves Jacobites, and one-third of the men were of the same persuasion." (Maxwell, 188).
1745 Edinburgh Volunteers (Maitland, 126; Maxwell, 190; Carlyle, 121; Williamson, 81; Steuart, 128).
1745 Lord Provost Stewart arrested in London and sent to Edinburgh for trial (Arnot, 222). There was no Town Council during 1745-6 (Arnot, 230).
1746 Lord Provost Stewart found not guilty of treason (Arnot, 222).

James Gillespie's Hospital (School)
1805 Built on the site of Wrychtis (Wright's) House (q.v.) as a hospital

for aged men and a separate free school for boys. Founded by James Gillespie (died 1797), tobacco merchant and owner of a snuff mill and a house at Spylaw, Colinton (Cockburn, 173; Keir, 797). The house is in Spylaw Park.

1870 New fee-paying school for boys and girls (Grant, III, 35; Keir, 797) in the vacated hospital (Smith, I, 71).

1904 Renamed James Gillespie's School (Keir, 797) and moved in 1914 to a site overlooking Bruntsfield Links vacated by the move of Boroughmuir School to Viewforth (Keir, 797).

1929 Warrender Park School, Marchmont Road, became James Gillespie's Boys' School (closed in 1975) and the other became James Gillespie's Girls' School.

1966 Girls' Secondary School moved to new buildings in Warrender House estate (see Bruntsfield House), and the Primary School for Girls is also sited there. Boroughmuir Primary School occupies the old buildings.

1972 Renamed James Gillespie's High School on becoming a co-educational comprehensive school.

James's Court, 501 Lawnmarket — north side.

1727 Court built by James Brownhill (Chambers, 55; Wilson, I, 207; Grant, I, 98; Malcolm, (b), 20, says 1720; W. Harrrison, 2, says that the date above the entrance was 1690; O.E.C., III, 247, says that it was 1723).

The most fashionable flats of the 18th century were in the court where the owners held private dances and employed their own scavenger to clean the Court. Among those living there were the Earl of Aberdeen, Ilay Campbell who became Lord President of the Court of Session, Sir John Clerk of Penicuik, Lord Bankton and Dr. James Gregory of Gregory's powder fame (Steuart, 24).

1762-71 Home of David Hume (Grant, I, 98).

1771 James Boswell lived here and entertained General Paoli, the Corsican chief (Grant, I, 299; Chambers, 172).

1773 Boswell entertained Dr. Johnson before their tour to the Hebrides (Grant, I, 99; Boswell, 11).

1790 Declined as a fashionable residence with the development of the New Town.

1857 Boswell's house burned (Grant, I, 98, says 1858). Savings Bank built on the site but later removed (Grant, I, 98) to Hanover Street and the building is now H.M. Commissary Office.

1861 Free Church Offices designed by David Cousin in James's Court extending to North Bank Street (Grant, I, 98).

1900's Patrick Geddes, pioneer in sociology, lived here (Keir, 47).

Now this court is approached by three closes, each labelled James's Court. The west block of buildings remains facing on to

North Bank Street, and there is considerable restoration of the remainder of the court at present.

Jeffrey Street, High Street — north side at Netherbow.
1867 Jeffrey Street built (Grant, I, 290) under the Improvement Act (q.v.) on the line of the old Leith Wynd.

Jock's Lodge, junction of Portobello and Willowbrae Roads.
"Long a wayside hamlet, on the lonely path that led to the Figgate Muir [see Figgate Whins], is said to have derived its name from an eccentric mendicant known as *Jock*, who built himself a hut there; and historically the name appears first in 1650." (Grant, III, 142).
1758 Louis Cauvin, teacher of French, owned the neighbouring farm (Grant, II, 318), and is buried in Restalrig Churchyard.

John Knox (1513-1572)
After taking orders he was captured by the French at St. Andrews in 1547; sentenced to labour in the galleys; released in 1549; and, after a ministry in Berwick and Newcastle, he fled to the continent. He returned in 1556; came to Scotland in 1559 and became minister at St. Giles, Edinburgh in 1560. Author of the *Book of Discipline*. Implacable opponent of Mary, Queen of Scots and Roman Catholicism, and saw Protestantism firmly established in 1561. Retired to St. Andrews in 1569 and returned to Edinburgh in 1572 where he died. Buried in St. Giles Burial Ground where the approximate site was marked in Parliament Square by a plaque engraved 'I.K. 1572' which was brought into St. Giles Church when the Close was covered by tarmacadam about 1970 (Fraser, 122).

John Knox's House, 45 High Street — north side.
Built not later than 1490 although the first mention of a house on this site was 1525 (R.C., 97). The Abbots of Dunfermline resided here (Steuart, 66).
1544 Partially destroyed by Hertford's troops.
1556 The home of James Mossman, goldsmith during the reign of Mary, Queen of Scots, who was imprisoned in the Castle for his allegiance (Steuart, 67) and was hanged in 1573. The house is regarded as the perfect example of domestic pre-Reformation architecture. It is four storeys high with timber projections and gables, of a later date, hanging over the street (*Edinburgh — An Architectural Guide*). The oak room dates from 1600.
Traditionally regarded as the dwelling house or manse of John Knox from 1560 to 1569 (R.C., 96) when he was minister at St. Giles (Grant, I, 212), but he lived in Warriston's Court from

John Knox's House and Moubray House (p. 152) to the left.

1560–66 (Catford, 28) and it seems likely that he lived in the house only for a short time before his death in 1572.
1849 Building condemned, but saved by the intervention of Lord Cockburn (Cruft, 23).

John's Coffee House
"A tavern, owned by John Row, under the piazzas at the entrance to Parliament Square, known, perhaps from the consumption of wine, as the 'Graping Office'." (Mackenzie, 223). An alternative suggestion for this name was that the tavern was celebrated by Dr. Archibald Pitcairne in his Latin lyric on Edinburgh Inns under the name of greppa — hence 'Greping Office', dubbed by the wits who groped their way down its dark stairs and underground passages (Stuart, 40).
1673 Coffee-house opened; closed by the Privy Council after a riot in 1677 (Sitwell and Bamford, 127).
1824 Building burned down in the great fire (Stuart, 40).

Johnston Terrace
1828 Johnston Terrace built (Robertson, 33), designed by Thomas Hamilton, its lower end crossing King's Stables Road by the King's Bridge. Living quarters for the families of the Castle garrison were built in 1873 on the south side, but these fell into disrepair and the building is now used as a workshop.

King's Buildings, see University of Edinburgh.

King's Park, see Holyrood Park.

King's Stables
The King's stables were at the foot of the Castle rock. There tournaments, weapon shows and other trials of arms were held, particularly in the reign of James IV (Williamson, 31).

c. 1663 City acquired the area (Grant, II, 225).

The modern road preserves the name of the royal mews which were situated here from the time of Robert II (1371-1390) (Smeaton, (b), 278). It is crossed by the King's Bridge at the lower end of Johnston Terrace.

Kirkbraehead
The site of St. John's Chapel which overlooked the rural parish of St. Cuthbert's (Wilson, II, 201). Grant (II, 136) puts the site as that of the Caledonian station (now demolished) and Forbes Gray (Scotsman, 16-1-1943) agrees.

Kirkbraehead was a three-storey mansion built in the middle of the 18th century (Grant, II, 136).

1776 Erection of Ranelagh Garden, a circular concert-room or rotunda with a ball-room (Forbes Gray, loc. cit.).

1790 Mansion occupied by Lord Elphinstone, Lieutenant Governor of the Castle (Forbes Gray, loc. cit.).

1869 Demolished for building of Caledonian station (Grant, II, 138).

Kirk o' Field
1275 The first record of the Collegiate Church of St. Mary-in-the-Fields which belonged to Holyrood Abbey (R.C., 125). It was founded by Alexander II (Steuart, 3).

The church was completely in the fields, beyond the wall of 1450, but within the Flodden Wall. The quadrangle of the University Old College occupies the exact site of the Church (Grant, III, 1).

1566 Kirk o' Field taken over by the Town for the Toun's College (Williamson, 245; Stewart, 8).

1567 Darnley murdered at Kirk o' Field (Arnot, 28; Chambers, 256; Wilson, I, 101; Grant, I, 263; II, 71; III, 3; Maxwell, 132).

1588 Church destroyed (Arnot, 243; Wilson, II, 246).

Krames
From German *Kramerei*— shopkeeping.

A low narrow arcade of booths along the north side of St. Giles Church, dating from 1550 or 1560 to 1817 (Maitland, 180;

Chambers, 102; Wilson, I, 256; Cockburn, 108; Dunlop and Dunlop, 79).

"A low arcade of booths, crammed in between the north side of St. Giles Cathedral and a thin range of buildings that stood parallel to the Cathedral, the eastmost of which buildings, looking down the High Street, was the famous shop of William Creech, the bookseller." (Cockburn, 108).

"Some roughly roofed over, others open to the sky, some tucked in between the buttresses and others pressed hard against the wall of the luckenbooths." (Catford, 44).

1817 Luckenbooths removed together with the krames (Cockburn, 109; Catford, 43).

Lady Stair's House, Lady Stair's Close, Lawnmarket — north side.

Lady Stair's Close was originally called Lady Gray's Close after the wife of the builder of the House (Chambers, 63, f.n.) which is the only remaining relic of the Close.

1622 House built by Sir William Gray of Pittendrum, and bears the date. (O.E.C., III, 243-252; XI, 13; Wilson, I, 212; Grant, I, 102).

18th century The house was the home of the widow of the first Earl of Stair. Lady Stair died in 1759 (Chambers, 69).

1781 When the Mound was begun a road was cut through the garden thus converting the Close into the "principal communication between the Lawnmarket and Hanover Street, then the western extremity of the New Town." (Chambers, 63, f.n.). This Close still opens into North Bank Street.

1895 Lord Rosebery purchased the House (Maxwell, 254).

1907 Lord Rosebery gave the House to the city (O.E.C., III, 244; Maxwell, 254).

The House is presently a museum of relics of Burns, Scott and Stevenson.

Laigh

Laigh — low. A laigh shop was a shop in a cellar. The Laigh Parliament Hall is the low-lying Parliament Hall below the main one. (See Advocates' Library).

Lamb's House, Waters Close, near Leith Harbour.

c.1550 Built by Andrew Lamb, a rich merchant, the house was "unequalled by any house in the Royal Mile." (Scotsman, 12-11-1948).

1561 Mary, Queen of Scots, spent her first hour here on arrival from France (Catford, 215; Scott-Moncrieff, 37).

18th century House renovated.

1930's House derelict with the roof off, and was bought by the Marquess of Bute who restored it.

1948 Plans to convert it into a maritime museum (Scotsman, 12-11-1948).

1958-60 Restored and presented to the National Trust for Scotland by Lord David Stuart, son of the 5th Marquess of Bute.

Now used as a day centre for old people.

Lampacre

"Ain aiker of land lying bewest the Cowes brigge [Coltbridge] upon the south side of the little house that stands by the wayside, commonly called the Lamp Aiker, within the parochine of St. Cuthbert's." It was gifted by Lord George Forrester as an addition to the emoluments of the schoolmaster of Corstorphine for supplying light to the lantern set in a niche in the east gable of Corstorphine Old Church (formerly the Church of St. John the Baptist, 1380). The light was for guiding travellers by boat across the marshes that lay between the Water of Leith and the village of Corstorphine. The old lamp is now replaced by an electric light. Murrayfield Parish Church was built upon the Lampacre (Grant, III, 118; *Historical Record of Murrayfield Parish Church* (1956)).

Lands

A land was, strictly speaking, a building in a tenement in the 16th century. It was "a building of several stories of separate dwellings, communicating by a common stair." (Wilson, I, 179, f.n.). The 16th century houses were less tall than 17th century ones.

"To-day, by the assistance of our friend, we were settled in convenient lodgings, up four pair of stairs, in the High Street, the fourth story being, in this city, reckoned more genteel than the first." (Smollett, 263).

The occupants of a land at the head of Dickson's Close, below Niddry's Wynd, in 1773 were, "First door upstairs, Mrs. Stirling, fishmonger; Mrs. Urquhart, who kept a lodging house of good repute, which was much resorted to by noblemen on occasions such as a peer's election. The Earl of Balcarres, when Lord Commissioner at the General Assembly, lived here; also, at different times, the Earl of Home, General Scott and Murray of Abercairney. Third flat, the Dowager Countess of Balcarres, mother of the ingenious authoress of 'Auld Robin Gray', and the rest of that family of talent. Fourth flat, Mrs. Buchan of Kelly. Fifth flat, the Misses Elliot, then milliners and mantua-makers of good figure. Garrets, a great variety of tailors and others." (Chambers, *Minor Antiquities of Edinburgh*, (1833), 227-8, f.n.).

"We then conducted him [Dr. Johnson] down the Post House

stairs, Parliament Close [i.e. Back Stairs, q.v.] and made him look up from the Cowgate to the highest building in Edinburgh . . . being thirteen floors or storeys from the ground upon the back elevation, the front wall being built upon the edge of a hill and the back wall rising from the bottom of the hill several storeys before it comes to a level with the front wall." (Boswell, 25).

"From confinement in space, as well as in imitation of their old allies, the French, (for the city of Paris seems to have been the model of Edinburgh), the houses were piled to an enormous height; some of them amounting to twelve stories. They were denominated *lands*. The access to the separate lodgings, in these huge piles, was by a common stair, exposed to every inconvenience arising from filth, steepness, darkness and danger from fire. Such, in good measure, is the situation of the *old town* at this hour." (i.e. 1779) (Arnot, 241).

1700 Previous to the great fire of 1700 some tenements were fifteen storeys high (Maitland, 140; Grant, I, 278).

1751 Tenement fell in the High Street near the Cross (Grant, I, 203).

1861 Collapse of tenement in or near Paisley's Close, known as 'Heave awa' Land' (q.v.) (Grant, I, 240; Grierson, 17; Livingstone, (b), 72; Catford, 191).

Lang Dykes (Gait)

The path or road following a line between the present Rose Street and Princes Street (O.E.C., XVII, 77; Maxwell, 191; Carlyle, 133). It ran from Kirkbraehead (q.v.) to St. Ninian's Row (below Regent Arch) and was named the 'Lang Dikes' in an 18th century map.

"Crossing Multrie's Hill [q.v.] and continuing westwards was a lane or roadway called the 'Lang Gait' or 'Lang Dykes', which, with its continuation along the North Bank of the Canongate, served as a somewhat primitive bypass linking the main roads from the west and north-west with the outlets from the city towards Leith and the east." (O.E.C., XXIII, 3).

1689 Claverhouse rode out by the Lang Gait (Chambers, 7; Wilson, I, 139).

Laundries

1908 Several public wash-houses in the city, known as 'steamies' by those using them for washing clothes.

1977 Last of the 'steamies' closed.

Lauriston

The district of Lauriston is named after the town house of the Laws of Lauriston which stood on the site now occupied by Chalmers Hospital (Smeaton, (b), 358).

Lauriston Castle and two distinguished residents.

Lauriston Castle, Cramond Road South.

1544 An earlier tower on this site destroyed in Hertford's raid (Geddie, 34) when the lands were owned by the Forresters of Corstorphine.

c.1593 Lauriston Castle built by Napier of Merchiston (Grant, III, 111).

1683 Castle bought by William Law, father of the financier John Law (Geddie, 33).

1823 Acquired and restored by Thomas Allan, a descendant of the Laws, who employed William Burn to enlarge the Castle in 1827. After this the Castle changed hands several times.

1926 Castle gifted to the nation by the owners, Mr and Mrs Reid.
The Trust is in the hands of the City of Edinburgh who have opened the Castle to the public.

1950 Edinburgh Croquet Club formed and rented the lawns of the Castle (Keir, 538).

Laverockbank, Trinity.
So called from the number of larks that used to frequent this area in times of deep snow (Mackenzie, 42).

Law Courts see Courts of Law.

Lawnmarket, from Castlehill to High Street at St. Giles Street.
Means 'Land Market' (O.E.C., XII, 50; Maitland, 181). It was the market in which landward (country) people sold their wares (Scott-Moncrieff, 41), but others consider that it was an open market for linen goods.

1477 The Cloth Market was here under James III's Charter (Fraser, 28; Steuart, 23).

Leith see also City of Queens

"In the reign of Alexander II [1214-49] the port belonged to the Logans, a family who owned extensive possessions in Midlothian, including the lands of Restalrig [q.v.] and took from it their patrimonial surname." (Wilson, II, 186).

The old road towards Leith from Edinburgh, Leith Wynd, is now Cranston Street (Williamson, 135).

North Leith belonged to the Abbey of Holyrood and South Leith to Restalrig.

1143 First recorded mention of Leith (Russell, 10; Geddie, 159, says 1128), when it was granted under the name of Inverlet by David I to the Holyrood monks.

1143-47 David I gave fisheries to Holyrood canons (Grant, III, 166).

1313 Edward II burned vessels in the harbour (Grant, III, 166).

1314 Edward II camped here on the way to Bannockburn.

1329 Robert the Bruce included the port of Leith in his Charter to Edinburgh (O.E.C., XX, app. 9; Maitland, 320; 485; Arnot, 570; Wilson, II, 185; Grant, III, 166; Robertson, 210; 239; Catford, 15; R.C., lv).

1380 Mariners' Incorporation instituted (Russell, 130). This became Trinity House in 1555.

1385 French troops in Leith to help the Scots (Maxwell, 42).

1398 and 1414 Edinburgh bought the Shore from Logan of Restalrig (Russell, 96).

1424 James I and his Queen, Jane Beaufort, landed (Sitwell and Bamford, 32).

1428 James I ordered enlargement of the port (Grant, III, 167) and about that time the King's Wark, used as an arsenal, naval yard, and later as a royal palace, may have been built near the shore, but the exact date is unknown (Grant, III, 236).

1428 James I granted to Edinburgh a Charter to uplift tolls from boats entering the port of Leith (Robertson, 85).

1435 Preceptory of St. Anthony (q.v.) founded by Sir Robert Logan of Restalrig (Arnot, 255; Wilson, II, 267; Grant, III, 215; Russell, 104; Geddie, 169; Keir, 437, and Steuart, 227, say 1430). It was off the Kirkgate.

1480 First mention of the Church of St. Mary (R.C., lvii) (*vide* 1485 *infra*).

1481 Town sacked by Edward IV (Smeaton, (b), 43).

1482 James III granted to Edinburgh certain customs from the harbour at Leith (Robertson, 86).

1483 Edinburgh citizens forbidden to have Leith business partners (Maitland, 10; 486; Arnot, 571; Grant, III, 167, says 1485).

1485 Church of St. Mary, later called South Leith Church, built in the Kirkgate (Geddie, 169; Keir, 437; Russell, 150, says before 1490;

Church notice-board says c. 1483).

1493 North and South Leith connected by Abbot Bellenden's (Ballantyne's) bridge (Grant, III, 167; R.C., lvii).

1502 Shipbuilding began (Russell, 191).

1544 and 1547 Leith burned by Hertford's troops (Catford, 237).

1548 French and Dutch troops help Scots (Wilson, I, 70; Smeaton, (a), 71).

1549 French fortify Leith (Maitland, 486).

c. 1550 Lamb's House built (q. v.).

1551 First recorded hanging in irons on the sands (Grant, III, 267).

1555 Trinity House built in Kirkgate (Grant, III, 223; Smeaton, (a), 350; Russell, 130).

1555 Leith erected into a Burgh of Barony (q. v.) (Maitland, 486).

1555 Old Mariners' Hospital erected (Maitland, 495).

1556 Mary of Guise bought South Leith (Russell, 97; Robertson, 82, says 1555).

1559 John Knox landed at Leith from exile (Geddie, 163).

1560 Siege of Leith (Maitland, 19; Arnot, 22; Wilson, I, 84; II, 199; Grant, III, 174; Geddie, 163; Russell, 267); fighting between French Roman Catholic troops under Mary of Guise and Protestant troops under Lord Grey. Two mounds in Leith Links, used as gun emplacements, are still visible.

1560 Preceptory of St. Anthony ruined (Wilson, II, 268).

1560 St. Mary's Church chancel destroyed (Wilson, II, 269). Excavations in 1848 disclosed shells, rings and coins of the period of Mary, Queen of Scots (Scotsman, 12-4-1848).

1561 Mary, Queen of Scots, landed (Wilson, I, 89; II, 138; Grant, III, 179; Maxwell, 116; Smeaton, (a), 81).

1565 Tolbooth and Town Hall built (Grant, III, 228; Geddie, 164).

1567 Edinburgh established superiority over South Leith (Smeaton, (a), 105).

1570 Leith made a base for blockading supplies to Edinburgh Castle which was holding out in favour of Mary, Queen of Scots, (R.C., lvi).

1584 Port made principal fish market (Grant III, 180).

1584 Preceptory of St. Anthony annexed by the Crown (Grant, III, 216).

1589 James VI sailed to Norway for his bride, Anne of Denmark (Maitland, 45; Wilson, I, 113; Grant, III, 180; Russell, 306), and landed at Leith in 1590.

1592 Body of murdered 'Bonnie Earl o' Moray' lay uncovered for months in South Leith Church (Geddie, 164).

1593 Golf Course on Leith Links (see Golf).

1593 Edinburgh Presbytery divided Leithers into four Incorporations, Mariners, Maltmen, Traders, Traffickers, each to pay one quarter of second minister's stipend at South Leith Church.

1594 Bothwell's third plot against James VI, the raid of Leith.

1606 North Leith erected into a parish (Wilson, II, 197; Russell, 172).

1609 Restalrig parish transferred to South Leith (O.E.C., IV, 153; Grant, III, 131; Russell, 155; Geddie, 169).

1614 King James Hospital, Kirkgate, founded (Maitland, 495; Grant, III, 217). The site is marked by a panel on the wall of South Leith Church (Russell, 130).

1618 Visit of John Taylor, the Water Poet (Grant, III, 183).

1619 Monopoly of soap-making granted to Leith for 21 years (J. S. Marshall, *Old Leith at Work*, (1977), 90).

1620 Beacons erected on rocks for shipping safety (Grant, III, 271).

1636 Royal Charter gave Edinburgh superiority over Leith which was erected into a Burgh of Barony (R.C., lviii).

1638 National Covenant signed on Leith Links (Geddie, 165).

1639 Edinburgh acquired North Leith from Earl of Roxburghe (Russell, 98; R.C., xlix).

1640 Charles I golfed on Leith Links (Marshall, 28; Grant, III, 260, says 1642).

1643 Solemn League and Covenant signed on Leith Links (Geddie, 165).

1645 Leith Links crowded with huts for plague victims (Catford, 237); less than one-third of the population surviving (Geddie, 165).

1650 Leith occupied by Cromwell's troops after Battle of Dunbar (Catford, 237).

1656 General Monk built Citadel on the site of St. Nicholas' Church (Maitland, 499; Grant, III, 187; Geddie, 165; R.C., 261; Keir, 437; Cruft, 91). Cruft and Geddie say 1653, but this is said to have been the date of Cromwell's plans for the Citadel which was not erected until 1656. It had largely disappeared by 1779 and now only the gate remains (Cruft, 92).

1663 Glassmaking begun in Leith (Marshall, *Old Leith at Work*, (1977), 81; Grant, III, 239, says 1682).

1669 Leith very opulent and a great fleet commonly lay at anchor (R.C., lvii).

1670 Major Thomas Weir hanged at the Gallow Lee (q.v.) (Chambers, 32). (See West Bow).

1676 Old Ship Hotel built (Russell, 406).

1677 Sugar refinery at Leith (Marshall, *Old Leith at Work*, (1977), 95).

1678 Tablet of Association of Porters above entry to the Old Sugar House (Geddie, 172). This was removed when Tolbooth Wynd was demolished.

1682 The Vaults rebuilt (Russell, 439).

1685 Windmill (later Signal) Tower built (Russell, 374).

1709 Royal Company of Archers shot for Silver Arrow on Leith Links (Marshall, 29).

1720 First dry dock (Grant, III, 259; Russell, 434).

The Shore, Leith, in the second half of the 19th century.

1726 Organisation of Carters — the stone is preserved in South Leith Churchyard.

1730 Stone pier erected (Grant, III, 271), a bit of bad construction (R.C., lviii).

1753 Act of Parliament to enlarge and deepen the harbours (Grant, III, 273).

c.1766 "There are a number of large sea-boats that ply . . . from Leith to Kinghorn." (Smollett, 280). They carried passengers and freight including horses and cattle.

1768 Honourable Company of Edinburgh Golfers built Golf House on Leith Links (Arnot, 361) and laid out a bowling green adjacent (Marshall, 13).

1775 Leith Street begun (O.E.C., XVII, 170; Wilson, II, 183).

1777 Council improved harbour (Arnot, 575) and Custom House quay erected (Grant, III, 273).

1779 Leith Fort built (Grant, III, 197), now demolished for high rise flats development (Keir, 385).

1788 Exchange Building, Constitution Street, erected (R.C., 260).

1789 Reflector light on pier head (Grant, III, 273).

1795 Royal Leith Volunteers established (Grant, III, 198).

1799 Rennie's report on the harbour (Grant, III, 273).

1801 Foundation stone laid for wet docks (Grant, III, 283).

1802 Edinburgh and Leith Shipping Company founded (Grant, III, 211).

1805 Five Leith vessels for whale fisheries (Grant, III, 278).

1805 St. James's Chapel, Constitution Street built (Russell, 396).

1806 East Old Dock opened (Smeaton, (a), 354).

1806 Bank of Leith opened in Bernard Street (Minto, 65).

1809 Martello Tower built (Grant, III, 274; Russell, 101).

1812 Custom House built in Commercial Street (Grant, III, 259; R.C., 260), designed by Robert Reid (*Edinburgh — An Architectural Guide*).

1814 North Leith Parish Church built to the design of William Burn (*Edinburgh — An Architectural Guide*).

1816 Trinity House demolished and reconstructed (Grant, III, 223; Russell, 127; Geddie, 170) to replace the 1555 House.

1817 Leith West (Queen's) Dock built (Grant, III, 283; Smeaton, (a), 354; Russell, 412).

1818 Tolbooth demolished (O.E.C., IV, 92; Geddie, 172, says 1819; Grant, III, 230, also gives 1819, but on p.193 illustrates 'The Old Tolbooth, 1820'). The Tolbooth was rebuilt between 1819 and 1822 (Grant, III, 230; Russell, 97).

1822 End of hanging in irons on the sands (Grant, III, 267).

1822 George IV landed at Leith (Grant, III, 208), marked by a plaque on the quayside, and by a painting by Alexander Carse which hangs on the wall of the old (1827) Town Hall.

1822 Preceptory of St. Anthony entirely removed (Russell, 117).

1826 Leith Dock Commission formed (Russell, 86; 413).

1827 Leith Town Council formed (O.E.C., XX, 75; Russell, 103). "Before 1833 the foreign trade of Leith was entirely controlled by the burgesses of Edinburgh." (O.E.C., XX, app. 9).

1827 Town Hall built at the corner of Constitution Street and Queen Charlotte Street (Grant, III, 243). It bears the date 1828.

1833 Leith became a Parliamentary Burgh with the right to have a Town Council (Robertson, 80), thus becoming independent of Edinburgh (R.C., lix).

1836 General Steam Navigation Company formed at Leith (Grant, III, 211).

1836 Dock Commission remodelled (Russell, 417).

1840 Leith Chamber of Commerce instituted (Grant, III, 245); chartered in 1852 (Keir, 645).

1846 Public Wells erected (Scotsman, 4-4-1846).

1848 South Leith Church restored (Grant, III, 219; Wilson, II, 270; Geddie, 168; Russell, 151; 162; Keir, 437, says 1847).

1850 Martello Tower erected (Scotsman, 5-4-1850).

1850 Leith Hospital built (Grant, III, 248).

1852 Victoria Dock opened (Grant, III, 284; Smeaton, (a), 354; Russell, 417).

1853 Roman Catholic Church of Our Lady, Star of the Sea, built (Grant, III, 244) in Constitution Street.

1855 Leith Nautical College established (Keir, 824); built in Commercial Street, 1903; enlarged in 1927.

1862 Watt's Hospital opened near the Links (Grant, III, 266).

1862 Corn Exchange opened at the corner of Constitution Street and Baltic Street. Now a paper merchant's office (Scotsman, 15-11-1978).

1863 St. James's Chapel rebuilt on a new site (Grant, III, 343; Russell, 396).

1869 Albert Dock opened (Grant, III, 286; Smeaton, (a), 354; Russell, 418).

1876 Post Office built (Grant, III, 243).

1881 Edinburgh Dock opened (Grant, III, 288; Russell, 419).

1888 Old Ship Hotel rebuilt (Russell, 406).

1898 Statue of Robert Burns at the north end of Constitution Street, designed by G. W. Stevenson.

1902 New Dock opened (Smeaton, (a), 354).

1904 Imperial Dock opened (Russell, 420).

1905 Electric tramcars running (Keir, 406).

1907 Statue of Queen Victoria at the foot of Leith Walk, designed by John Rhind.

1920 Act to amalgamate Leith with Edinburgh (Russell, 454; Geddie, 158, says 1922).

1932 Town hall and Library erected in Ferry Road; later rebuilt after severe damage in air-raid.

1936 Dock extension towards Newhaven planned, and further extensions in 1949-54.

1971 There has been a progressive depopulation from some 80,000 in the 1920's to 51,000 in 1971.

Leith Walk

1650 Originally called Leith Loan (Grant, III, 151) the new road was laid on a line of fortifications raised by General David Leslie (Wilson, II, 183) to check Cromwell's march on Edinburgh.

"The principal approach to Leith continued for nearly a century after this [1680] to be the Eastern Road through the Watergate, and the present broad and handsome thoroughfare which still retains the name Leith Walk was then simply an elevated gravel path." (Wilson, II, 183).

1748 Even as late as this "no horses were suffered on it" (Wood *et al.*, 149).

1774 Leith Walk formed (Lindsay, *Georgian Edinburgh*, (1973), 49).

1835 Tolls on Leith Walk abolished (Grierson, 12).

Leith Wynd

The main road to Leith from the Netherbow Port around the west flank of the Calton Hill. Replaced under the Improvement Act (q.v.) and now represented by Cranston Street (Williamson, 135).

Liberton

The name is thought to derive from Lepers Town as there was a leper hospital in the vicinity (Keir, 86).

1143-7 Church at Liberton referred to (Grant, III, 326) and granted to the Monks of Holyrood.

15th century Liberton Tower, believed to have been the residence of Macbeth of Liberton (Grant, III, 327) still stands near Braid Hills Drive.

17th century Liberton House, south-east of the Tower, off Liberton Drive, is still occupied.

1815 New Church built (Grant, III, 327; Geddie, 125, says 1825); renovated in 1882.

1920 Liberton became part of Edinburgh.

Liberton's (Libberton's) Wynd, Lawnmarket — south side.

Contained John Dowie's Tavern (see Inns), and Twelve Apostles' House (q.v.).

1477 Mentioned in James III's Charter as the meal market (Grant, I, 120).

1745 Henry Mackenzie, author of *Man of Feeling* and *Anecdotes and Egotisms* born here (Grant, I, 120).

1817 Partly demolished during building of the County Hall (q.v.) (Grant, I, 123).

1828 Houses pulled down for proposed George IV Bridge (Scotsman, 21-6-1828).

1829 William Burke executed here (Grant, II, 228; Scotsman, 31-1-1829). The Wynd was the last place of execution after the demolition of the Tolbooth in 1817. There is a plaque on the County Buildings to this effect.

1834 Gallows socket removed (Grant, I, 120) but by this date Liberton's Wynd had been demolished for George IV Bridge (q.v.).

1864 Last public hanging in Edinburgh — opposite present Sheriff Court (Keir, 52).

Little Jack's Close, 229 Canongate — north side.

The Close was next to Shoemakers' Land (q.v.). General Dalzell (Dalyell) of the Binns, who defeated the Covenanters at Rullion Green in 1666, lived here (Steuart, 85).

1753-62 David Hume lived in Jack's Land while writing his *History of England* (Chambers, 56).

1912 "The land is still standing as it was when Hume lived there." (Chambers, 56, f.n.).

1956-8 Area rebuilt and no trace of the Close remains.

Lochend

The loch of Restalrig, vulgarly Loch-end; or else a corruption of

Logan of Restalrig (O.E.C., XII, 101; Maitland, 502). Here James IV indulged his sport of wildfowling (Fraser, 44).

Lochend House was built in the 16th century and was occupied by the Logans of Restalrig (Grant, III, 132). It was partially destroyed later that century. A further building was added and the house is now occupied as a Health Centre overlooking Lochend Loch.

1511 First cannon factory built at Hawkhill (Lochend) (O.E.C., X, 77).

Lodging (Lugeing)
In the 16th century this meant an individual house in a land (q.v.).

Lord Provost
The title of Lord Provost, as opposed to Provost, has remained since 1487 (Robertson and Wood, 175) although Charles II only granted this title in 1667 (Wilson, I, 187; Grant, II, 281). Since the regional government reorganisation of 1975 Edinburgh is the only Scottish city legally permitted to retain the title. The Lord Provost's emblems of authority, the Mace and the Sword date respectively from 1617 and 1627. His chain of office and badge have been used since 1899, while the Lady Provost wears a chain of garnets and Scottish pearls presented in 1935 by the women citizens of Edinburgh (Keir, 284).

The Lord Provost is entitled to have two special lamp-posts at the door of his house, while Bailies have one. The Lord Provost is now chairman of the Edinburgh District Council, the Town Council having been abolished in 1975. He is styled the 'Right Honourable' and is Lord Lieutenant of the County of the City of Edinburgh and Lord High Admiral of the Firth of Forth.

Lorimer
A lorimer was a craftsman in iron work in saddlery (Chambers, 233).

Lothian Hut, foot of the Canongate — south side.
c.1750 Hut erected by 3rd Marquis of Lothian and was occupied by the wife of the 4th Marquis.

1790's Leased to Professor Dugald Stewart (O.E.C., XII, 123; Chambers, 323; Wilson, II, 108; Grant, II, 39; Smeaton, (a), 231).

1825 Pulled down to make way for a brewery (Grant, II, 39; Chambers, 323).

Lothian Road
1788 Road formed (O.E.C., XVIII, 178) on the site of the Castle Barns

(Grant, II, 138). There was a story that the road was built in a single day as the result of a wager (Geddie, *Romantic Edinburgh*, 212) but this is considered to be legendary.

1822 Canal basin formed (see Union Canal) (Grant, II, 215).
1913 Usher Hall, gifted by Thomas Usher, built (Robertson, 174).
1922 Canal basin cleared and later built upon.
1936 Lothian House, a Government office, built (Keir, 1008).
1962 Bell Tower Clock, at the Usher Hall, presented to the city.

Lothian Street, Bristo Street.
In Lothian Street lived Thomas de Quincey, whose house at No. 42 (Steuart, 156, says No. 44) no longer exists; and Charles Darwin, who attended medical classes (W. Harrison, 28).

Luckenbooths see also Shops.
Luckenbooths contained closed or locked shops (O.E.C., XII, 65; Maitland, 180; Chambers, 95). Booth is said to derive from the Norse word for a stall, and 'booth' is found in the Bible (Leviticus, XXIII, 42, *et al.*) meaning a shelter.

The Luckenbooths

"The Magistrates in 1450 built a line of houses and booths along the south side of the High Street, hard by the Church, from the 'Lady Steps' at the east end to the Tolbooth at the west end, to help meet the expenses [i.e. of building St. Giles]. That line of booths is called the Buith Raw [Booth Row], and in the eighteenth century the Luckenbooths." (C. A. Malcolm, S.M.T. Magazine, 1941).

"A four storey tenement, timber fronted for the most part" (R.C., 127) separated from the Church by the 'Stinking Style' (Fraser, 42).

1434 Luckenbooths, joined to the Tolbooth, (O.E.C., XIV, 12) dealt in a wide range of domestic goods and services (Catford, 44).

1817 Luckenbooths demolished (Cockburn, 109; Catford, 43).

Lyon Court

The exact date of origin is unknown, but it is of great antiquity, and heraldry has existed since the 12th century. There is mention of the office of King-of-arms in the time of James I (1406-37) and the succession has never failed since 1452. The Court consists of the Lord Lyon, three heralds, Marchmont, Rothesay and Albany, and three pursuivants, Falkland, Unicorn and Carrick, all of whom are royal appointments, and a number of messengers. The Court met in May and November under an Act of Parliament in the reign of James VI.

The principal of the Lyon Court or College of Heralds is the Lord Lyon King-at-Arms (Maitland, 375; Arnot, 492; Grant, I, 370). In 1681 Sir Alexander Erskine of Cambo was crowned Lord King-of-Arms, the last to be crowned (Grant, I, 371). "Of old, and before it degenerated into a mere legal sinecure, the office was one of great dignity." (Grant, I, 371). While this may have been true of the Victorian age, the frequent appearances of the Lord Lyon and his heralds on state occasions, the marshalling of which has devolved on the Lyon Court, would suggest that Grant's strictures are no longer justified.

The duties of the Lord Lyon, which were established by an Act of Scots Parliament in 1672 and confirmed in 1867, include to marshal ceremonies at coronations and other state occasions; or at funerals of royalty and nobility; to take cognizance of the arms of nobility and gentry; and to grant supporters to arms of newly created peers (Maitland, 375).

The Lyon Court is in New Register House.

Lyon's Close, High Street — north side.

c.1750 The millinery shop of the Misses Ramsay, one of the earliest in the city, was in the Close (Steuart, 59).

McEwan Hall, University Medical School.

1897 Built on the site of the mansion called Ross House (Catford, 68) as a gift from Sir William McEwan, and designed by R. Rowand Anderson. The Hall seats 2200 and is used for University of Edinburgh graduations and other functions. It contains a fine organ (Stewart, 13). The monument to the donor is on the island site opposite.

Magdalen Chapel, Cowgate.

The Chapel, visible from George IV Bridge near the Central Library, was founded by Michael Macquhen, who died in 1537 and who was probably a goldsmith (Fraser, 64), and his wife Janet Rhynd (Rynd) (Chambers, 248, f.n.). She died in 1553 and was buried in the Chapel. Magdalen Chapel may have been built on the site of an ancient church, the Maison Dieu (Grant, II, 261).

1540-44 Chapel built (O.E.C., VIII, 1-78; Maitland, 189; Arnot, 245; Wilson, II, 251; Grant, II, 261; Smeaton, (a), 254; Cruft, 13; Fraser, 64). Fraser adds that Macquhen founded a neighbouring house for the bedesmen (q.v.).

1553 Chapel managed by the Hammermen after the death of the foundress, and a stained glass window was inserted (Fraser, 70). This window still exists as four panels or shields embodied in one window, and is the oldest example of pre-Reformation Scottish stained glass.

1578 General Assembly of the Church of Scotland met in the Chapel (Grant, II, 262).

1618 Steeple added (Cruft, 13); completed in 1628.

1625 Tower of the Chapel built (O.E.C., VIII, 33) as part of the steeple.

1634-5 Bell placed in the tower (O.E.C., VIII, 35; *Booklet of the Chapel* says 1632).

Sculpture above the entrance to Magdalen Chapel showing the initials of the founders and the insignia and figure of the Hammermen.

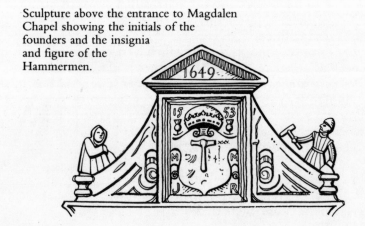

1685 Headless body of Earl of Argyle brought to the Chapel (Grant, II, 262).

1765 Baptists met in the Chapel (Keir, 185).

1858 Chapel sold to the Protestant Institute of Scotland (O.E.C., XIV, app. 18; VIII, 77, says 1863; *Booklet of the Chapel* says 1857).

1951 Regarded by the Royal Commission on Ancient Monuments as one of the three most important surviving buildings in Edinburgh (R.C., 105).

1965 The Protestant Institute was amalgamated with the Scottish Reformation Society who still own the Chapel.

1966 Used as Chaplaincy Centre for Heriot-Watt University, and is still used for this purpose for that part of the University remaining in Chambers Street, although the main Chaplaincy Centre was dedicated at Riccarton in 1978.

Mahogany Land, West Bow.
A very old house, the date of erection of which is unknown, which stood in the West Bow. The outer side was protected by a screen of wood (Grant, I, 319; Chambers, 47).

The Maiden
The Maiden was the Scottish guillotine (Maxwell, 298), and is now in the National Museum of Antiquities. It is said to have been the prototype of that designed by Dr Guillotine (Sitwell and Bamford. 89).

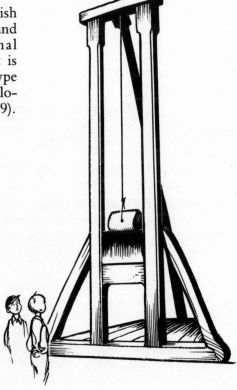

1564 The Maiden was made in Halifax, Yorkshire (Maxwell, 299).

1565-1710 Used for executions (Williamson, 60).

1565 First execution by the Maiden (Maxwell, 298; Wilson, I, 113, says 1566).

1581 Ex-Regent Morton executed by the Maiden (O.E.C., IV, 100); Chambers, 71; Wilson, I, 226; Maxwell, 137; 298). The suggestion that Morton designed the instrument is not based on fact. "Earl Morton hath brought you down a Maiden from Halifax, you never saw the like of her, and she'll clasp you around the neck, and your head will remain in her arms." (Scott, *The Abbot,* chap. 18).

1661 Marquis of Argyle executed (O.E.C., IV, 101; Grant, I, 58; Maxwell, 173).

1710 Executions ceased.

Manor Place

1829-33 "A pleasant row of houses, then the extreme west end of Edinburgh, which looked into the grounds of the old Manor House of Coates [i.e. Easter Coates House (q.v.)] and afforded lazy access into the country." (John Veitch, *Memoir of Sir William Hamilton, Bart.* (1869), 138).

Maps and Directories

1647 Gordon of Rothiemay's panoramic views (Grant, II, 280; Fraser, 103-9).

1670 Wenceslas Hollar's pictorial map (Fraser, 149).

1742 William Edgar's Survey, the first reliable map of the city (O.E.C., XII, 209).

1773-4 Peter Williamson's *Edinburgh Directory* (Gray, 45; Grant, I, 122, says 1784).

1807 *Edinburgh and Leith Post Office Directory* published annually until 1974-5.

1852 First Ordnance Survey map of Edinburgh.

Mark (Merk, Merck) see also Coinage.

The mark was a silver coin worth 13 shillings and 4 pence Scots, or 1 shilling 1⅓d sterling (5½p). The Scots pound had depreciated to one-twelfth of its sterling value by 1350 (Scott-Moncrieff, 32).

Markets

See Wood *et al.* 179-195; Keir, 657-663.

1477 James III ordained sites to various markets (Maitland, 8; Grant, II, 230; Robertson and Wood, 268).

There were fifteen different markets in the Old Town, each with its traditional stance in 1477. Cottons and linens were sold in the Lawnmarket; dairy produce and wool near the upper (butter) tron (q.v.) at the Upper (Over) Bow; meal between Liberton's Wynd and the Tolbooth; cordiners sold shoes west of the Tolbooth; poultry near the Cross; hatmakers and skinners on the north side of the High Street opposite the krames; meat and fish near the lower tron — meat between the tron and Blackfriars Wynd and fish from there to the Netherbow; salt in Niddry's Wynd; hammermen (cutlers, locksmiths, lorimers etc.) in St. Mary's Wynd; corn sold in the Cowgate between Forester's and Peebles Wynds; timber nearer the Greyfriars monastery; second-hand goods ('ald girth and geir') in front of the monastery; cattle were sold in the region of King's Stables Road, the sale of live animals being forbidden in the town (from Fraser, 28-30).

Corn and Meal
1477 Corn and grain sold in the High Street from the Tolbooth to Liberton's Wynd.
1540 Meal and victual market removed from High Street.
1560 Corn market built at the foot of the Bow, at the east end of the Grassmarket (Grant, II, 231).
1587 Corn market in the nether kirkyard of St. Giles.
1602 Halls built in the nether kirkyard and the meal market was accommodated south of Parliament House.
1716 Corn market in Marlin's Wynd (q.v.) (Grant, I, 374).
1840 Meal, corn and grain in the Grassmarket corn market building (Keir, 657). Straw in the Grassmarket (Keir, 657).
1849 Corn exchange opened (Gilbert, 120).
1903 Corn market in Gorgie.
1910 Corn Exchange in New Market Road, off Slateford Road (Keir, 1008).

Cattle and Horses
1477 James III's Charter stipulated particularly that cattle be not brought into the burgh but sold in the market under the wall "far west at our stable" i.e. Grassmarket and King's Stables Road.
1840 Cattle in the west end of the Grassmarket, West Port and King's Stables Road; horses in the west end of the Grassmarket (Keir, 657).
1843 Cattle market in Lauriston Place (Minto and Armstrong, 44) but the horse market continued in the Grassmarket.
1843 Site of Ramsay Lodge (at the top of Lady Lawson's Wynd — not that in Ramsay Garden) used as a cattle market (O.E.C., XVIII, 166).
1900 Cattle market in Lauriston partly demolished for building of the Fire Station (Smeaton, (a), 335; (b), 361), and the remainder removed for the College of Art in 1907 (Minto and Armstrong, 44). Auction sales of horses, cattle and sheep by private companies in

Haymarket and in Valleyfield Street (beside King's Theatre).
1911 Slaughterhouse and cattle market moved to Gorgie (Keir, 658).

Flesh and Poultry

1477 James III's Charter placed the meat market from the lower (salt) tron (q.v.) to Blackfriars Wynd.

The fleshmarket in the mid-17th century was just south of the Tron Church. Fleshmarket Close (q.v.), opposite the Tron Church, ran north downhill to a Fleshmarket in the valley of the Nor' Loch at the foot of the present Scotsman offices, and eventually below the south span of the North Bridge.

The retail poultry market was also in Fleshmarket Close; but the wholesale poultry market, together with eggs, butter and cheese stood nearer the Tron Church, where the tron weighing machine was situated.

1840 The poultry, flesh and meat market was between the North Bridge and the Fleshmarket Close (Keir, 657). Sheep, lambs and pigs were sold between Fountainbridge and Cowfeeder Row (High Riggs, q.v.) (Keir, 657).

1851 The municipal slaughterhouse was in Fountainbridge before its removal to Gorgie in 1910 (Minto and Armstrong, 44).

1883 A private 'dead meat' market was in Fountainbridge (Keir, 663).

The meat market is now in New Market Street, Slateford (Keir, 1008).

Fish

1477 Under James III's Charter fish was sold between Blackfriars Wynd and the Netherbow.

The Fishmarket Close, east of Parliament Close, which ran south to the Cowgate, led to a fish market.

1675 Fish to be kept in creels at the head of Fishmarket Close, beside the Cross (Robertson, 126).

1684 All fish sold in the fish market except oysters and shellfish (Robertson, 126).

1822 There was no fish shop in Edinburgh before this date.

1840 The fish market was in Market Street area and shared a corner of the fruit and vegetable market until it was excluded from the Waverley Market (Keir, 661).

1845 The fish market was sited below the span of the North Bridge nearest the Waverley Station (Scotsman, 19-11-1845).

1845 The fish market was allocated the exclusive sale of shellfish in the city (Scotsman, 19-11-1845).

c.1870 Fish market in MacDowall Street, east of the North Bridge (Keir, 661), until 1895.

1896 The principal fish market was at Newhaven — and still is.

Fruit and Vegetables

1513 No fruitsellers to sell fruit at the 'mercat croce'.

1745 Green market in the High Street between Hart's Close and the Cap and Feathers Close (q.v.), roughly opposite Hunter Square.

1800's In the early 1800's fruit and vegetables were sold along the north side of the High Street from the North Bridge to the Royal Exchange, when the High Street was a continuous market from top to bottom.

1840 Fruit and vegetables sold in Market Street area near the old Physic Garden (see Botanic Garden) (Keir, 657).

1868 Waverley Market built as a fruit and vegetable market but, with the growing diversity of uses of the Waverley Market, the sale of fruit and vegetables returned to Market Street. There was another fruit market on the site of the present King's Theatre.

The fruit and vegetable market is now in Chesser Avenue, Gorgie.

Market Street

1867 Built as a result of the Improvement Act (q.v.). Originally it was a flesh market, and then a fruit and vegetable market on the south side of the Waverley Station, but later Market Street extended further westwards to meet the Mound.

The offices of the Edinburgh Evening News were in this extension of Market Street.

Marlin's Wynd, Blair Street.
The Wynd led from the High Street between Peebles Wynd and Niddry's Wynd (Fraser, 61) to the Cowgate. It contained the corn market and led to the poultry market (Grant, I, 374). It was named after a Frenchman, Jean Marlin, who was reputed to have paved the High Street (O.E.C., XII, 76) although Chambers (209) states that this was done by two French brothers called Jean and Bartoulme Foliot.

Marlin's Wynd was uncovered inside the Tron Church at diggings during the recent (1974) renovations.

Mary Erskine School see Merchant Maiden Hospital.

Mary of Gueldres see Trinity College Church.

Mary of Guise see Oratory.

Mary King's Close, High Street — north side.
The Close, which was also known as Brown's Close or Touris Close, was abandoned after the plague of 1645 in which most of its

143

inhabitants perished (Nimmo, 77). It became a place of terror to the superstitious (Grant, I, 227) and was sealed off to prevent the disease spreading.

1845 The northern part was an open ruin with massive vaulted lower storeys while the southern part had been damaged by a fire in 1750 (Grant, I, 227).

The Close was covered by buildings of the Royal Exchange (City Chambers) (Grant, I, 227) beneath which the Close may be visited by arrangement. It is partly used for storing Town Council documents.

Mary, Queen of Scots

8-12-1542 Born at Linlithgow Palace (Scott, *Tales of a Grandfather,* chap. XXIX, says 7-12-1542).

14-12-1542 James V died at Falkland Palace (Scott, loc. cit., chap. XXVIII). Mary of Guise became Regent.

9-9-1543 Crowned on 30th anniversary of Flodden (Sitwell and Bamford, 47).

24-6-1548 Agreement that Mary should marry the Dauphin of France, and she left for France in the following month.

24-4-1558 Married Francis, Dauphin of France, at Notre Dame, Paris.

10-6-1560 Death of Mary of Guise.

5-12-1560 Death of Francis II (Scott, loc. cit., chap. XXIX).

14-8-1561 Mary left France (Scott, loc. cit., chap. XXX, says 15-8-1561).

19-8-1561 Arrived at Leith (Grant, III, 179, says 20-8-1560, but in I, 45, says August, 1561).

1-9-1561 State entry into Edinburgh (Grant, II, 66; Catford, 28; Sitwell and Bamford, 64, say 2-9-1561).

9-4-1563 — 15-4-1563 Mary at Lochleven Castle.

9-7-1565 Betrothed to Henry, Lord Darnley.

22-7-1565 Banns of marriage published (Sitwell and Bamford, 68).

29-7-1565 Married Darnley at Holyrood (Steuart, 108; Grant, II, 68, says at Stirling Castle); ceremony conducted by the Bishop of Brechin (Steuart, 109).

1-3-1566 Darnley signed a bond against David Rizzio (Sitwell and Bamford, 69).

9-3-1566 Rizzio murdered at Holyrood Palace.

19-6-1566 James (VI) born in Edinburgh Castle (O.E.C., V, 58; Arnot, 291; Maitland, 161; Wilson, I, 100; 164; Maxwell, 146).

31-1-1567 Darnley arrived in Edinburgh and went to Kirk o' Field.

9-2-1567 Darnley murdered at Kirk o' Field.

12-4-1567 James Hepburn, Earl of Bothwell, tried and acquitted of murder.

21-4-1567 Mary went to Stirling to see her son, James, for the last time.

24-4-1567 Mary taken to Dunbar by Bothwell.

3-5-1567 Bothwell's Catholic divorce from Lady Jean Gordon.

6-5-1567 Mary went from Dunbar to Edinburgh (Sitwell and Bamford, 78, say 3-5-1567).

7-5-1567 Bothwell's Protestant divorce from Lady Jean Gordon.

15-5-1567 Mary married Bothwell at Holyrood Abbey; ceremony conducted by Bishop of Orkney (Steuart, 111).

15-6-1567 Mary surrendered at Carberry and taken to the Black Turnpike (q.v.).

16-6-1567 Mary taken to Holyrood, and thence to Lochleven Castle in disguise.

21-6-1567 'Casket Letters' opened (Sitwell and Bamford, 82).

24-7-1567 Mary abdicated.

29-7-1567 James VI crowned at Stirling.

25-3-1568 Mary's unsuccessful attempt to escape from Lochleven.

2-5-1568 Mary escaped from Lochleven.

16-5-1568 Mary left for England where she was shortly made prisoner.

22-11-1586 Mary sentenced to death.

8-2-1587 Mary executed.

Meadows, see South Loch and Public Parks.

Melbourne Place, George IV Bridge north of Victoria Street.
1852 Housed Royal Medical Society (of medical students) (Grant, II, 303, says 1853) until 1966; and Edinburgh Chamber of Commerce and Manufacturers (q.v.) (Grant, I, 123).
1974 Lothian Region Offices occupy the whole site.

Mercat Cross, see Cross.

Merchant Company, (Company of Merchants)
1514 Edinburgh Merchants drew up rules for their Guild to prevent illegal trading (Fraser, 60).
1681 Company instituted by Royal Charter (Maitland, 319; Arnot, 530; Grant, I, 376; Cockburn, 350; Robertson, 127; J. Harrison, 9).
1691 Merchants' Hall in house once belonging to Tam o' the Cowgate (q.v.) at the corner of Candlemaker Row and Cowgate (Grant, I, 378). The Merchants left in 1726 and were housed in the High Street. The Cowgate building was demolished in 1829 (O.E.C., XXIX, 11) but the association is perpetuated in Merchant Street, off Candlemaker Row.
c.1788 Merchants' Hall built at No. 4 Hunter Square (Grant, I, 376), designed by John Baxter. Now a branch of Royal Bank.
1870 Merchant Company converted its foundations into day schools (Grant, II, 359).
1879 Company's Hall in Hanover Street (Grant, II, 162); reconstructed in 1902.

Merchant Maiden Hospital (Mary Erskine School).

1694 The Mary Erskine School for Merchant Maidens met in Merchants'
Hall, Cowgate (*vide supra*) (O.E.C., XXIX, 11). Smith (I, 15) says
it was founded in 1677.

1702 Merchant Maiden School incorporated by Act of Scots Parliament
(Grant, II, 362).

1707 School built in Bristo Street, outside the Bristo Port (Maitland, 460;
Arnot, 564; Grant, II, 324).

1818 School moved to a site south of Archibald Place (off Lauriston
Place) (J. Harrison, 15; Grant, II, 362, says 1816). Building designed
by William Burn.

1871 Site vacated for George Watson's Hospital (q.v.) (O.E.C., XXIX,
27) and the school moved to Hopetoun Rooms, Nos. 70-72 Queen
Street (O.E.C., XXIX, 80). It came under the Merchant Company
and was renamed Edinburgh Ladies' College in 1889, then Queen
Street School, and later, in 1944, Mary Erskine School (Keir, 777).

1966 Moved to new buildings in grounds of Ravelston House (q.v.).

1978 Proposal to join its primary classes with those of Stewart's-Melville
College.

Merchiston Castle, Colinton Road.
An ancient Castle, the date of building unknown, but is thought to
be 15th century (R.C., 233). The Tower was recorded in 1436
(Minto and Armstrong, 52); and references to Merchiston occur in
Exchequer Rolls of 1266 (Smith, I, 91).

1438 Merchiston Tower acquired by Alexander Napier (Smith, I, 91).

1572 Castle occupied as a blockhouse to prevent supplies reaching
Edinburgh Castle, then holding out for Mary, Queen of Scots
(R.C., 233).

Merchiston Castle — yesterday and today, showing Napier
College.

The Castle belonged to the Napiers of Merchiston. John
Napier, the inventor of logarithms in 1614, was born in the Castle
in 1550 (O.E.C., XXXI, 7; Grant, III, 35), and died in 1617 (Smith,
I, 94).
1833 Merchiston Castle School built in the grounds (O.E.C., XV, app.
24), remaining there until its move to Colinton in 1930 (Keir, 985).
1964 Castle restored and incorporated in the newly built Napier College
of Commerce and Technology (q.v.) (Minto and Armstrong, 52).

Merk, see Mark.

Mills
1140 Charter granted by David I to the Monks of Holyrood for grinding
grain.
1329 Charter by Robert the Bruce making over the mills of Leith to the
citizens of Edinburgh for services to the national cause in the Wars
of Independence (Grant, III, 166).
1650 Leith mills burned by Cromwell's troops (Grant, III, 174).
1722 Mills of Leith sold to Edinburgh.
1828 There were 71 mills driven by the motive power of the Water of
Leith (q.v.). Fourteen corn mills, 12 barley mills, 20 flour mills, 7
saw mills, 5 snuff mills, 5 cloth-fulling mills, 4 paper mills, 2 lint
mills and 2 leather mills were all in a ten mile stretch of the river
from Balerno to Leith (Scotsman, 6-11-1828).
1855 First rubber mill in the city (Grant, II, 219).

Milne's Court; **Milne Square**, see Mylne.

Milton House, Canongate — south side.
c.1742 Milton House built (Wilson, II, 104; Carlyle, 272, f.n.) in the
gardens of Lord Roxburgh's house (Grant, II, 15; 34) by Andrew
Fletcher of Milton.
    The house was occupied in the 19th century as a Roman
Catholic school (Grant, II, 34) and is now the site of Milton House
Primary School.

Mint, see Cunzie House.

Minto House, Chambers Street.
18th century House in Argyle Square (q.v.) opening from Horse Wynd
(q.v.) and occupied by the Minto family (Grant, II, 272; Daiches,
211, says 1720's).
19th century Early in this century the house was divided into small
apartments (Grant, II, 274).
1829 House fitted up as a surgical hospital for street accident cases by

Professor James Syme, Professor of Surgery (O.E.C., XXX, 144; Grant, II, 274; Catford, 189).

1871 House demolished during building of Chambers Street, but a new Minto House was built facing on to the Street, and became the Extramural School of Medicine (Stewart, 30; Guthrie, 23).

1926 House acquired by the Faculty of Arts of Edinburgh University (Stewart, 30).

Miscellaneous Dates

(A heterogeneous collection of dates which do not fit in elsewhere).

1253 Church Synod in town (Smeaton, (a), 12).

1437 Murderers of James I tortured before their execution (Williamson, 25).

1530 Pillory and other punishments in use (until 1728) (Wilson, II, 297).

1543 Act allowing people to read the Bible in their own tongue (Maxwell, 110). (See Carving on Houses).

1554 First manufacture of soap in town (Grant, II, 266).

1574 Teacher of French opened a school in town (Maitland, 34).

1580 Bible to be kept by each householder (Maitland, 39).

1583 Town divided into four parishes, St. Giles, Magdalen, New, and Trinity (Maitland, 42).

1586 First reference to locksmiths in town (Chambers, 233, f.n.; Grant, II, 263).

1587 All ecclesiastical property alienated to the King (O.E.C., XVIII, 14; Maitland, 45).

1588 Town armed against the Spanish Armada (Maitland, 45), 736 merchants and 717 craftsmen called up.

1588 First pewterer in town (Grant, II, 263).

1599 Privy Council ordained a new Calendar; the year to begin on 1st January, 1600 instead of 25th March, 1600 (O.E.C., III, 104, f.n.; Arnot, 49; Smeaton, (a), 102).

1641 City divided into six parishes (Maitland 141; Arnot 261).

1643 Solemn League and Covenant signed in St. Giles Church (Maitland, 282; Arnot, 125; Maxwell, 168).

1659 Dromedary seen in city for the first time (Wilson, II, 88; Grant, II, 15). "Ane great beast calit ane drummondary, cleven futted like unto a Kow." (Nimmo, 78).

1660 Restoration excitement (O.E.C., III, 218; Maitland, 95; Grant, I, 55; 159).

1666 Battle of Rullion Green (Maitland, 506; Grant, III, 30; Maxwell, 175; Geddie, 101).

1679 257 Covenanters shipped as slaves to Barbados (Grant, III, 189).

1691 First surgical instrument maker in city (Grant, II, 263).

1702 East India Company vessel seized in River Thames (Wilson, I, 141).

1705 English vessel seized in Forth as reprisal (Arnot, 186).

1717 Last riding of the city marches (Maitland, 178). This was not the last 'beating of the bounds' — it was revived symbolically and on a smaller scale in 1946 to celebrate victory in World War II (Smith, I, 133).

1726 Gladiatorial show behind Holyrood (Grant, II, 75).

1750 First teaching of English in the city (Grant, I, 252).

1764 First edge-tool maker and first manufacturer of fish-hooks in the city (Grant, II, 263).

1780 First umbrella seen in the city (Creech, 91), carried by Alexander ('Lang Sandy') Wood, the surgeon.

1785 and 1786 Lunardi's balloon ascents from the garden of Heriot's Hospital (O.E.C., XIV, 154, f.n.; Grant, II, 371).

1788 Circus opened (Creech, 75).

1793-4 Sedition trials in city (Smeaton, (a), 135). "In order to find a match for the judicial spirit of this court, we must go back to the days of Lauderdale and Dalziel." (Cockburn, 101). Braxfield was "the Jeffreys of Scotland" (Cockburn, 116).

1814 Meeting against West Indian slavery (Cockburn, 282).

1845 Bonaly peel tower completed by Lord Cockburn (Grant, III, 326).

1886 Edinburgh International Exhibition held in the Meadows (Smeaton, (a), 143).

Mons Meg, Castle.
The inscription says that it was forged at Mons in 1476, but this has probably nothing to do with Mons in Belgium. James II gave Brawny Kim, the smith, the lands of Mollance in Galloway, and the gun was named after Kim's wife, Meg — thus Mollance Meg, later contracted to Mons Meg (Williamson, 89). The gun weighs 6½ tons (6630 kg.).

1455 Given to James II to attack Threave Castle (Williamson, 89).

1489 Used by James IV at the siege of Dumbarton (Smeaton, (b), 144).

1558 Fired at the occasion of the marriage of Mary to Francis, Dauphin of France (Smeaton, (b), 144). The ball which was fired was found on Wardie Muir, two miles away (F. Watt, *The Book of Edinburgh Anecdote*, (1912), 113).

1650 'Muckle Meg' delivered up to General Monk (Williamson, 89).

1682 Mons Meg burst during the salute to the Duke of York (James VII (II)) (Wilson, I, 137; Williamson, 77).

1754 Mons Meg removed to London (Williamson, 90; Smeaton, (b), 145; Wilson, I, 169, says 1754 or 1759).

1829 Sir Walter Scott secured its return (Wilson, I, 169; Grant, III, 209; Maxwell, 67; Smeaton, (a), 148; Russell, 299; Williamson, 90).

Monuments
1951 The Royal Commission Inventory of the Ancient and Historic

Monuments of Scotland (Cmd. 7967) lists as most worthy of
preservation in the City of Edinburgh (R.C., xxxi) —

Burgh of Edinburgh
Edinburgh Castle; St. Giles Church; Tron Church, Magdalen
Chapel; Greyfriars Church; Cannonball House; Milne's Court;
Gladstone's Land; Lady Stair's House; 300-302, 306-310, 312-328
Lawnmarket; City Chambers; Parliament House; Moubray House;
'John Knox's House'; 1 and 74-78 Grassmarket; Candlemakers'
Hall; Heriot's Hospital; Old University; Surgeons' Hall; fragments
of Flodden Wall and Telfer Wall; Mercat Cross; Statue of Charles II.

Burgh of Canongate
Palace of Holyroodhouse and remains of Holyrood Abbey;
Canongate Church; Abbey Strand; White Horse Close;
Queensberry House; 82, 82a, 142, 167-169, 194-198 Canongate;
Acheson House; Huntly House; Canongate Tolbooth; Moray
House; Bible Land; Chessel's Court; Canongate Burgh Cross.

New Town and Inner Suburbs
St. Cuthbert's Church; Register House; Assembly Rooms;
Charlotte Square; remains of George Square.

Outlying Districts
St. Anthony's Chapel; Pilrig House, Drylaw House; Easter Coates
House; Murrayfield House; Ravelston House; Beechwood House;
Roseburn House; Merchiston Castle; Bruntsfield House; Braid
House; Duddingston House.

Leith, Newhaven and Restalrig
St. Triduana's Well; Lamb's House; National Bank of Scotland,
Bernard Street, Leith; Craigentinny House.

Moray House, 174 Canongate — south side.
1628 Built by Dowager Countess of Home (O.E.C., XI, 11, says 1618;
XII, app. 2, is undated; XVII, 27, quotes Chambers; Chambers,
306, says 1628; Wilson, II, 99, says 1628; Grant, II, 31, says before
1633; W. Harrison, 22, says 1618; Steuart, 89, says 1623; *Edinburgh
— An Architectural Guide*, 1628).
1645 House passed to Margaret, Countess of Moray (Grant, II, 31;
Williamson, 128; R.C., 174, says 1643).
1648 and 1650 Cromwell occupied the house (O.E.C., III, 217; XVII, 28;
Maitland, 91; Arnot, 135; Wilson, I, 122).
1707 Earl of Seafield (Lord High Chancellor) occupied the house. "It is
said that the Commissioners [for the Union of 1707] met in a

summer house in the grounds of Moray House, meaning to sign the Treaty there, but the violence of the mob compelled them to withdraw to a house in the High Street near the Tron." (Williamson, 79).

1753 British Linen Company occupied Moray House for 40 years (C.A. Malcolm, *The British Linen Bank*, 1746-1946, 161).

1846 United Free Church Training College for teachers in the House (O.E.C., XII, app. 23; Smeaton, (a), 227).

1907 Two training colleges for Protestant teachers combined as the Edinburgh Provincial Committee for the Training of Teachers in Moray House (Keir, 818).

1959 College of Education in the House, and the College has spread to Holyrood Road.

Morningside

1846 No conveyance ran to Morningside from Edinburgh, and the want of an omnibus was felt by residents and summer visitors (Scotsman, 15-4-1846).

A detailed history of Morningside is to be found in C.J. Smith, *Historical South Edinburgh, (1978)*.

Morocco Land, 273-77 Canongate — north side.

The story of Morocco Land (O.E.C., XII, 92; Grant, II, 6; Wilson, II, 80; Williamson, 133; Chambers, 299; Nimmo, 81; Catford, 83; Steuart, 77; R.C., 182).

1950 Buildings demolished and reconstructed with the figure of a Moor on the wall.

Morrison Street

"Once covered by orchards, nursery gardens and farms connected with the Castle." (Minto and Armstrong, 37). The last vestige of this was Castle Barns (R.C., 232) which, in 1798, was a small hamlet on the Falkirk Road. A building with an outside wooden stair stood until some 30 years ago opposite the north end of Semple Street. when it was demolished, and is now an area for the sale of used cars. Morrison Street was built from about 1825.

Mortality Rate

Previous to 1818 the lower classes paid tolerable attention to cleanliness and health and over the period 1780-1819 mortality decreased from 1:34 (29.7 per 1000) to 1:40 (25 per 1000) annually. In the period 1820-1839 mortality returned to 1:34, the increase being ascribed to the importation of Irish labourers to work on the construction of the Union Canal (Wood *et al.*, 19).

Statistically, per 1000 of the population, the death rate fell from

27.8 in 1871 to 18.8 in 1881 (Grierson, 17) and to 13.1 in 1961 (Keir, 101).

Mortonhall, Braid Hills.
1641 The Trotters bought Mortonhall estate (Geddie, 116; Smith, II, says 1635).
1769 Morton Hall built (R.C., 236). The house lies north of Frogston Road East, and the grounds are now occupied by a nursery garden and a site for caravans.

Morton House, the dower house of the estate, bears the date 1709 (R.C., 236), and lies south of Frogston Road West.

Morton House, Blackfriars Wynd — west side.
(As distinct from Morton House (*vide supra*) in Mortonhall).
16th century House built and additions made in the 17th century (R.C., 100). It was the ancient residence of the Earls of Morton and traditionally of the Regent Morton (Grant, I, 259).

The house has been restored and still stands in Blackfriars Street, being used as an examination hall by University of Edinburgh (Stewart, 17).

Motor Cars
1903 First private car was registered in Edinburgh — S 1 — which was allocated to the Lord Justice-Clerk (Robertson, 176). The number of the official car for the use of the Lord Provost is S O.

Moubray House, Trunk's Close, 53 High Street — north side.
This four-storey house is probably Edinburgh's oldest dwelling, being built in c. 1472 by Andrew Moubray (Scotsman, 18-8-1951), or in 1477 by Robert Moubray (R.C., 94).
1910 House bought by public subscription (O.E.C., V, 157-162).
1975 House restored.

Mound
Originated in provision made by George Boyd, a tailor, to cross the semi-fluid quagmire of the half-drained Nor' Loch — 'Geordie Boyd's Mud Brig' (Grant, II, 82).
1781 Mound begun (Grant, II, 82; Maxwell, 201, f.n.) on an artificial accumulation of earth. By 1783 there had been deposited 1800 cartloads removed from the foundations of the New Town (Creech, 65) and at the completion of the Mound in 1830 it was estimated to contain 2 million cartloads.

During the building there were rotundas on the Mound used by showmen for menageries etc.
1798 Bank Street formed (Grant, II, 93).

1822 Royal Institution built at the foot of the Mound and offered jointly to the Royal Society of Edinburgh, the Society of Scottish Antiquaries, the Institute for the Encouragement of Fine Arts and the Board of Trustees for Manufacturers and Fisheries. The feu was taken by the Board whose tenants the other three became (Youngson, 162).

1823 Royal Institution, designed by William Playfair, completed (Grant, II, 83; Cockburn, 464, f.n.; Smeaton, (a), 271; Malcolm, (b), 65, says 1824).

1826 Royal Institution became the home of the Royal Scottish Academy of Painting, Sculpture and Architecture, and has housed annual Exhibitions since 1827.

1827 Royal Institution for the Promotion of Fine Arts chartered (Cockburn, 356), having been established in 1819.

1830 Mound completed (Grant, II, 82).

1836 Royal Institution enlarged (Smeaton, (a), 271) and the statue of Queen Victoria by John Steel was erected on the portico (Grant, II, 83) in 1844.

1850 Mound reconstructed (Malcolm, (b), 65).

1850 National Gallery, designed by William Playfair, founded (Grant, II, 88; Smeaton, (a), 272; Malcolm, (b), 66).

1859 National Gallery opened (Grant, II, 88).

1910 Memorial to the Black Watch erected at the top of Market Street.

1960's The Mound was liable to icing during winter and an electric blanket was underlaid, but this has since been discontinued owing to maintenance problems.

Multrie's Hill
Alternatively spelt Moultrie's, Moultrey's, Multree's, Moultray's and Multersey's, it was later known as Bunker's Hill. It was originally a village where French weavers attempted unsuccessfully to make silk.

It was the site of the Register House (q.v.) and St. James's Square (q.v.) at the east end of Princes Street (O.E.C., XVII, 77; Wilson, II, 41; 203).

1734 John Cleland, who owned land on the north slope of the hill, built his house (O.E.C., II, 167-176), which was still standing in 1909 but has now vanished.

Murrayfield House, Murrayfield Avenue.
1734 House built on Nisbet Park, bought by Archibald Murray and was renamed Murrayfield. This house is the west part of the present building (R.C., 227).

1773 Succeeded by the future Lord Henderland who built the east wing. The house is still in private ownership.

Museum see Royal Scottish Museum.

Mushat's Cairn
The cairn, which stands near the Willowbrae entrance to Holyrood Park, is the scene of a murder in 1720 when Nicol Mushat killed his wife (Grant, II, 310; Smeaton, (b), 261.

Music Hall see Assembly Rooms.

Mylne (Milne) Square, High Street — north side.
It lay opposite the north part of the Tron Church (Chambers, 204, f.n.) and was built as an 'Old Town improvement' (Wilson, II, 29) in an effort to escape from overcrowded closes.
1684-88 Mylne Square built (O.E.C., XIV, 45-8). Named after its architect, Robert Mylne, the last of seven royal master-masons of that family (Williamson, 207, who dates it 1690).
1787 Square partly demolished and rebuilt to give a uniform width to the North Bridge (O.E.C., XIV, 48).
1896 Remains of Mylne Square removed when North Bridge was further widened (O.E.C., XII, 38).

Entrance to Mylne's Court.

Mylne's (Milne's) Court, 517 Lawnmarket — north side.
1690 Designed by Robert Mylne, it was a block of tenements, the first to be symmetrically planned (Grant, I, 96). The first example of the modern square (Williamson, 207).
1883 Buildings on the west side of the Court demolished.
c.1910 Tolbooth Mission set up to look after the needs of local children in Mylne's Court (Cruft, 5); abolished in 1956 (Keir, 47).
1960 Buildings condemned (Cruft, 6).
1967-70 Restored and used as residences for the University of Edinburgh — Salvesen and Henman Halls (Stewart, 19).
     A close leads from the Court to Mound Place between H.M. Commissary Office and New College.

Napier College of Commerce and Technology
1964 Buildings enclosing Merchiston Castle (q. v.) opened (Keir, 817) as a College of Further Education now under Lothian Regional Council. The official opening ceremony was in 1965.

National Gallery see also Mound.
1850 Built to the design of William Playfair (Grant, II, 88; Smeaton, (a), 272; Malcolm, (b), 66).
1859 Building shared with Royal Scottish Academy (Keir, 871).
1910-12 Building wholly used for National Collection (Keir, 871).
1978 Gallery extended.

National Gallery of Modern Art
1960 Housed in Inverleith House, Botanic Garden (q. v.) (Keir, 875).
1977 The buildings of John Watson's School (see Dean Lands), Belford Road, acquired as the site.

National Library, George IV Bridge.
1925 Arose from gift of Advocates' Library (q. v.) (O.E.C., XVIII, app. 24; Keir, 912), and building presented by Sir Alexander Grant.
1937 Frontage built on site of demolished Sheriff Court in George IV Bridge. Previous entry had been from the Laigh Parliament Hall until the new façade was erected.
1956 National Library opened by Queen Elizabeth (Keir, 912).
     The Library is entitled to a copy of every book published under copyright privilege since 1709 (the privilege formerly of the Advocates' Library).

National Museum of Antiquities of Scotland, Queen Street.
1780 Founded as an integral part of the Society of Antiquaries of Scotland (Keir, 928).
1827 After being housed in many places the museum moved to the Royal

Scottish Academy, Mound (Scotsman, August, 1827).

1891 Moved to No. 1 Queen Street (Keir, 928) which it shares with the National Portrait Gallery (*vide infra*).

National Portrait Gallery, Queen Street.

1882 National Portrait Gallery of Scotland founded (Keir, 874).

1889 Gallery opened in No. 1 Queen Street, which it shares with National Museum of Antiquities, in the building designed by Rowand Anderson with sculpture by Birnie Rhind (*Edinburgh — An Architectural Guide*).

Navy (Scottish) see also Defence Forces.

It was not until the reigns of James III and IV that Scotland possessed any ships for purely warlike purposes (Scotsman, 11-2-1950). This was the period of Sir Andrew Wood and the brothers Barton (Grant, III, 200). Andrew Barton was slain in 1511; John died in 1513 (Grant, III, 202); and Robert was captain of the 'Great Michael' in 1511 (Grant, III, 204).

1482 Andrew Wood knighted (Grant, III, 200).

1489 Wood defeated English off Dunbar (Grant, III, 201).

1490 Wood victorious again in Firths of Forth and Tay (Grant, III, 202).

1505 The 'Great Michael' built at Newhaven (Smeaton, (a), 355). She was the 'biggest ship in the world' and was built on the orders of James IV of wood from the Fife forests which were extensively stripped for the purpose (Catford, 22). There is a model of it in the museum in the Castle.

1510 Wood created 'Admiral of the Seas' (Grant, III, 298).

1511 'Great Michael' launched (Grant, III, 298; Russell, 201). Robert Barton was made her captain (Grant, III, 204).

1513 Ship sold to Louis XII of France after Flodden (Scotsman, 11-2-1950).

1515 Death of Sir Andrew Wood (Russell, 201; Grant, III, 202, says c.1540).

The "Great Michael."

Netherbow Port

A bow was an arch (O.E.C., XII, 50). The Netherbow Port was the city gate in the Flodden Wall opening towards the Canongate. Its position is marked by brass blocks in the roadway between St. Mary's Street and Jeffrey Street. "The Netherbow Port might be called the Temple Bar of Edinburgh . . . it divided Edinburgh from the Canongate, as Temple Bar separates London from Westminster." (Scott, *Heart of Midlothian,* chap. 6).

1514–60 Flodden Wall built (see Town Walls).

1538 Netherbow Gate repaired (Grant, I, 217).

1544 Gate blown open by cannon-fire from Hertford's troops (Grant, I, 217).

1571 Netherbow Port rebuilt (Maitland, 140).

1606 New Netherbow Port built (O.E.C., XI, 11; Maitland, 140; Arnot, 238; Wilson, I, 150; Grant, I, 218; Smeaton, (a), 212). "Almost a duplicate of Porte St. Honoré in Paris." (Dunlop and Dunlop, 4; 6).

1764 Port demolished (O.E.C., IV, 50; Arnot, 238; Grant, I, 218; Smeaton, (a), 212, says 1760) and its clock was given to the Orphan Hospital (q.v.).

New Assembly Close, High Street — south side.

c.1580 The Close was the home of Murray of Blackbarony.

1766–84 Dancing Assembly in the Close.

Cameron of Lochiel's men take Edinburgh at the Netherbow Port in the Rising of 1745.

1814 House of the Assembly used by Commercial Bank until 1847.
It is now the Wax Museum and the Close continues past the Museum and ends blindly.

New College see Assembly Hall.

New Street, Canongate — north side.
c.1760 New Street built as a private roadway (O.E.C., XII, 95; Wilson, II, 85; Grant, II, 18) on the site of the demolished Kinloch's Close. Here lived the Lords Kames and Hailes.
1786 Street declared public.
1819 Street became public in effect.
It still exists, but not as private housing. The Eastern Scottish bus garage fills the east side, and there is a disused school in the west side. New Street leads to East Market Street and Calton Road.

New Town
(See A. J. Youngson, *The Making of Classical Edinburgh*, (1968)).
"Edinburgh is considerably extended on the south side, where there are divers little elegant squares built in the English manner: and the citizens have planned some improvements on the north, which, when put into execution, will add greatly to the beauty and convenience of this capital." (Smollett, 286).
1752 Publication of 'Proposals for carrying out certain Public Works in the City of Edinburgh' (Youngson, 3).
1767 Act for extending the Royalty of the City (Chambers, 6; Maxwell, 238). George Drummond (d. 1766), six times Lord Provost, "changed the face of the metropolis, and from a mass of ruinous and neglected buildings brought it into rivalship with the first cities of Europe." (O.E.C., IV, 54, quoting from the *Scots Magazine* of 1802).
1767 James Craig's plan for the New Town, submitted in 1766, was finally adopted (O.E.C., I, 146; XXIII, 1-37; Arnot, 316; Wilson, II, 204; Grant, II, 117; Smeaton, (a), 133; Youngson, 106-9).
1767 Thistle Court, reputedly the first finished building in the New Town (O.E.C., XXIII, 15; R.C., 204). Two of the houses are now lawyers' offices and two form an electricity sub-station.
1767-81 St. Andrew Square (q.v.) built. Building proceeded westward in George Street under increasingly stringent building restrictions.
1780 Town Concil ordered naming of the streets (O.E.C., XII, 2).
1784-90 Princes Street, George Street and Queen Street built up to and including Hanover Street.
1785 Rose Street and Thistle Street named (O.E.C., XXIII, 19).
1786-93 Streets built up to and including Frederick Street.
1790 New Town built west to Castle Street (Maxwell, 240).

1792 Castle Street built. Sir Walter Scott lived in No. 39 North Castle Street from 1797.

1792-1810 Charlotte Square (q.v.) built.

1802-22 Building of northern New Town, i.e. from Queen Street Gardens (1823) to Fettes Row (1819), westward to Queensferry Street (1823) and eastward to York Place (c.1798), Picardy Place (c.1800), Forth Street (c.1805) and Albany Street (c.1805) (Grant, II, 185).

1803-17 Heriot Row (1803), Abercromby Place (1804), Northumberland Street (1810), Great King Street (1817) area was designed by William Sibbald and Robert Reid (Lindsay, *Georgian Edinburgh* (1973) 50).

1813 Shandwick Place planned.

1813 Coates Crescent, William Street, Walker Street, Manor Place and Melville Street planned (Lindsay, Georgian Edinburgh, (1973), 53).

1817 Streets to be named and numbered.

1817-25 Ann Street, St. Bernard's Crescent area developed by Sir Henry Raeburn to the design of James Mylne (Youngson, 214).

1820-26 Melville Street built, designed by Robert Brown (*Edinburgh — An Architectural Guide*).

1822-3 Moray Place to Randolph Crescent built (Grant, II, 200) to the design of Gillespie Graham (Youngson, 222); completed in 1855.

1823 Drumsheugh estate laid out for building (Smeaton, (a), 291).

1823 Queen Street Gardens laid out (Grant, II, 158).

1823 Royal Circus built (Grant, II, 199), planned by William Playfair (Lindsay, *Georgian Edinburgh*, 1973, 51).

1824 Atholl Crescent begun, arthitect Thomas Bonnar (*Edinburgh — An Architectural Guide*).

1829-33 Manor Place the western extremity of the city (Smeaton, (b), 326).

1830 Rutland Square built, designed by Archibald Elliott and built by John Tait (*Edinburgh — An Architectural Guide*).

1850 New Town extended across the Dean Bridge, built in 1832 (Robertson, 159; Scotsman, 13-4-1850).

1855 Melville Crescent built, designed by John Lessels (*Edinburgh — An Architectural Guide*). John Steell's statue of the second Viscount Melville was added later.

Newhaven

Formerly called 'Our Lady's Port of Grace' (Maitland, 500; Russell, 221; Geddie, 16). The title derived from a chapel dedicated to the Virgin Mary and St. James (Grant, III, 295; Wilson, II, 200).

1504 James IV founded Newhaven (O.E.C., XX, app. 22; Russell, 95; 220).

1505 'Great Michael' built (Smeaton, (a), 355); launched, 1511 (see Navy).

1506 James IV erected a shipyard (Grant, III, 297).

1510 Edinburgh bought Newhaven (Grant, III, 168; 297; Russell, 95; 231; R.C., v) from James IV (Cruft, 93).

1513 Ropeworks in Newhaven (J. S. Marshall, *Old Leith at Work*, (1977), 75).

1550 Mary of Guise sailed from Newhaven to visit her daughter Mary (later Queen of Scots) in France (Grant, III, 298).

1793 Herring fishery begun at Newhaven (Grant, III, 301).

1797 Pier destroyed by violent storm (Grant, III, 302).

1812 Slip built.

1821 Chain pier built (Grant, III, 303; Russell, 404).

1848 Newhaven ferries transferred to Granton.

1864 Breakwater planned (Grant, III, 303).

1920 Newhaven taken into Edinburgh.

Newhaven is the main fish market for Edinburgh, but the Newhaven fishwives, once a common sight in their distinctive clothes selling fish in the streets, have disappeared.

Newhaven fishwives in their 19th century dresses. The unmarried ones went bare-headed — these two differ little from fishwives of recent times.

Newington House

1805 Newington House built in the region of the present Blacket Avenue.

1808 Stone pillars and gates erected at the ends of the Blacket Avenue and Mayfield Terrace entrances to Newington House (Smith, I, 26).

1865 Newington was the most densely populated of Edinburgh's southern suburbs (Smith, I, 28).

1915 Scottish National Institute for War Blinded acquired Newington House.

1966 House demolished and estate bought by the University of Edinburgh (Smith, I, 28).

Newspapers and Periodicals

1651 First newspaper, *Mercurius Scoticus*, published (Arnot, 454). Grant (I, 286) says that the paper was started in 1652 by Cromwell's troops who had brought a printer with them. Keir (695) says that it was issued in Leith. Sitwell and Bamford (123) say that it was a reprint, made at Leith in 1652, of the London publication *A Diurnal of Passages and Affairs*.

1660 *Mercurius Caledonius*, Scotland's first indigenous newspaper, lasted only ten issues (Keir, 696).

1699 *Edinburgh Gazette*, first city newspaper (Gray, 32; Keir, 696, says 1680).

1705 First number of the *Edinburgh Courant* (Grant, I, 203) issued from an office at the Cross.

1708 *Scots Postman* or *New Edinburgh Gazette* — a Government publication.

1718 *Evening Courant* printed thrice weekly (Maxwell, 273).

1720 *Caledonian Mercury* appeared in the Jacobean interest (Gray, 31), published from No. 265 High Street.

1739 *The Scots Magazine* began (Arnot, 453); still continues.

1763 *Edinburgh Advertiser* published (Chambers, 49; Grant, I, 318, says 1764).

1779 First number of *The Mirror* (Wilson, I, 359).

1783 *The Edinburgh Magazine* published by James Sibbald (Grant, I, 181).

1792 Six newspapers in the city — *Courant, Mercury, Herald, Advertiser, Caledonian Chronicle* and *Gazetteer* (Creech, 76, f.n.).

1802 First number of *Edinburgh Review* (Maxwell, 267; Cockburn, 166); lasted until 1929.

1817 First publication of *The Scotsman* (Grant, I, 283; Cockburn, 308; Smeaton, (a), 136; Maxwell, 273). It was published from No. 347 High Street; moved in 1842 to No. 257 High Street; to Cockburn Street in 1860; and to its present site in 1904.

1817 *Blackwood's Edinburgh Magazine* began (Maxwell, 268); still in publication.

1823 *Scotsman* published twice weekly (Maxwell, 273).

1832 *Chambers Journal* founded (Smeaton, (a), 194).

1855 *Scotsman* began daily issues (Maxwell, 273). Bought by Lord Thomson in 1953.

1873 *Edinburgh Evening News* published (Keir, 697).

1886 *Edinburgh Evening Dispatch* printed (Keir, 697). This paper was discontinued in 1963, having been gradually replaced by the *Evening News*, which Lord Thomson had also acquired.

Nicolson Square
c.1770 Houses were occupied by nobility.

1814 Wesleyan Methodist Church built (Grant, II, 335; Keir, 184); the date 1815 is carved on the frontage.

1847 Public baths opened (Scotsman, 1-12-1847).

1886 Monument by brassfounders of Edinburgh for the International Exhibition which formed part of the sundial in the Meadows (Smith, I, 23) was later erected in Nicolson Square Gardens.

Nicolson Street
c.1760 Nicolson Street formed through the grounds of Lady Nicolson's estate, east of Potterrow (Grant, II, 334).
1763 Riding School built, a block of buildings and stables, called the Royal Menage (Grant, II, 335; Scotsman, 24-5-1828).
1806 Royal Blind Asylum tranferred from Shakespeare Square (Grant, II, 336), and built on the site now occupied by St. Cuthbert's Co-operative shop.
1832 College of Surgeons (q.v.) built their Hall on the site of the Riding School (Grant, II, 335; Scotsman, 24-5-1828).

Niddrie Marischal, Craigmillar
"The Wauchopes have occupied Niddrie Marischal . . . since the twelfth century." (O.E.C., XVIII, app. 32; Cockburn, 16, f.n.).
1633 Niddrie Marischal mansion built (Geddie, 147).
    It is now a housing estate. The House was demolished some ten years ago.

Niddry's Wynd, 80-86 High Street — south side.
1477 The salt market was here under James III's Charter.
1505 St. Mary's Chapel built (Arnot, 246).
1762 St. Cecilia's Hall (q.v.) built at the corner of Niddry's Wynd and Cowgate (Arnot, 379; Chambers, 249; Wilson, II, 207; Grant, I, 251; O.E.C., I, 19; Cockburn, 29; Williamson, 312).
1788 Wynd partly demolished for building of South Bridge. Now Niddry Street (Grant, I, 245).

Nor' Loch
The Nor' Loch was an artificial defence created by damming the Craig Burn (Fraser, 28). The dam crossed the valley where the North Bridge now stands (Wood *et al.*, 389), and the loch covered the site of the present Princes Street Gardens. It extended from Lochbank or Bearford's Parks (q.v.) in the north to the Castle rock in the south, and from Trinity College Church in the east to the West (St. Cuthbert's) Church in the west. Prior to its creation the ground was the King's Garden and a tournament ground.
1396 Tournament held on the site (Chambers, 117).
1450 Nor' Loch planned as part of the town's defences (Grant, II, 80; Smeaton, (a), 29; Robertson and Wood, 4). (See Town Walls).
1460 Nor' Loch formed (O.E.C., XI, 12). It was 1700 feet (523m) long and 400 feet (123m) wide (Grant, II, 82).

1499-1500 In time of pestilence cleansing was not to be done in the Loch but in the Water of Leith (Robertson and Wood, 6).

1501-1750 Upwards of 150 suicides in the Loch (Roberston and Wood, 6).

1552, 1593, 1728 Proposals to bring the Water of Leith or the sea into the Loch (Robertson and Wood, 8).

1554 Sluice installed at the east end to regulate the height of the Loch (Robertson and Wood, 6).

1556 Butchers and slaughterers not to deposit offal etc. in the Loch (Robertson and Wood, 7).

1562 Breakers of the seventh Commandment to be 'dookit' in the Loch (Robertson and Wood, 10).

1589 Oats ordered for feeding of swans in the Loch (Robertson and Wood, 7).

1589-1670 Many witches ducked in the Loch before being burned on Castlehill (Robertson and Wood, 14).

1655 Storms cast thousands of eels upon the banks of the Loch (Robertson and Wood, 7).

1663 Much smuggling into town over the Loch (Robertson and Wood, 20; 23).

1682 Three persons drowned in frozen Loch (Grant, II, 81).

1685 Duckings ceased because the wood of the beam and stool became rotten (Robertson and Wood, 13).

Ducking a witch in the Nor' Loch.

1716 Town purchased Lochbank from Loch to Lang Dykes (q.v.)
(Robertson and Wood, 22).
1763 Nor' Loch partly drained for foundations of the North Bridge
(O.E.C., XI, 12; Arnot, 313; Grant, I, 336; Robertson and Wood,
24).
1790 Drain from St. Cuthbert's Church through the Loch bed
(Robertson and Wood, 25).
1820 Loch west of the Mound finally drained (Cockburn, 370).

North Bridge
Scheme proposed by Duke of York (later James VII) (c.1681), Earl
of Mar (1728) and Lord Kames (1754) to erect a bridge but this was
opposed by builders who were extending the city southwards.
1763 North Bridge begun (O.E.C., I, 139; IV, 49; Arnot, 313; Maxwell,
238; Smeaton, (a), 133) to the design of William Mylne. The
foundation stone was laid by Lord Provost Drummond who had
pressed for the erection of the bridge.
1769 Arch of Bridge fell (O.E.C., XXII, 197; Arnot, 314; Grant, I, 338;
Creech, 63, f.n.; Youngson, 63); due to an error in digging the
foundations (Steuart, 165).
1771-76 Quarrels regarding building west of the North Bridge, on the
south side of Princes Street.
1772 Bridge reopened for traffic (O.E.C., IX, 211; Wilson, II, 172).
1873 Bridge widened (Grant, I, 340; Maxwell, 238, f.n.).
1894-5 Bridge demolished for reconstruction.
1896 Foundation stone laid for new bridge.
1897 Bridge reopened.
1904 *Scotsman* offices built at south-west end of bridge.

North Foulis Close, 231 High Street — north side.
At the entrance to the Close there is a medallion portrait (erected in
1885) of James Gillespie who had a shop here. It shows him with a
large nose, said to suggest that the source of his fortune came from
snuff.
1826 John Kay, the caricaturist who published *Old Edinburgh Portraits*,
died in the Close (Steuart, 58).
    North Foulis Close now leads, together with Geddes' Entry
and Old Stamp Close (q.v.) to a modern courtyard.

Observatory, see Calton Hill and Blackford Hill.
1776 Old Observatory on Calton Hill (Grant, II, 104; Smeaton, (b), 374).
1818 New Observatory on Calton Hill (Grant, II, 106; Smeaton, (b),
374).
1846 Short's Observatory in Ramsay Lane (Grant, I, 87); (see Outlook
Tower).

1894-5 Royal Observatory on Blackford Hill (Smeaton, (b), 369; Keir, 938).

Old Assembly Close, High Street — south side.
Formerly called Steel's Close (Stuart, 58). "Of old this almost deserted alley formed the most common access betwixt the High Street and the southern suburbs." (Scott, *Redgauntlet*, letter V, note).
1720-66 Its Assembly Rooms were the centre of fashionable dances (see Dancing Assemblies).
1824 Close extensively damaged in the great fire which started in the Close (Grant, I, 244). (See Fires).

Later in the 19th century one of Heriot's Free Schools was built between Old Assembly Close and the neighbouring Borthwick's Close (q.v.).

The Close now leads to a children's playground (see Bell's Wynd).

Old Bank Close, Lawnmarket — south side.
Formerly called Hope's Close in 1637 when Thomas Hope, the King's Advocate, lived there (Chambers, 70).
1569 House of Robert Gourlay, messenger-at-arms, was in the Close (Chambers, 70).
1581 Ex-Regent Morton confined in Gourlay's house while awaiting execution (Chambers, 71).
1593-4 James VI stayed in the house (R. T. Skinner, *The Royal Mile*, (1947), 25).
1637 House passed to the family of Hope of Craighall, later Lord Kerse (Chambers, 72).
1689 Sir George Lockhart, Lord President of the Court of Session, murdered by Chieslie of Dalry at the head of the Close (Chambers, 75).
1700-1805 Bank of Scotland at the foot of the Close after a fire in Parliament Close in 1700 destroyed the Bank's premises there. (Chambers, 70; Grant, II, 95, says from 1695).
c.1827 Demolished for building of George IV Bridge.

Old Fishmarket Close, 190 High Street — south side.
Reached through an archway in Salamander Land (q.v.) (Grant, I, 242), it contained the fish market in the 17th century.

Among those living in the Close were George Heriot, Daniel Defoe, Lord President Dundas and the public hangman (Wiliamson, 230). It contained the offices of the *Courant* newspaper. Several editions of the *Encyclopaedia Britannica* were printed in the Close.

1708 The Post Office was sited at the foot of the Close.
1824 Severely destroyed in the great fire.
  The Church of Scotland's People's Palace, a day centre for homeless and a night shelter for those unable to secure admission to a lodging house, is in the Close near the Cowgate.

Old Playhouse Close, 194–198 Canongate — south side.
17th century Tenement built (R.C., 179).
1746 First regular theatre in Edinburgh (q.v.) established (Grant, II, 23).
  John Home's *Douglas* was produced here in 1756 (Grant, II, 24).
1769 Theatre discontinued when Theatre Royal opened in Shakespeare Square.
1960's Close renovated.

Old Post Office Close, High Street — north side.
The Post Office was housed on the first floor of a house in the Close in the first half of the 18th century (Grant, I, 358).
  The Close was absorbed in the enlargement of the City Chambers buildings in 1932 and the site of the Close is marked by a plaque on the City Collectors's Office.

Old St. Paul's Church, Jeffrey Street.
In 1689 Episcopalians left St. Giles Church with the Bishop of Edinburgh on account of their Jacobite allegiance and their refusal to accept the succession of William of Orange. They were disestablished, and worshipped in a wool-store at the junction of Leith Wynd and Carrubber's Close for nearly 200 years until the Church was built in 1883.

Old Stamp Office Close, High Street — north side.
Here lived the Earl of Eglintoune (Chambers, 192) whose house became Fortune's Tavern (see Inns).
  The Close contained the office of the Scottish Inland Revenue until 1821.
  Old Stamp Office Close now leads, together with Geddes' Entry and North Foulis Close (q.v.) into a modern courtyard.

Old Town, see also Architecture and Early Houses.
The original extent was from the Castle to the Netherbow with wynds and closes opening to either side. The Cowgate and Canongate were added later to the Old Town. It lay within the Town Walls (q.v.) until the Canongate was absorbed. The earliest town was some quarter of a square mile (65 hectares).
  "Even in 1700 some of the tenements built on a slope reached fourteen storeys . . . one such monster, nicknamed 'Babylon', and

The Old Town of Edinburgh at sunset from the Salisbury Crags.

described as 'ane immense heap of combustible material'." (Smout, 343).

"The forty years between 1760 and 1800 saw the Old Town thoroughly changed in respect of population." (Wood *et al.*, 13). (See Population).

1820-30 'Improvements' in the Old Town (O.E.C., XII, 249).

1860 "Since 1860 two-thirds of the ancient buildings in the Old Town of Edinburgh have been demolished." (O.E.C., I, 1 — dated 1908; Chambers, 10, f.n.). This process continued and eventually led to a protection order after the report of the Royal Commission on Ancient and Historic Monuments (1951).

1866-7 City Improvement Trust resulted in the destruction of much Cowgate property including High School Yards and Wynd (O.E.C., V, 90; Grant, II, 251; Wood *et al.*, 33).

1902 Further demolition of old houses (O.E.C., I, 8).

1951 Following the preservation measures for Ancient and Historic buildings the Town Council has restored considerable parts of the Old Town, especially in the Lawnmarket and Canongate. Maintenance of structural appearances has been achieved, notably in White Horse Close, Huntly House and Chessel's Court.

Oratory and Palace of Mary of Guise, Castlehill — north side. Built after 1544 (Dunlop and Dunlop, 62) and taken down in 1845 for the building of the Assembly Hall and New College of the Free Church (Dunlop and Dunlop, 73; Chambers, 25, says 1846; R.C., 126, says 1861; Nimmo, 66, also says the Palace was demolished in 1861). The Laus Deo house bears the surprising date 1591 in an illustration in Chambers (22), Grant (I, 92) says that it bore the

inscription *Laus honor Deo* and the initials I.R. (James V).
Mary died in 1560.

Orphan Hospital
1733 Erected to the design of William Adam near Trinity College
Church (q.v.) on the site now covered by Waverley Station. It was
built by private donations helped by the Society for the Propagation
of Christian Knowledge (O.E.C., XXVII, 155; Grant, I, 359).
1738 Seal of Cause granted by the Town Council (Grant, I, 359).
1742 Royal Letters Patent created it a corporation (Grant, I, 359).
1764 Clock from the demolished Netherbow erected (Grant, I, 218).
1845 Hospital demolished during the development of the railways, and
rebuilt at Dean (q.v.).

Outlook Tower, 549 Castlehill — north side.
1846 Maria Theresa Short's Observatory built (Grant, I, 87) in a 17th
century building through the ground floor of which Skinner's
Close passed (R.C., 72). A camera obscura which she devised,
affording a panoramic view of the city, was installed about 1855.
1891 Acquired by Patrick Geddes.
1950's Outlook Tower sold to the University of Edinburgh.

Oysters
1592 Records of oyster fishing at Newhaven date from 1592 (J. S.
Marshall, *Old Leith at Work*, (1977), 44).
1773 Oysters were sent from the Forth to London for the first time
(Arnot, 586). "From their beds in the Forth, they are taken to the
Medway and other rivers not distant from London, where they are
deposited to fatten for the consumption of the great metropolis . . If
the oyster-banks on the Forth are not dragged more sparingly, this
commodity will be speedily exhausted." (Arnot, 586).
At one time its was estimated that six million oysters were
landed in one year from the beds between Newhaven and
Inchkeith, but they rapidly disappeared owing to lack of control.

Paisley Close, see Heave Awa' Land.

Palace of Mary of Guise, see Oratory.

Panmure House, Canongate — north side.
c.1691 House built and was the residence of the Earls of Panmure (Keir,
32).
1778-90 Occupied by Adam Smith, author of *Wealth of Nations*
(Chambers, 318).
1957 House restored by Town Council with a donation from Lord

168

Thomson and used as the Canongate Boys' Club (founded in 1927) (Keir, 43).

1973 A social training centre for young people (Catford, 93). It is now reached only through Little Lochend Close.

Paper-Making

Paper-making is a trade long associated with the Water of Leith, and its history is discussed in O.E.C., XXV, 46-70 from which the following dates are taken —

c.1591; 1675; 1679 Mills opened at Dalry.

1659; 1681 Mills opened at Canonmills.

1681; 1716; 1717; 1742; 1770 Mills opened at Colinton.

1681; 1693 Mills opened at Restalrig.

1709; 1716; 1727; 1766; 1779 Mills opened at Penicuik.

1714 Mill opened at Slateford.

Parliament Close (Square), High Street — south side.

"Which new-fangled affectation has termed a square." (Scott, *Redgauntlet*, chap. 1).

Before the 17th century the ground occupied by Parliament House and adjacent buildings was St. Giles Churchyard which extended down to the Cowgate. After the Reformation St. Giles Church became "the place of sepulture." (Chambers, 109).

Parliament Close was not formed until after the Restoration as a line of private buildings forming a square with the Church (Chambers, 110). The inhabitants and shopkeepers formed themselves into the Parliament Close Council of 50-100 members who dined together (Chambers, 115).

1676, 1700, 1824 Fires in Parliament Close (see Fires).

1685 Statue of Charles II erected in the Close (O.E.C., III, 218; XVI, 141; XVII, 82-90; Maitland, 105; 185; Arnot, 297; Wilson, I, 265; Grant, I, 176; R.C., 122). The statue was repaired in 1824 and 1972.

1707 Following the Union of Parliaments, Parliament House was used for the Court of Session. Previously the private dwellings had given place to various courts, the High Court of Justiciary, the Court of Session, the Court of Exchequer, and the requisite adjoining rooms.

1753 Description of Parliament Close (O.E.C., III, 228).

1817 County Buildings (q.v.) erected (Grant, I, 123); rebuilt in 1905 (Keir, 1008; Cruft, 2, says 1907).

1820's A symmetrical façade, designed by Robert Reid, was applied to the front of previously individually styled buildings, and this took some years to erect.

1888 Statue of 5th Duke of Buccleuch unveiled in the Close.

1965 Statue of John Knox removed from St. Giles Church and erected in Parliament Close (Evening News, 15-3-1978).

1977 Major resurfacing on the west side of the Close.

Parliament House (Hall), Parliament Close (Square).
The early Parliaments were held in the Great Hall of the Castle, and later in the Tolbooth (Grant, I, 157).

1632 On the suggestion of Charles I the Collegiate buildings of St. Giles were demolished for the building of Parliament House (O.E.C., III, 219; XIII; 1-78; Maitland, 185; Smeaton, (a), 179). It was designed by John Mylne.

"The only reasons given for the undertaking were that the accommodation for Parliament, the Court of Session, the Exchequer and other Crown officials was inadequate, and that it was unseemly that part of St. Giles should be set aside for secular purposes." (Extracts from the Records of the Burgh of Edinburgh, 1626-41, xi). But the Council had put the Church to many uses, and the Church had to be closed if Charles I were to make it a Cathedral for the bishoprics he wished to erect.

The Hall lies north and south at the west end of Parliament Close (Square).

1639 Parliament House occupied (O.E.C., III, 221; XIII, 50; Arnot, 293; Maxwell, 165).

1639-1707 Parliament Hall used for meetings of the Three Estates (i.e. the Scottish Parliament) (Grant, I, 157).

1640 Parliament House completed (O.E.C., III, 221; Maxwell, 165).

Parliament Hall.

The only parts of this Hall remaining are the Great Hall, the west half of the First Division Court, the Lobby from Parliament Close and the Advocates' Robing Room (O.E.C., III, 221). The Laigh Hall of 1636 is still in the original form.

1642 College of Justice asssembled in Parliament Hall, and has remained there.

1656 General Monk feasted in Hall (O.E.C., III, 223; Wilson, I, 265).

1680 Duke of York (later James VII (II)) entertained in Hall (O.E.C., III, 223; Wilson, I, 135; Grant, II, 75; Arnot, 177, says 1685).

1705 Parliament took steps towards a union with England (Wilson, I, 141).

1707 Last meeting of the Scottish Parliament (Grant, I, 163; Maxwell, 184) before the Union of Parliaments (Arnot, 189; Wilson, I, 280; Grant, I, 163). "The Union of the Crowns had but complicated existing evils; the only remedy lay in legislative fusion." (Maxwell, 184).

1707 Scenes over the Union (O.E.C., III, 224; IV, 4; Maxwell, 185; Wilson, I, 142, says 1706).

"By the middle of the eighteenth century the people of Edinburgh, recognising the chief reason for the increasing wealth of the country, had well-nigh laid aside their resentment against the Union." (Maxwell, 222).

1753 Description of Parliament Close (O.E.C., III, 228).

1808 Extension of Law Courts (O.E.C., III, 237; Wilson, I, 154; Cockburn, 110).

1844 New suite of rooms built to south of Hall (O.E.C., III, 210).

1868 Stained glass window placed in Hall (Smeaton, (a), 181).

1889-92 William Nelson restored old Parliament Hall, now only used regularly by advocates.

1963 Two new courtrooms added, making twelve in all (Keir, 193).

Particate
A particate is a rood or one-fourth of an acre (approx. $1000m^2$) (O.E.C., X, 97, f.n.; Maitland, 148).

Paul's Work (Wark), foot of Leith Wynd — east side.
1479 Hospital of Our Blessed Lady founded (O.E.C., XVII, 49-75; Maitland, 468; Grant, I, 300; Robertson, 278). R.C. (184) calls it the Hospital of St. Paul, and gives the date as 1469.

1582 Town Council became proprietors of this charity (Grant, I, 301), and the building was reconstructed (Smeaton, (a), 217).

1601 Seven Flemings brought to work a woollen factory here (Maitland, 55).

1619 Buildings reconstructed and renamed Paul's Work, a charitable work factory (O.E.C., XV, 133; Arnot, 248; Wilson, II, 180;

Grant, I, 301; Dunlop and Dunlop, 53; Robertson, 278), and Dutch workers brought to teach children the manufacture of woollen stuffs (Grant, I, 301; Smeaton, (a), 217).

1632 Converted into a Correction House for idle vagabonds (Dunlop and Dunlop, 54; Robertson, 279).

1636 Used as a temporary prison while still taking apprentice weavers.

1650 Used as a hopital for wounded soldiers of David Leslie's army (Grant, I, 302).

1683 Linen manufacture in Paul's Work (Grant I, 302).

1731 Charity Workhouse opened nearby, but superseded by a new Charity Workhouse near Bristo Port (built in 1743 south of Greyfriars Kirkyard) (Robertson, 279).

1750 This building sold and inmates transferred to the new Charity Workhouse (R.C., 184).

1779 Manufacture of broad cloths (Grant, I, 302).

1843 Used as Canongate Free Church (Scotsman 19-9-1849).

1849 Paul's Work demolished during North British Railway workings (Grant, I, 302).

Paving of Streets

1532 First paving of High Street (O.E.C., XIV, 84; Maitland, 12; Grant, I, 192; Smeaton, (a), 65). This was reputedly done by a Frenchman, Jean Marlin, but Chambers (209) says that the Foliot brothers were responsible. (See Marlin's Wynd).

1535 Canongate paved (R.C., liii).

1543 West Bow to West Port paved (Grant, II, 230).

Late 16th century Granite setts (q.v.) laid down in the mud of the causeways.

1688 Royal Charter compelled proprietors to construct walks of hewn stone in front of their tenements (R.C., xlix).

'Pear-tree House'

The name given to a house at the junction of West Richmond Street and Chapel Street from the pear-tree in the garden.

1756 House built (O.E.C., XXII, 88), and was owned by Sir James Ferguson, Earl of Glencairn, and, later, Andrew Usher, father of the donor of the Usher Hall (O.E.C., XXII, 88).

Until recently owned by a distillery company, but now is becoming derelict.

Peebles Wynd, High Street — south side.
Peebles Wynd was one of the corn markets under James III's Charter.

A favourite dwelling place for bakers, the Wynd was demolished during the construction of Hunter Square c.1788. The

Quaker Meeting House in the Wynd moved to the Pleasance (Keir, 183).

Peffermill House, Duddingston.

1636 Peffermill House built by Edward Edgar of Wedderlie in the Merse (Geddie, 133) and is thought to have been where Braidwood taught deaf children (see Dumbiedykes).

The mill at the house was recently removed, but the house, approached from Peffermill Road, is still occupied.

Pend

A pend was an archway.

Photography

There were many enthusiastic photographers in Edinburgh from 1843 with the invention of the Calotype process by Robert Adamson, and its use by David Octavius Hill in his Calton Hill studio.

1861 Edinburgh Photographic Society formed (Keir, 560). It holds an exhibition annually during the Edinburgh International Festival.

Physic Garden see Botanic Garden.

Picardy

Picardy was situated in the area enclosed between the modern Picardy Place and Union Street, and now only remains as Picardy Place, the continuation of York Place to the east.

1685 French artisans, having left Multrie's Hill (q.v.), settled in Picardy after the Edict of Nantes was revoked (Wilson, II, 213).

1725 Colony of French weavers in 'Little Picardy' (Grant, II, 85).

1730 Governors of Heriot's Hospital sold part of Broughton Loan to the city for the use of the French refugees who colonised the Picardy village (Grant, II, 186) and ran a spinning school in Gray's Close (O.E.C., XXV, 13) until 1739.

1776 All the original settlers had died by this date (O.E.C., XXV, 27).

c.1800 Picardy Place built, designed by Robert Burn.

Piershill

Piershill and the Three Steps were two lands of the Barony of Restalrig. Piershill was "a distinct heritable subject at the very beginning of the sixteenth century" and the name occurs in a feu charter of 1580 (O.E.C., XXIII, 63-81). The Three Steps lay immediately west of Piershill, roughly south of the former St. Margaret's repair sheds and the old Piershill suburban railway line station.

Grant's (III, 142) account of an 18th century Colonel Piers as the founder of Piershill is unsubstantiated, nor has any Colonel Piers been traced.

1753-60 Piershill belonged to the Earl of Moray.

1758 The Three Steps purchased by Louis Cauvin who lived near Jock's Lodge (q.v.) and whose school was in Bishop's Close (q.v.).

1774-93 Lands held by Lord Elliot.

1793 Plans for Piershill Barracks (Grant, III, 142; Minto and Armstrong, 29).

1934 Barracks demolished for tenement dwellings (O.E.C., XXIII, 78; Minto and Armstrong, 29).

Pilrig

Pilrig means the peel (i.e. tower) on the ridge (O.E.C., XXII, 161).

1623 Gilbert Kirkwood acquired the lands of Pilrig (R.C., 220).

1638 Pilrig House built (O.E.C., XXII, 160-166; Grant, III, 91; Russell, 386).

1828 Additions to the house by William Burn. The house is still standing in Pilrig Park, but is derelict.

1849 Pilrig Model Buildings Association formed for research into working-class houses (Grant, III, 92).

Pinkie House, Musselburgh.

1617 Pinkie House built by Lord Seton.

1745 Prince Charles slept in the house after the Battle of Prestonpans (Grant, I, 331).

It is now part of Loretto School.

Plack see also Coinage.

A plack = two bodles = fourpence Scots = one third of one English penny in the old currency.

Plague and Pestilence see also Street Cleanliness.

1475 Outbreak of plague in Edinburgh (Sitwell and Bamford, 36).

c.1500 Description of two outbreaks of plague (Fraser, 48-50).

1513 Plague in town (Maitland, 11; Maxwell, 202).

1517 Pestilence in town (O.E.C., IX, 26; Fraser, 61).

1519 Return of pestilence (O.E.C., IX, 27). Fraser (61) says that this was leprosy and that a leper colony was set up at Greenside (q.v.).

1530 Plague in town (Wilson, II, 125; Grant, I, 298; Maxwell, 202). It was also in Leith (Grant, III, 168).

1568 Plague in town (Maitland, 23; Wilson, I, 264; Grant, III, 29; Maxwell, 202).

1574 Plague in town (J. Stark, *Picture of Edinburgh* (1806), 9).

1585 Plague in town (O.E.C., X, 184; XVI, 26; Maitland, 43). 1400 citizens died (Smout, 152). Patients and convalescents were evacuated to the Burgh Muir (q.v.).

1645 Plague in city (Maitland, 85; Arnot, 259; Wilson, II, 81; Grant, II, 6; Maxwell, 202; Russell, 329; Geddie, 165; Stark, loc. cit., 39, who said that it was the last visitation). The worst affected area was Mary King's Close (q.v.) from which the few left alive fled (Nimmo, 77). Plague also in Leith (Grant, III, 186; 263) from which only 40 per cent survived (Fraser, 113). There was a similar evacuation of the sick to the Burgh Muir, and to Leith Links from Leith.

"All business in the Town came to a standstill. The High School and the College were dismissed, the Court of Session and Parliament left the city, and the trade, as is shown by the Common Good's yield, diminished by one half where it did not utterly disappear." (Extracts from the Records of the Burgh of Edinburgh (1642-1665), lvii). The University went to Linlithgow for a year (Fraser, 111).

The plague was eliminated by flea and rat control at Leith and other ports (Keir, 347).

1831 Cholera in city (Livingstone, (a), 11).

1848 Cholera in city (Grierson, 17; Scotsman, 7-10-1848; 8-11-1848).

Pleasance

Formerly Dearenough (Wilson, II, 128; Grant, I, 382). The name Pleasance was given to the site of the Priory of Nuns dedicated to St. Mary of Placentia (Maitland, 176; Arnot, 252; 328), but R.C. (216) doubts whether such a nunnery ever existed.

1636 Portion of the village of 'The Pleasants' purchased by the city from the Earl of Roxburghe (Smeaton, (b), 103; R.C., xlix, gives 1639).

The Pleasance is in process of demolition; some of the west side has been built as flats; some of the east side is University of Edinburgh buildings; the rest is derelict and the church is an organ store.

Police see also Town Guard.

1771 Police commissioners for suburban areas (Robertson, 155).

1805 Act to set up one group of police commissioners for the town (Grant, II, 120). A police court erected in Riddle's Court.

1812 Police system introduced. Police court discontinued and work returned to the Burgh Court.

1817 Town Guard (q.v.) disbanded (O.E.C., XIV, 170; Wilson, II, 38; Maxwell, 218; Cockburn, 197; 339; Smeaton, (b), 206; Robertson, 263).

1848 Police Office in High Street on the site of Salamander Land (q.v.)

(Grant, I, 242; Scotsman, 23-2-1848).

1904 Police telephone boxes introduced at 24 points throughout the city (Keir, 214).

1926 Traffic department created.

1928 Automatic signals on some crossroads.

1933 Police box system introduced — 141 boxes in the city (Keir, 214).

1977 Lothian Region budgets an expenditure of £7½m on police for the year.

Poliomyelitis

1936, 1941, 1947 and subsequently until 1959 — small outbreaks in the city (Keir, 348).

1956 Poliomyelitis vaccination scheme launched with a successful control (Keir, 349).

Population

These figures are not strictly comparable as they refer to different areas, and the city was growing by the acquisition of neighbouring districts — but they convey the general growth.

1660 City and Leith 35,372 (Smeaton, (b), 108).

1707 City 20,000 (Maxwell, 199).

1760 City 60,000.

1775 City 80,836 (Arnot, 339; Creech, 88, f.n.).

1791 New Town 7,206 (Gray, 17).

1811 Edinburgh and Leith 102,987 (Grant, II, 120).

1831 Greater Edinburgh 175,407 (Keir, 99).

1881 Greater Edinburgh 320,549 (Keir, 99).

1931 Greater Edinburgh 439,101 (Keir, 99).

There were some 450,000 inhabitants of Greater Edinburgh before the intake, after the local government reorganisation of 1975, of West Lothian, Midlothian and East Lothian into the

THE REGENT'S BRIDGE
WATERLOO PLACE

This sketch affords a good specimen of the style of architecture in the New Town of Edinburgh. The objects discernible in it are:— The Regent's Arch, the Theatre, New Buildings, the Royal Institution. St. John's Chapel, and St. Cuthbert's Church. The Regent's Bridge is a stupendous Arch thrown across one of the streets below, leading to the old town; the foundations of the houses in the foreground being on a level with the base of the arch, and these houses being in height eight stories. In the sketch are introduced a Newhaven fish-woman, and a Highland piper and soldier.

Lothian Region which now has a population of some 740,000.

Between 1951 and 1971 there has been an extraordinary movement of population away from the central area of the city which has lost 43 per cent of its population in twenty years (Peacock *et al.*, 3).

Porteous Riots

1736 Porteous riots (O.E.C., IV, 22; Maitland, 123; Arnot, 206; Wilson, I, 143; 252; Grant, I, 128-131; Maxwell, 215; Carlyle, 38; Smeaton, (a), 125; 257; Catford, 38). The story is told in Scott's *Heart of Midlothian.*

The grave of Captain John Porteous in Greyfriars Churchyard was marked only by a post inscribed 'P.1736', but this was replaced in 1973 by a headstone and an inscription (Catford, 40).

Portobello

1739 Portobello founded. House built on Figgate Lands (q.v.) in 1742 and named Portobello after Puerto Bello in Panama which was captured in 1739 (Russell, 380; Smeaton, (a), 361).

1742 Portobello Hut built (Grant, III, 144); demolished in 1851.

1763 Feuing began (Grant, III, 144).

1765 Bed of clay discovered (Grant, III, 144) west of the town.

1785 Tower built (O.E.C., XIV, 84) as a summer house; it was restored in 1864.

1795 Bathing machines on the sands.

1806 Salt water baths built (Grant, III, 147).

1822 George IV reviewed Yeomanry on the sands (Grant, III, 146).

1825 St. Mark's Episcopal Chapel built (Grant, III, 147).

1825 Relief Chapel built (Grant, III, 147).

1826 St. John's R.C. Chapel built (Grant, III, 147).

THE ROYAL INSTITUTION, CASTLE, &c., PRINCES STREET

This magnificent structure, commenced in 1825, from the designs of Mr Playfair, was erected at the joint expense, and for the mutual accommodation of, the Royal Society, the Society of Antiquaries, and the Society for the Encouragement of the Fine Arts, in Scotland; and is one of the most attractive buildings in Edinburgh.

1827 John G. Lockhart lived in Portobello while writing his *Life of Burns.*
1833 Portobello a Parliamentary Burgh (Grant, III, 146).
1834 United Secession Chapel built (Grant, III, 147).
1856 Hugh Miller, the geologist, committed suicide in his house in Tower Street (Grant, III, 148).
1860 Building of Promenade begun. Pulled down in 1916.
1871 Iron pier constructed (Grant, III, 148), demolished in 1916.
1876 Free Church built (Grant, III, 147).
1876 Marine Parade planned (Grant, III, 147).
1878 Town Hall built.
1880 U.P. Church built (Grant, III, 147).
1896 Portobello incorporated into the city (Chambers, 332, f.n.).
1914 New Town Hall built (Keir, 1008).
1923 Power Station opened (Keir, 1008); closed in 1977.
1936 Open air swimming pool opened (Keir, 1008; Catford, 234, says 1939). Closed in 1979.

Ports or Gates
c.1560 Ports for entry or exit through the town walls (q.v.).
They were all ruinous by 1745 (Grant, I, 38).
West Port, Grassmarket (Maitland, 139; Grant, II, 222).
Greyfriars Port or Bristo Port on the site covered by the New North Church (Maitland, 139).
Potterrow Port, between the Old College of the University of Edinburgh and the Royal Scottish Museum (Grant, II, 330).
Cowgate Port, at the foot of St. Mary's Wynd (now Street) (Maitland, 140; Wilson, II, 127; Grant, I, 298).
Netherbow Port, at the junction of the High Street and St. Mary's Wynd (Street) (Grant, I, 217).
New Port or Halkerston's Wynd Port, at the south end of the foundations of the North Bridge (Chambers, 117, f.n.).

Portsburgh
A suburb to the west of the West Port, extending to Tollcross (Smeaton, (a), 260), owned by the Touris of Inverleith. "The trade suburb of Old Edinburgh, as the Royal Burgh of Canongate outside the Netherbow was its Court suburb." (quoted by Williamson, 258; Wilson, II, 169).
Easter Portsburgh comprised Potterrow and Bristo; Wester Portsburgh contained West Port and Lauriston. Main Point, Wester Portsburgh, or Port Hopetoun, was the terminus of the Union Canal (q.v.) (Youngson, 179).
1648 City bought the superiority of Portsburgh (Maitland, 110; Grant, II, 222; Smeaton, (b), 276) from Hepburn of Humbie to whom the

Touris family had sold the land (R.C., lix).
1856 Portsburgh merged into the city under the Edinburgh Municipal
Extension Act.

Post Office
"The Post-Office was in the first floor of a house near the Cross,
above an alley which still bears the name of the Post-Office Close.
Thence it removed to a floor in the south side of the Parliament
Square, which was fitted up like a shop, and the letters were dealt
across an ordinary counter, like other goods. At this time all the
out-of-door business of delivery was managed by only one
letter-carrier . . . From the Parliament Square the office was
removed to Lord Covington's house [behind the Parliament
Close] . . . thence, after some years, to a house in North Bridge
Street; thence to Waterloo Place; and finally to a new and handsome
structure on the North Bridge." (Chambers, 129, f.n.).
1635 Post Office first established in Edinburgh; mails to London twice
weekly; postage 8 pence [presumably Scots] (Smeaton, (b), 103).
1695 Act for General Post Office in city (Arnot, 538; Grant, I, 354).
1710 General Post Office subordinated to London (Grant, I, 355).
1715 First mounted post — Edinburgh to Stirling (Maxwell, 189).
1774-5 Penny post established by Peter Williamson in the Luckenbooths
(Edinburgh Tatler, January, 1978, 71; Grant, I, 356, says 1776;
Scotsman, 5-7-1978, says 1773-4).
1793 Penny post to Leith, Musselburgh, Dalkeith and Prestonpans
(Grant, II, 283).
1821 General Post Office moved to Waterloo Place (O.E.C., XII, 35;
Grant, I, 234; 358). The building now houses the Excise Office (C.
McWilliam, *New Town Guide,* (1978), 16).
1848 Delivery of letters from London and the South commenced at 7
a.m., 11 a.m., 3 p.m., and 6 p.m., and "should be completed in
about two hours" (Scotsman, 4-3-1848).
1861 Prince Consort laid foundation stone of General Post Office in its
present site (Grant, I, 358; Smeaton, (a), 142).
1866 General Post Office opened (Grant, I, 358; Smeaton, (a), 344).

Post Office Close see Old Post Office Close.

Potterrow, from South College Street to West Nicolson Street.
The Potterrow Port stood at the north end of the present
Potterrow.
1582 Occupied by Lennox's troops intending to seize Holyrood Palace
(Grant, II, 330).
1639 Gun foundry established in Potterrow to cast cannon for Leslie's
troops in the first Covenanting War (Chambers, 247; Grant, II, 330).

179

1673 Tailors' Hall built (O.E.C., XXII, 63; Grant, II, 331). This was demolished with much of the Potterrow during the 1970 development of the University of Edinburgh, but the lintel is preserved in Huntly House Museum.

18th century In the late 18th century Mrs Flockhart's ('Lucky Fykie's') Tavern (Chambers, 168; Stuart, 90).

Pound Scots
One pound Scots = one-twelfth of £1 stg. = 1/8d = 8p.

Poverty Relief
1576 Tokens provided for the poor (Robertson, 281).

1592 Council ordered a tax or levy for the poor (Robertson, 282).

1596 Council spent £100 on food for the poor (Robertson, 282).

1630 Church collections for the poor (Robertson, 283).

1695-1813 Percentage of property rates levied went for poor relief (Robertson, 283).

1738 Proposed Charity Workhouse at Bristo (Robertson, 284).

1743 Workhouse opened (Robertson, 287).

1762 St. Cuthbert's Poorhouse opened (Robertson, 304).

1772, 1783, 1813 Shortage of Workhouse funds (Robertson, 291; 292; 293).

1842 Removal of Bedlam (q.v.) and patients transferred to Morningside Asylum (Robertson, 297; Grant, II, 324, say Bedlam demolished in 1871).

1845 Poor Law Act (Robertson, 303).

1868 Craigleith Poorhouse opened (Robertson, 304), now the Western General Hospital.

1870 Craiglockhart Poorhouse opened (Robertson, 303), now Greenlea Old People's Home.

Powderhall, Broughton.
18th century Mansion built and was the residence of the Mylnes of Powderhall (Grant, III, 89).

1870 Powderhall Stadium housed the New Year professional sprint handicap until the 1950's (Keir, 536); (see Sports).

The stadium now houses greyhound racing (since 1927) and speedway racing (since 1977).

President's Steps
The name given to a flight of steps from the east end of Parliament Close to the Old Post Office Close (O.E.C., XII, 131). These should not be confused with Back Stairs (q.v.).

President's Steps no longer remain.

Prestonfield House

The estate belonged to the Hamiltons, but the date of building is uncertain. The house was sometimes called Priestfield House (Grant, III, 56).

1677 Sir James Dick bought Prestonfield (R.C., l).

1681 Prestonfield House burned (Grant, III, 56) by students of Edinburgh University (Smith, I, 33).

1687 House rebuilt to the design of William Bruce. Description of the house and grounds (Cockburn, 17).

    The grounds are now covered by a golf course and a housing scheme, and the house is a hotel.

Princes Street

Originally intended to be called St. Giles Street but George III objected. The name was changed to Prince's Street after the Prince Regent, and the present plural form was adopted in 1848 (Malcolm, (b), 26).

    It began as a residential street (Steuart, 167-175) as may be seen in old prints.

1769 First house in Princes Street built by John Neale, a silk mercer, on the site of the present Woolworth's (Edinburgh Evening Dispatch, 20-6-1949). It was No. 10 and was to be free of burghal taxation for all time. Neale's daughter married Archibald Constable, the publisher, who bought the house in 1822.

    No. 17 became Blackwood's bookshop in 1816, then Elliott's bookshop and later another bookshop.

    No. 21 was built by Shadrach Moyes, now a multiple tailoring store.

    No. 27 was occupied by Henry Erskine after he left George Square, now R. W. Forsyth's store. Another source says he lived in No. 53 which is now an hotel.

    No. 31 was owned by Lord Hermand, and is also part of R. W. Forsyth's shop.

    No. 37 was the house of John Clerk of Eldin, father of the lame lawyer of the same name, and is now a clothes shop.

    No. 40 was built by a lawyer called Wight who owned the house in St. Andrew Square just north of it, and built the Princes Street house low and flat-roofed so that he could still see the clock in St. Giles Tower. The Sun Life Insurance occupied the first floor; now a fashion shop.

    No. 84 was a Tax Office and was later owned by James Donaldson who founded Donaldson's Hospital (q.v.). The New Club occupied Nos. 84 and 85 from 1834. No. 84 is a shop for children's clothes.

    No. 100 was owned by Lady Mary Clerk of Penicuik, and is

now the Overseas League Club.

No. 106 belonged to a friend of Sir Walter Scott, John Irving, and has recently been opened as a bookshop.

No. 108 was Lord Woodhouselee's house; later Mackie's baker's shop and tearooms, now a bookshop.

No. 126 was owned by James Skene of Rubislaw who designed Princes Street Gardens after the Nor' Loch was drained. It is a shop for woollen goods.

No. 139 housed Lord Braxfield's widow, Mrs Orde, and is now the American Express office.

(The information regarding the owners is taken from Steuart, 167-175).

1771 David Hume's house built in St David's Street (Wilson, I, 209).

1786 Hanover Street built (Grant, II, 162).

1795 Frederick Street built (Grant, II, 162).

1805 Princes Street completely built (Malcolm, (b), 35).

1821 Shops and flats began to be built (Robertson, 8).

1827 Act to prevent building at the east end of the south side of Princes Street (Robertson and Wood, 33), i.e. west of the site for the North British Hotel, and above ground level.

1834 New Club, designed by William Burn, opened (Cruft, 65).

1850 Princes Street becoming a business quarter (Robertson, 52).

1866 University Club opened (Grant, II, 125).

1876 The Arcade completed (Grant, II, 125) — vanished in 1950 in shop development.

1877 Princes Street widened.

1896 Site cleared for North British Railway Hotel (O.E.C., I, 149).

1902 North British Railway Hotel opened (O.E.C., XXIII, 152; Malcolm, (b), 49). The tower rises to 195 feet (60m) above the pavement, and there are four storeys below and six storeys above ground level. The four clock faces are each 13 feet (4m) in diameter, each minute hand being 6ft. 3in. (1.9m) long and each hour hand 4ft. 6in. (1.4m).

1903 Jenner's store absorbed the old Stock Exchange (q.v.) (Grierson, 40).

1904 Caledonian Station Hotel built (*Edinburgh Weekly*, 7-10-1966).

1923 Council purchased Nos. 10-15 Princes Street and imposed rates (Malcolm, (b), 27). Now Woolworth's store.

The water supply to Princes Street derived from the reservoir on Castlehill (see Water Supply).

New building in Princess Street must now conform to the requirements of a statutory panel regarding the provision of an upper level pedestrian walk-way, while there are other regulations regarding displays in the shops.

Princes Street Gardens see also Nor' Loch.

1816-20 West Princes Street Gardens laid out (Grant, II, 98; Smeaton, (a), 273).

1816 Building prohibited on south side of Princes Street (O.E.C., I, 148).

1827 Act prohibiting for 21 years building in East Princes Street Gardens (Robertson and Wood, 33).

1830 East Princes Street Gardens laid out (Grant, II, 100).

1831 Act making the 1827 prohibition perpetual (Robertson and Wood, 33).

1836 Proposed railway through the Gardens successfully opposed (Robertson, 37).

1840 Foundation stone laid for Scott monument, (200ft. (61m) high) designed by George Meikle Kemp, in East Gardens (Grant, II, 126; Gilbert, 99, says 1838). Repair to deteriorating stone, 1974-7.

1845 Railway begun through the Gardens (Robertson, 45). (See Railways).

1846 John Steell's statue of Sir Walter Scott placed in the monument (Grant, II, 127).

1849-50 East Gardens remodelled following the building of the railway (Grant, II, 100).

1850 First move to make the Gardens public (Robertson, 52).

1853 First band concerts in the Gardens (Robertson, 47; Grierson, 5).

1854 Statue of John Wilson ('Christopher North') by John Steell erected in East Gardens (Grant, II, 127).

1862 Crown won a lawsuit against Town Council over the ownership of the land in the West Gardens used for the railway (Robertson and Wood, 45).

1867 Allan Ramsay statue by John Steell in West Gardens (Robertson, 50).

Detail from Scott Monument showing the "Lady of the Lake."

1868 Two dozen seats bought for band performances (Robertson, 48).
1869 Ross fountain sanctioned (Robertson, 51).
1872 Iron bridge erected over the railway (Robertson, 46).
1872 Proposed bandstand for Gardens (Robertson, 48), erected in 1878 (Malcolm, (b), 73).
1872 Waverley Market (q.v.) built (Smeaton, (a), 269).
1872-3 Waverley Bridge built (Grant, II, 100; Smeaton, (a), 269), enlarged in 1894–5 (Smeaton, (a), 269).
1873 Well House Tower restored (Robertson, 49). (See Castle).
1876 West Gardens acquired by Town Council (Grant, II, 98; Robertson, 58).
1876 Statue of David Livingstone, by Mrs D. O. Hill, in East Gardens (Grant, II, 130).
1877 Statue of Adam Black, by John Hutchison, in East Gardens (Grant, II, 128).
1877 Statue of Sir James Y. Simpson, by William Brodie, in West Gardens (Grant, II, 130).
1879 Dean Ramsay Memorial, by Robert Anderson, in West Gardens (Grant, II, 206) next St. John's Church.
1903 Floral Clock in West Gardens electrically worked (Malcolm, (b), 73).
1906 Royal Scots Greys Memorial, sculptor Birnie Rhind, in West Gardens.

Kettledrummer of the Royal Scots Greys (2nd Dragoons) and an officer of the Royal Scots in full dress as they would have paraded in the 1930's. The War memorials of both regiments stand in West Princes Street Gardens.

1910 Statue of Dr Thomas Guthrie by F. W. Pomeroy in West Gardens (Evening News, 15-3-1978).

1927 Scottish American War Memorial in West Gardens unveiled (Evening News, 15-3-1978).

1935 Ross bandstand to replace previous one (Robertson, 61; Malcolm, (b), 73), which had been erected in 1877, and was moved to the Meadows.

1952 Memorial to the Royal Scots, the First or Royal Regiment of Foot, unveiled in West Gardens.

1977 Threat of Dutch elm disease to elms in the Gardens and elsewhere in the city.

1978 Stone erected by the Norwegian Brigade in gratitude for Scottish hospitality during World War II.

Princes Street Proprietors
Feuars of property to the west of Hanover Street who resolved to act together to prevent building on the south side of Princes Street. It was formed in 1801; held its first meeting in 1811; and was disbanded in 1881 (Robertson, 1-61).

Printing
(A concise summary of printing and publishing in Edinburgh will be found in Keir, 686-695).

1507 Walter Chepman and Andro Myllar introduced printing to the town (Wilson, I, 40; II, 57; Grant, I, 255; Maxwell, 82; Keir, 686; Arnot, 432, says 1509). Their press was at the foot of Blackfriars Wynd in the Cowgate (R.C., xlviii).

1508 First book published in Scotland — *The Knightly Tale of Gologras and Gawane* (Grant, I, 255).

1540 Acts of Parliament ordered to be printed (Arnot, 65).

1574 Bassandyne's Bible printed (Wilson, II, 68; Grant, I, 207).

1610 Hart's Folio Bible printed (Arnot, 433).

1721 Allan Ramsay published books in No. 153 High Street, and had moved to the Luckenbooths by 1728 (Minto and Armstrong, 8; Sitwell and Bamford, 163, say 1725).

1749 Neill and Company, the first Edinburgh printers, opened in Canonmills (Keir, 688).

1760 David Willison opened a printing press in Craig's Close (Keir, 687).

1763 There were six printing houses in Edinburgh (Creech, 82).

1771 First edition of the *Encyclopaedia Britannica* printed in three volumes, edited by William Smellie (Anderson, 240). This encyclopaedia was later printed by T. & A. Constable and A. & C. Black.

1775 Pillans and Wilson opened in Riddle's Close (Keir, 687); now in Bernard Terrace.

1775 The most profitable trade in Edinburgh was that of a bookseller which included printing (Topham, 179; 181).

1779 There were 27 printing offices in the city (Chambers, 49; Keir, 686).

1795 T. & A. Constable took over Willison's printing works and moved them to the High Street, from where they removed in 1833 to Thistle Street (Keir, 687), and are now in Hopetoun Street.

1798 Thomas Nelson opened his printing business in the West Bow (Grant, II, 355; Keir, 688), moving later to Hope Park and thence to Dalkeith Road (Grant, II, 355).

1806 Oliver and Boyd opened their business in Tweeddale Court (Grant, I, 281; Keir, 56), and are now in Stevenson House, Baxter's Place, part of the Longman Group.

1816 William Blackwood opened a printing business in No. 17 Princes Street (Edinburgh Evening Dispatch, 20-6-1949), moving later to No. 45 George Street and recently to Thistle Street.

1848 James Thin opened a bookshop opposite the University (Keir, 704).

1868 W. & R. Chambers opened in Warriston's Close (Grant, I, 224; Williamson, 224), and are now in Thistle Street.

Public Baths (including Swimming Baths).

1696-1714 College of Physicians bath-house opened near the Cowgate at a charge of 12 shillings Scots and one penny to the servant, or at an annual subscription of one guinea (Grant, II, 147; Turner, 106; O.E.C., XXXIV, 61, says 1712).

1707-40 Baths near the College of Surgeons in Black Friars Land (Turner, 105; O.E.C., XXXIV, 59, says 1704).

1736 Baths at the foot of Carrubber's Close. (O.E.C., XXXIV, 62).

1756 Bath, or Bagnio, at Royal Infirmary affording sweating or massage treatment at an annual subscription of one guinea or life membership at ten guineas. A cold bath cost one shilling, a hot bath two shillings and sweating treatment four shillings (Turner, 106).

1806 Salt water baths at Portobello.

1813 Bath at Seafield House, Leith. (O.E.C., XXXIV, 65).

1844 Baths for working classes on the site of the present General Post Office.

1847 Public baths in Nicolson Square (Scotsman, 1-12-1847).

1887 Warrender swimming baths, purchased by the city in 1908.

1887 Infirmary Street swimming baths.

1897 Dalry swimming baths.

1900 Glenogle Road swimming baths.

1901 Baths at Melville House, Portobello.

1936 Portobello open-air swimming baths.

1969 Royal Commonwealth Swimming Pool, Dalkeith Road.

1977 Edinburgh District Council spends nearly £1m. annually on baths.

Public Health see also Birth Rate and Mortality Rate.

1832 Board of Health set up (Grierson, 17).

1862 Dr Henry Littlejohn appointed first Medical Officer of Health for the city (Keir, 338), and he served until 1908.

1863 Rates per 1000 of population — Birth 36.24; Death 25.88; Infant mortality per 1000 live births 145; Deaths from tuberculosis per 1000 of population 6.23 (Keir, 341).

1961 Comparable rates — Birth 17.7; Death 13.1; Infant mortality 23; Tuberculosis deaths 0.03 (Keir, 341).

Public Libraries

1725 Allan Ramsay's Circulating Library — the first in Britain (Graham, 96; Pennycook, 35, says 1728). It contained some 30,000 volumes (Scott-Moncrieff, 56).

1890 Free Carnegie Library in George IV Bridge, now the Central Library, was established by a gift from Andrew Carnegie.

1897 Fountainbridge Library from a bequest by Thomas Nelson.

1900 Stockbridge Library.

1904 Morningside Library (Smith, I, 148).

1914 St. Leonard's Juvenile Library.

1977 Apart from the Central Library, Mobile Library and Hospital Libraries there are nineteen public libraries in the city on which the Edinburgh District Council spends £1½m per annum.

Public Parks

In 1940 the city listed 68 public parks under its control, including 36 bowling greens, 80 tennis courts, 6 golf courses, 14 putting greens and 96 football pitches; while by 1963 there were 56 bowling greens, 134 tennis courts, 23 putting greens, over 120 football pitches, 11 for rugby, 10 for hockey, 8 for cricket, 10 badminton courts and 4 running tracks (Keir, 543). Among the many parks are:

David I is said to have granted the Burgh Muir to the community in 1128.

James II gifted Greenside to the citizens in 1456.

Blackford Hill bought by the town in 1884 (Gilbert, 162).

Braid Hills acquired in 1890.

Bruntsfield Links, long used as a quarry; as a golf course 1695-1890; as a short-hole golf course since that date to the present time.

Calton Hill acquired by the town in 1722.

Corstorphine Hill.

Craiglockhart and Colinton Dell acquired in 1872.

Inverleith Park acquired in 1876 and pond created.

Leith Links have long been open to the citizens.

Meadows reclaimed from Burgh (South) Loch in 1722, opened as a pleasure ground in 1860.

Portobello Park opened in 1898.
Princes Street Gardens opened 1816-1830.
Roseburn Park opened in 1898.
Saughtonhall acquired in 1900.
1977 The upkeep of public parks cost the ratepayers nearly £1m annually.

Publishing, see Printing.

Queen Mary's Bath
This small building, erected probably in the 16th century (*Edinburgh — An Architectural Guide*) near Holyrood House (Wilson, II, 120) was "actually one of the turrets along the Abbey wall." (Scott-Moncrieff, 28). Malcolm ((a), 64) says that it was a miniature tower at the north-west of the Abbey wall, while Grant (II, 41) describes it as a squat corbelled tower north-east of the tennis courts. Keir (39) comments that the debate as to what was the purpose of the Bath House still continues. The building was repaired in 1852 (Grant, II, 41) and in the 1960's the approach to Holyroodhouse was renovated and a garden laid out to include the Bath House (Minto and Armstrong, 14).

Queen Street
In Craig's plan for the New Town it was called Forth Street and was to be a mirror image of Princes Street with houses on one side only and gardens on the other.
1770 Houses built from the east end (Catford, 119).

No. 8 was the first house completed and was designed by Robert Adam; was occupied by Edinburgh Institution (Grant, II, 153); in 1955 it became the new Library of the Royal College of Physicians (Keir, 325).
1844 College of Physicians, designed by Thomas Hamilton, built at Nos. 9 and 10 (Grant, II, 153; Youngson, 275).

No. 1 Philosophical College, founded in 1848 (Grant, II, 152), now is occupied jointly by the National Portrait Gallery (q.v.) and the National Museum of Antiquities of Scotland (q.v.).

No. 5 is presently the Edinburgh studio of the British Broadcasting Corporation, which is scheduled to move to a new centre at Greenside.

No. 52 Home of Sir James Y. Simpson, Professor of Midwifery, where, in 1847, he discovered the anaesthetic properties of chloroform (Grant, II, 154). It is now a Church of Scotland Counselling Centre, but Simpson's room remains unchanged as a museum.

No. 53 Home of Professor John Wilson ('Christopher North') for eight years (Pennycook, 101).

Nos. 70-72 Hopetoun Rooms where Chopin gave his last recital in Edinburgh in 1848, and where the Merchant Maiden Hospital (q.v.) occupied the building from 1871 to 1966 (O.E.C., XXIX, 80). Now a block of offices.

Queen Street Gardens
1823 Gardens laid out and enclosed by a parapet wall (Grant, II, 158).

Queensberry House, Canongate — south side.
Built in 1634 (Scotsman, 26-1-1945); 1680 (O.E.C., XV, app. 19; Chambers, 336); 1681 (Williamson, 123); 1681-2 (O.E.C., I, 14); Wilson (II, 106) gives no date, and Grant (II, 35) says that the 1st Duke of Queensberry bought it in 1686.
1729 The poet John Gay, author of the *Beggar's Opera*, was entertained by the 3rd Duke of Queensberry (Grant, II, 38; Graham, 112).
1801 The house, stripped of its ornaments, was sold to the government by the Duke of Queensberry (Williamson, 124), the original marble staircase being transferred to Gosford House, East Lothian.
1848 Used as an annexe for the Royal Infirmary during the cholera outbreak (Scotsman, 26-1-1945).
1853 Purchased as a House of Refuge (O.E.C., XV, app. 21; Grant, II, 38). It was used as a barracks, then as a hospital, in 1906 as a House of Refuge for the destitute and a home for inebriate women (Williamson, 124).
1945 Became Queensberry House Hospital for the Elderly.

Radical Road, Arthur's Seat.
1820 Road constructed at the foot of Salisbury Crags by unemployed workmen who had been influenced by Radical notions (Smeaton, (a), 247; (b), 261; Grant, II, 311; O.E.C., XVIII, 182).

Railways
No railway entered the town before 1840 (Robertson, 37-46).

(1) The earliest line was the Edinburgh-Dalkeith, commissioned by Act of Parliament in 1826 to reduce carriage charges on coal from the Lothian coal-fields. Horses provided the motive power, one horse being sufficient until the gradient at Portobello where two were required. Between St. Leonards tunnel and Duddingston vehicles were drawn up the steep incline by a rope worked from a stationary engine.

It was called the 'Innocent Railway' because it never killed anybody, but Youngson (314) points out that this referred only to passengers.

1831 Line opened (O.E.C., XXX, 153) from St. Leonards to South Esk (i.e. Newtongrange).

1834 Passenger services to Dalkeith — 300,000 per annum travelled by the 1840's.

1838 Line extended from Niddrie to Leith.

1845 Acquired by North British Railway Company (Maclean, 6) who soon converted it to steam locomotion.

(2) Local railway lines to carry freight, and later passengers, included —

1836 Edinburgh, Leith and Newhaven railway incorporated, with an extension to Granton in 1846 (O.E.C., XXXIII, 159).

1842 Line opened from Scotland Street to Trinity (Gilbert, 100) with plans for later extension south to the site of the present Waverley Station and north to Granton (O.E.C., XXXIII, 159).

1847 North British Railway Company acquired the Edinburgh-Leith-Granton railway and extended this by train ferry to Burntisland, across Fife to Tayport and by train ferry to Dundee.

1847 Branch line to Musselburgh from North British Station (Scotsman, 17-7-1847).

1848 480,808 passengers used the Edinburgh–Leith–Granton line in six months (Scotsman, 2-2-1848).

1877 Tay Bridge built and carried trains (Scotsman, 23-9-1877) until its collapse in 1879. Rebuilt in 1887.

1877 Edinburgh-Queensferry-Dunfermline line instituted, taking 1½ hours including 12 minutes for the Queensferry passage (Scotsman, 1-11-1877).

1890 Forth Railway Bridge built thus obviating the need for a ferry.

(3) Suburban lines. There were two lines opened in 1884 (Gilbert, 163), the one owned by the North British Railway Company and the other by the Caledonian Railway Company. These lines were closed for passengers in 1962.

The North British route was Waverley, Haymarket, Gorgie, Morningside, Blackford, Newington, Duddingston, Portobello, Abbeyhill. It carried freight and passengers, but now only occasional freight. Craiglockhart Station was opened in 1887.

The Caledonian route was Princes Street, Dalry, Murrayfield, Craigleith (with a branch to Barnton opened in 1891 (Gilbert, 173)), East Pilton (with a branch to Granton), Newhaven and Leith. This line is now closed.

(4) North British lines to the west and south. In 1838 a proposal was made to run a line from Glasgow to Haymarket (Gilbert, 93) but a suggestion that this might be extended to the North Bridge was successfully opposed by the Princes Street Proprietors (q.v.) who owned the land on the south side of Princes Street as their gardens. In the 1840's trade revival renewed interest in the possible

extension, but it was insisted that the railway occupy the lowest lying land in the valley of the Nor' Loch, and be enclosed on each side by a wall and embankment with trees and shrubs to conceal it.

About this time the North British Railway Company was embarking on lines to Berwick and thence to London. These projects necessitated the construction of a tunnel from Haymarket to Princes Street (about 1000 yards (0.9km)), one through the Mound and one through Calton Hill (some ¼ mile (0.4km) in length).

1842 The Edinburgh and Glasgow Railway Company opened a line to Haymarket (O.E.C., XIV, app. 10; Smeaton, (a), 139). This had taken three years to build (Gilbert, 107).

1842 The North British Railway Company was founded to connect Haddington and Berwick to Edinburgh (Gilbert, 104).

1845 Tunnel through the south flank of the Calton Hill completed (Scotsman, 20-12-1845).

1846 Haymarket tunnel completed.

1846 Tunnel through the Mound completed (Scotsman, 21-2-1846).

1846 Telegraph on Glasow-Edinburgh railway line (Scotsman, 17-1-1846).

1846 Carriage run experimentally from Haymarket to the new station at North Bridge (Scotsman, 9-5-1846).

1846 Train from Glasgow with twenty carriages "drawn by a locomotive emerged from the tunnel at the West Church [i.e. St. Cuthbert's] Manse and rolled slowly along the valley of the Nor' Loch, through the tunnel under the Mound, to the station of the North British Railway Company in the old Physic Garden." (Scotsman, 20-5-1846).

1846 North British Railway Company opened a line to Berwick (Gilbert, 115; Maclean, 6).

1847 Petition for Sunday trains(Scotsman, 24-4-1847).

1847 North British Railway service Edinburgh-London in 14 hours (Scotsman, 3-7-1847).

1848 Waverley Bridge Station, designed for Edinburgh and Glasgow Railway Company, opened after the union of that company with the North British Railway Company (Scotsman, 4-3-1848).

1848 Direct access made from Princes Street to the station (Scotsman, 20-12-1848).

1848 Line to Hawick opened as far as Galashiels (Scotsman, 14-6-1848).

1849 Line reached Hawick (Maclean, 6).

1850 First public train from London to Edinburgh by the east coast route (Scotsman, 8-8-1950).

1862 'Flying Scotsman', the oldest named train in the world, completed the run to London in 10½ hours .

1862 Edinburgh-Hawick line extended to Carlisle using part of the

Caledonian track (Maclean, 6).

1865 Edinburgh-Glasgow line acquired by North British Railway Company.

1875 Sleeping car on North British line to London (Maclean, 12).

1892 New tunnels to Haymarket for increased traffic (Maclean, 12).

1900 Restaurant cars on London trains for the first time.

1923 East Coast Joint Stock, jointly owned by North British, North-Eastern and Great Northern Railway Companies, amalgamated as the London and North-Eastern Railway Company.

(5) Caledonian lines to the west and south. The connection between Edinburgh and London via Beattock and Carlisle, called the Caledonian Railway Company which was formed in 1845, was later named the London Midland and Scottish Railway Company. During its construction there was need for an Edinburgh station which was built at Kirkbraehead (q.v.).

1848 Caledonian Railway Company opened the Edinburgh-Carlisle-London line (Gilbert, 119; Smeaton, (a), 141) from Lothian Road Station.

1848 Express trains from London (Euston) to Edinburgh via Beattock took 12½ hours (Scotsman, 3-5-1848).

1869 Caledonian Station built (Grant, II, 138; Gilbert, 146 and Malcolm, (b), 74, both say that it was opened in 1870).

1876 Through train from Caledonian Station to Glasgow (Maclean, 12).

1902 Caledonian Station rebuilt (Malcolm, (b), 74).

1965 Caledonian Station demolished, all trains going to Waverley Station. Caledonian Station is now a car park.

(6) Railways were nationalised as British Railways (later called British Rail) in 1948 and unprofitable lines closed during the next sixteen years, and especially in 1964.

1957 Diesel engines on Edinburgh-Glasgow line.

1962 Diesel engines on Edinburgh-London line.

THE UNIVERSITY, SOUTH BRIDGE
This justly famed University was founded by James VI in 1582. The present building was commenced in 1789, under the auspices of Robertson the historian, after a design of Mr Robert Adam, upon the site where formerly stood Kirk of Fields, the scene of Lord Darnley's murder. The sketch also comprises the Tron Church, and the Register Office in the distance.

1977 London–Edinburgh run in 5 hours 22 minutes, with a further
reduction to 4 hours 40 minutes in 1978.

Ramsay Garden, Castlehill — north side, off Ramsay Lane.
Incorporates the site of Allan Ramsay's villa, erected in 1751 (see
'Goose Pie'). Allan Ramsay died in 1757 and the house passed to his
son, Allan Ramsay, portrait-painter to George III (Chambers, 16)
who enlarged the house (Steuart, 22). John Galt wrote much of his
Annals of the Parish (published in 1821) in the house (Steuart, 23).

1845 The property passed to Murray of Henderland (Grant, I, 83), (see
Murrayfield House).

1892 Buildings erected in Ramsay Garden by Patrick Geddes (Keir, 50).
One, now called Ramsay Lodge, Allan Ramsay's house, became a
University of Edinburgh Hall of Residence and is now the staff
college of a Financial Company. Other houses are much
sought-after flats (Keir, 370).

Rates
Rates are levied on the rateable value of lands and heritages, except
such buildings or lands as those used by police, justices, churches,
roads, parks etc. The University, the Royal Infirmary and similar
institutions are partially exempt from the payment of rates. In 1940
the rates yielded nearly £2½m which was expended on watching,
lighting, cleansing, parks, drainage, public amenities (baths,
wash-houses etc.) and public assistance. In 1977 the nett amount to
be raised by Edinburgh District rates (excluding a Government
grant of £5½m.) was over £16½m., and by the Lothian Regional
Council a further £67½m. The District is responsible for planning,
housing, recreation, baths, museums and libraries, cleansing and
public health as major items; and the Region supports education,
social work, highways, drainage, police, fire stations and water
supply etc.

NORTH BRIDGE STREET
One of the leading features of Edinburgh, as connecting the old and new
portions of the city. The sketch
exhibits in a striking manner the
difference between the ancient and
modern style of building. The Tron
Church appears in the distance, the
Old Town forming the background.

Ravelston House

1622 Ravelston House built, the home of the Foulis family (Grant, III, 106; R.C., 228). According to Geddie (54) only a trace of the original house remained in 1926.

1726 Property acquired by the Keiths of Ravelston and Dunnottar (Grant, III, 106; Geddie, 54).

1966 House left unchanged when the newly built Mary Erskine School moved into the grounds (see Merchant Maiden Hospital).

Regalia see also Castle.

The 'Honours Three' are the Crown, the Sceptre and the Sword of State (Williamson, 93). The Crown is generally believed to include the circlet of Robert the Bruce, and is thought to have been made after 1314 and to have been used at the coronation of David II in 1329. It is thought that it has been altered at the wish of successive kings. The Sceptre was presented to James IV by Pope Alexander VI and it was remade for James V. The Sword of State was presented to James IV by Pope Julius II in 1507 (Weirter, 193-201).

The National Service of Thanksgiving and Dedication in St. Giles Church, June, 1953. It shows H.M. Queen Elizabeth preceded by the Honours of Scotland in procession to the nave.

The regalia were removed to Dunnottar Castle in 1651 during Cromwell's occupation (Cochrane, 35) and were lodged in 1707 in the Crown Room of Edinburgh Castle (Cochrane, 60).

In the Castle "are carefully preserved the regalia of the Kingdom, consisting of the crown, said to be of great value, a sceptre and a sword of state adorned with jewels. Of these symbols of sovereignty the people are exceedingly jealous. A report being spread, during the sitting of the Union Parliament, that they were removed to London, such a tumult arose that probably the lord commissioner would have been torn in pieces if he had not produced them for the satisfaction of the populace." (Smollett, 273).

1779 "In one apartment [of the Castle] called the *crown-room*, it is pretended that the regalia of Scotland are deposited. That they were lodged there with much formality, on the 26th March, 1707, is certain. Whether they be there still, is very problematical. If they be, nothing, at least, can be more absurd than the way in which they have been kept. The way to preserve an object of great value is not to lock it up for ever from the eyes of the public; quite the reverse . . . If the officers of state and governor of Edinburgh Castle will not make personal inquiry whether the regalia of Scotland be still in the Castle, the public will be entitled to conclude *that they are no longer there,* and that they have been carried off by private orders from the Court." (Arnot, 291).

1794 Crown Room opened for the first time since 1707. An oak chest there was shaken and assumed to be empty (Grant, I, 71).

1818 Warrant from the Prince Regent, later George IV, to reopen the Crown Room, and the regalia were found in the oak chest. Grant (I, 71) quotes Sir Walter Scott's emotions on the occasion at which he was present, "The joy was therefore extreme when, the ponderous lid having been forced open . . . the regalia were discovered lying at the bottom covered with linen cloths, exactly as they had been left in 1707." (O.E.C., VIII, 205; Wilson, I, 166; Cockburn, 348; Gilbert, 65; Smeaton, (a), 136; 152).

Regality
A territorial jurisdiction conferred by the king in Scotland.

Regent Bridge see Waterloo Place.

Register House
c.1540 Register House established in the Castle (O.E.C., XVII, 148).
1662 Register House transferred to the Tolbooth (O.E.C., XVII, 149).
1765 £12,000 granted from forfeited estates for building the Register House (O.E.C., XIII, 6; XVII, 147-175).

Register House from the General Post Office.

1774 Foundation stone of Register House, designed by Robert Adam, laid at the east end of Princes Street (O.E.C., XVII, 162; Arnot, 230; Grant, I, 367; Smeaton, (a), 267).

1788 Register House built (O.E.C., XVII, 165; Creech, 75).

1822-27 Enlargement of Register House (R.C., 195, says completed in 1834).

1850 Iron railing erected in front of Register House (Scotsman, 18-12-1850).

1852 Statue of Duke of Wellington, designed by John Steell, erected in front of Register House (Grant, I, 372).

1857-60 New Register House added partly behind the old one (Grant, I, 372).

1902-4 Wing added to the west of the House.

1923 Public Search Room opened (O.E.C., XVII, 165, f.n.).

1971 West Register House opened in former St. George's Church, Charlotte Square (q.v.).

Religion see also Assembly Hall and Churches.
(This information is extracted from Keir, 164–192).

A list has been given under Churches of places of worship erected in Edinburgh until the late 19th century. The number was increased with the expansion of the city during the first half of the

20th century, and in the 1950's the Church Extension scheme of the Church of Scotland saw a further development and the demolition or conversion for other use of many churches in the narrower confines of the city, while unions of congregations resulted in one of the churches concerned becoming available for other use. This process continues.

In 1963 (Keir, 173) the Presbytery of Edinburgh embraced 137 churches. This number had been reduced to 110 by 1976 in spite of a geographically widened Presbytery.

There were eight Burgh Churches — St. Giles, Greyfriars, West St. Giles, Highland Tolbooth St. John's, St. Andrews and St. George's, St. Stephens, St. Mary's (Bellevue) and Greenside. From the Reformation to the Act of Union (1929) the Burgh was responsible for providing places of worship and paying the stipend, and in 1925 a sum was handed to the General Trustees of the Church of Scotland for investment to this end.

Regarding the other denominations in 1963, the Free Church had 3 charges; the United Free Church had 7 charges and a membership of 2,000; the Roman Catholic Church had 20 churches with some 46,000 members; the Scottish Episcopal Church (which was the official religion in Scotland for 72 years between 1560 and 1690) had 34 churches with nearly 10,000 communicants; the Quakers had 125 members; the Methodists had 6 churches and 1,700 members; the Baptists had 16 churches for their 2,400 members; the Congregationalists had 11 churches and nearly 3,000 members; 200 Unitarians met in St. Mark's, Castle Terrace; and there were some 300 Jewish families attending the Synagogue in Salisbury Road, which was built in 1931; the Church of Christ, founded in 1839, had 200 members who have met since 1933 in St. Leonard's Street.

Restalrig

Restalrig was formerly called Lestalric. The Barony of Restalrig extended eastward from the Shore of Leith to the Fishwives' Causeway, and westward to Calton Hill and the Canongate boundary embracing the lands of Lochend, Barbersburn, North Park, Craigentinny, Fillyside, Wheatfield, Cow Park, Piershill and Three Steps (O.E.C., XXIII, 63; Wilson, II, 186).

1198 The De Lestalrics owned Restalrig (Russell, 27).

1365 Restalrig referred to as a Burgh of Barony (q.v.) (R.C., lx).

Late 14th century Restalrig was owned by the Logan family (Grant, III, 132).

1487 The Parish Church, which had existed from the 12th Century, was rebuilt (R.C., 253) and made Collegiate (R.C., lxi).

1560 Restalrig Church largely destroyed (Arnot, 256; Wilson, II, 249).

The parishioners, having been ordered by the Assembly of that year to join St. Mary's, South Leith, the church was "utterlie casten doune" (Grant, III, 130; R.C., 253).

1605 James Elphinstone, Lord Balmerino, obtained a Crown Charter of lands and Barony in succession to the Logans who forfeited them for their share in the Gowrie conspiracy (O.E.C., XXIII, 64).

1609 Restalrig Parish transferred to South Leith (O.E.C., IV, 153; Grant, III, 131; Russell, 155; Geddie, 169).

1650 Restalrig Church destroyed (Arnot, 573).

1745 Lord Balmerino lost possession of Restalrig because of his Jacobite sympathies, and the Earl of Moray bought the lands.

1837 Church reopened for services (O.E.C., IV, 153).

1908 Earl of Moray restored St. Triduana's Well (q.v.) which is in the Churchyard. (O.E.C., IV, 153).

1912 Restalrig Church became the Parish Church again.

Riddle's Close, 312-28 Lawnmarket — south side.
"In Riddell's Close there is an enclosed court, evidently intended to be capable of defence." (Chambers, 76).

1591 Riddle's Close built (Catford, 51). Bailie John MacMorran carried on his business in a large mansion in Riddle's Court until he was shot, in 1595, by a High School boy during a protest when the town refused the scholars a holiday (Maitland, 421; Arnot, 423; Grant, I, 110). This mansion, where James VI and his Queen were dined by the Town Council in 1598, is well preserved (Chambers, 77). The

James VI arrives for a banquet
in Riddles's Court.

ceiling of the inner room bears the date 1678, while that in the upper room, redecorated in 1897, bears the City Arms and the dates 1582-1897 (Letter in Scotsman, 26-10-1946).

1726 Building of flats near the Close entrance (Scotsman, loc. cit.).

1751 First Edinburgh house of David Hume, the historian (Chambers, 55; Catford, 55).

1775 Messrs Pillans and Wilson opened a printing works (Keir, 687).

1805 First Police Court held in the house; abandoned in 1812.

1850/89 MacMorran's house used as Edinburgh Mechanics' Library (Catford, 54).

1889 Converted by Patrick Geddes into one of the earliest students' residences (Scotsman, loc. cit.).

1893 Renovations under the Improvements scheme (Cruft, 11).

1903 Occupied by Free Church of Scotland (Scotsman, loc. cit.).

1936 Used as Fettesian-Lorettonian Boys' Club (Scotsman, loc. cit.).

1946 House bought by Town Council (Catford, 54).

1958-9 Property restored as flats and offices while retaining much of the original structure (Cruft, 11).

1964 Adapted as Adult Education Centre and Workers' Educational Association (Keir, 51).

Risp

A risp, also called a tirling-pin, crow or ringle, was the predecessor of the outside door knocker. A vertical iron bar with serrated edges and an iron ring which produced a harsh grating sound when drawn over the serrations (Chambers, 207; Wilson, II, 133; Russell, 275; Graham, 85; Dunlop and Dunlop, 60).

Robberies

Robberies were common in the High Street and Closes occasioned through poverty and heavy burdens on the people — "the haill money of the kingdome being spent by the frequent resoirt of our Scottismen at the Court of England." (O.E.C., XVI, 69, from the *Diary of John Nicoll, 1650-1667*).

1763 Housebreaking and robbery rare; 1783 housebreaking and robbery common (Creech, 105).

Roseburn House

"Small, quaint, and very massively built, with crow-stepped gables and great chimneys, it exhibits marks of very great antiquity, and yet all the history it possesses is purely traditional." (Grant, III, 102).

It bears elaborately decorated lintels with the date 1562, the Royal Arms, and the initials M.R. thus leading to the theory that Mary, Queen of Scots, lived here. This supposition was examined

(Weekly Scotsman, 29-7-1948) and was refuted, the M.R. being the
initials of Mungo Russell, a former owner (R.C., 230).

1650 Cromwell lived in the house (Grant, III, 103; Smeaton, (b), 328).
It is still in private occupation.

Royal Botanic Garden see Botanic Garden.

Royal College of Physicians see College of Physicians.

Royal College of Surgeons see College of Surgeons.

Royal Exchange, 249 High Street — north side.
The Royal Exchange was designed by John Adam, and is now the
City Chambers whose buildings rise from Cockburn Street to a
height of twelve storeys.

1753 Foundation of Royal Exchange (O.E.C., IV, 45; Arnot, 311;
Grant, I, 183). The subsoil dug for the foundations was used to
construct the Castle Esplanade (Wilson, I, 160; Smeaton, (a), 144).

1761 Royal Exchange completed (Grant, I, 183) at the expense of Mary
King's Close (q.v.) and some others opposite the Cross. The
Exchange was created for lawyers and merchants to conduct their
business, but was not a success as such.

1811 Buildings taken over as City Chambers (Minto and Armstrong, 6).
There were shops in the arches, except for the central arch, and in
the forecourt, but these were removed by the end of the century.

1901 City Chambers enlarged (Smeaton, (a), 195) and north-west wing
built.

1904 Larger Council Chamber constructed in new west wing (Catford,
63).

1908 City Chambers extended to include Writers' Court (q.v.) and
Warriston's Close (q.v.) (O.E.C., I, 7).

1916 Statue of Alexander and Bucephalus moved from St Andrew
Square (q.v.) to the forecourt.

1927 Stone of Remembrance laid beneath central arch.

1932-4 Further extension of City Chambers area at the expense of Allan's
Close, Craig's Close (q.v.) and Old Post Office Close (q.v.)
(O.E.C., XXIII, 149, f.n.).

Royal High School
1519 Earliest reference to Grammar School (Arnot, 420; Grant, II, 287).

1529 James V granted to the headmaster the sole privilege of instructing
the youth of Edinburgh at this school.

1554 Cardinal Bethune's (Beaton's) House (q.v.) in Blackfriars Wynd
rented for the Grammar School (Grant, II, 287).

1555 School moved to a house near the head of High School Wynd
(Grant, II, 287).

1567 Town Council resolved to build their High School in the lands of the Black Friars Monastery, and the royal patronage of James VI gave it the title of *Schola Regia Edinensis* (Grant, II, 287). The building bore the date 1578 (O.E.C., V, 71; Maitland, 421; Arnot, 422; Grant, II, 288; Chambers, 76, f.n.). The school was run jointly by the City and the Presbytery of Edinburgh. After their first year the pupils spoke only Latin. The Royal High School had a monopoly to teach Latin, and pupils from other later schools, e.g. Heriot's, were sent to the High School for classes in this.

1587 Revolt among pupils (Maitland, 44; Grant, II, 289, says 1580).

1595 Bailie MacMorran shot dead by a pupil (Maitland, 421; Arnot, 423; Grant, I, 110) during a 'sit-in' protest in demand of a holiday. The school met six days each week from 6a.m. to 6p.m., and the only holidays were Saints Days and one week in May and in September.

1657 Building reconstructed and a library added in the following year.

1777 Foundation of new school at the High School Yards (at the foot of the present Infirmary Street) designed by Alexander Laing (O.E.C., V, 85; Arnot, 422, f.n.; Chambers, 76, f.n.; Grant, II, 293).

1825 Foundation of new school at Calton Hill, designed by Thomas Hamilton (Smeaton, (a), 137).

1829 The new Royal High School opened (O.E.C., V, 87; XXX, 144; Grant, II, 110; Smeaton, (a), 137). The old building became the surgical house of the Royal Infirmary, and is now used by the Geography Department of the University of Edinburgh.

1969 New co-educational Royal High School opened at Barnton. The Calton Hill building was used as the Civic Art Centre, but in 1977 work started to convert it for the proposed Scottish Assembly.

Royal Highland and Agricultural Society

1784 Highland Society of Scotland founded (Grant, I, 294).

1787 Incorporated by Royal Charter (Grant, I, 294).

1822 Society held its first show in a site off the Canongate (Keir, 734).

1856 By a Charter under the Great Seal the Society was empowered to grant diplomas and certificates in agriculture (Grant, I, 294), and had its headquarters in George IV Bridge (Grant, I, 295).

1948 Became the Royal Highland and Agricultural Society (Keir, 734).

1958 Society bought a permanent site at Ingliston, on the western outskirts of the city (Keir, 735) with a view to holding its annual shows there rather than moving from place to place. This has taken place for the past fifteen years, and the Society has developed the use of the site by commercial enterprises, including car races etc. at weekends.

1978 Plans proposed to build a Conference Centre at Ingliston to be run by the Society.

Royal Infirmary of Edinburgh

1721 Lord Provost George Drummond pressed for an Infirmary.

1729 First Infirmary at the head of Robertson's Close contained six beds (O.E.C., IV, 15; V, 79; XV, 135-163; Maitland, 450; Arnot, 546; Grant, II, 298; Maxwell, 142; Turner, 50). The site is marked by a plaque on the south wall at the top of Infirmary Street.

1736 Royal Charter secured (O.E.C., IV, 16; Arnot, 547; Grant, II, 298; Maxwell, 142; Turner, 69).

1736 Surgeons opened a Hospital in College Wynd in opposition (O.E.C., XV, 148; Turner, 66).

1738 Agreement reached between Surgeons and Infirmary (Turner, 66).

1738-41 Second Royal Infirmary erected, on land belonging at one time to the Black Friars, to the design of William Adam. The buildings were in what is now Infirmary Street, but was formerly called Jamaica Street (O.E.C., IV, 16; V, 81; XV, 135-163; Grant, II, 298; Smeaton, (a), 319; Turner, 80).

1745 Infirmary opened (O.E.C., II, 9; Maitland, 182). Turner (147) gives the date as 1741 and says that the number of beds, initially 60-70, was increased as funds permitted.

1748 Infirmary completed (O.E.C., V, 83).

1762-75 15,600 patients admitted; 11,700 (75%) discharged cured; 1,500 relieved; some 750 died; and the remainder discharged themselves (Smout, 257).

1763 One hundred students attending the Infirmary each year (Turner, 150).

1785 First Infirmary pulled down during the building of the South Bridge.

1791 323 students at the Royal Infirmary.

1800 Changes to make staff appointments permanent (Cockburn, 105).

1832 Surgical block opened in the vacated Royal High School building (q.v.) (O.E.C., XXX, 144; Turner, 183), making the bed complement 228.

1835 Royal Maternity Hospital opened in St. John Street, Canongate (Grant, II, 27).

1853 Further surgical beds provided by building on a vacant site east of the main hospital (Turner, 193).

1870 Foundation stone of third Infirmary, designed by David Bryce, laid by Prince of Wales (later Edward VII) (O.E.C., XV, 163; Grant, II, 259; Turner, 234). This was built on the site of George Watson's Hospital (q.v.) and adjacent to the proposed site for the University Medical School. The statue by Robert Hill of George II, who gave the Royal Charter in 1736, stands at the main entrance.

1873 End of second Royal Infirmary.

1879 Third Royal Infirmary enlarged (Maxwell, 143).

1879 Edinburgh Royal Maternity and Simpson Memorial Hospital opened in Lauriston Place (Grant, II, 362, says 1878).

1884 Second Infirmary building demolished for the erection of two schools and Infirmary Street baths (Catford, 62).

1885 Old surgical block of second Infirmary used as a Hospital for Infectious Diseases (Gilbert, 164) until the City Hospital was built in 1903-4. It is now the Geography Department of the University of Edinburgh.

1903 Royal Infirmary enlarged by the removal of buildings in Lauriston Lane, including the Dental Hospital, the Royal College of Physicians' Laboratory, George Watson's juvenile school and the Royal Hospital for Sick Children, all of which were re-sited (Turner, 282-3).

1930 Further growth of the Royal Infirmary when the second George Watson's Boys' College site was bought.

1935 Foundation stone laid for the Royal Simpson Maternity Pavilion within the enlarged Royal Infirmary, opened in 1939.

With advancing knowledge, techniques and investigation procedures the Royal Infirmary has enlarged to the limit of its confines. In spite of the growth of other hospitals within the city, particularly the Western General Hospital, the City Hospital, and the Northern and Eastern General Hospitals, and the transfer of specialised units to each, the clamant need for a fully modern centre of medical care and teaching is being met. The complicated procedure of demolition and rebuilding in a piecemeal fashion proceeds on the restricted site, although the Royal Infirmary owns much of the property to Tollcross.

Royal Institution see Mound.

Royal Mile
From the drawridge of the Castle to Holyroodhouse door is just over one mile in length.

1523 People referred to the Lawnmarket, High Street and Canongate as the King's Road (Fraser, 61).

Royal Occasions see also Castle and Holyrood.

1215 Alexander II's first parliament in town (Arnot, 5; Wilson, I, 6; Smeaton, (a), 11).

1449 Mary of Gueldres, James II's bride, arrived at Leith (O.E.C., III, 46; Wilson, II, 166; Grant, II, 54; Maxwell, 64; Russell, 137).

1454 James II fixed the town as a seat of Court (Maxwell, 24).

1461 Henry VI of England sought refuge (Maitland, 8).

1466 James III brought to town by nobles (Maxwell, 73).

1469 Margaret of Denmark, James III's bride, arrived at Leith (Grant, II, 55; Smeaton, (a), 40).

1488 James IV crowned (Wilson, I, 32; Maxwell, 79, f.n., says at Scone).
1503 Princess Margaret Tudor entered the town by Bristo Port for her marriage to James IV (O.E.C., II, 70; III, 50; X, 62; Wilson, I, 35; Grant, II, 60; 230; Maxwell, 84). This marriage resulted in the Union of the Crowns in 1603.
1528 Plot to assassinate James V (Wilson, II, 129; Grant, I, 383).
1537 Madeleine (Magdalene) de Valois and her husband, James V, arrived at Leith (O.E.C., X, 158; Grant, II, 63; Maxwell, 102; Geddie, 162).
1538 Mary (Marie) of Guise, second wife of James V, entered town by the West Port after their marriage in St. Andrews (Grant, II, 64).
1561 Mary, Queen of Scots, arrived at Leith (Wilson, I, 89; II, 138; Grant, III, 179; Maxwell, 116; Smeaton, (a), 81), and later made her public entry into the town (Wilson, I, 90).
1579 James VI's first public entry (Wilson, I, 112; II, 169; Maitland, 37; Arnot, 35).
1590 Anne of Denmark and her husband, James VI, arrived at Leith (Wilson, I, 113; Smeaton, (a), 95).
1596 James VI moved Court to Linlithgow (Maitland, 50; Arnot, 46; Smeaton, (a), 100).
1603 James VI set out for London (Wilson, I, 117; Maxwell, 151; Williamson, 63).
1617 James VI revisited town (O.E.C., III, 216; Chambers, 246; Grant, II, 73; Maxwell, 158; Wilson, I, 117; Maitland, 58; Smeaton, (a), 106).
1633 Charles I entered Edinburgh through the West Port (O.E.C., I, 106; III, 217; XVIII, 12; Wilson, I, 119; Grant, II, 58; 73; Maxwell, 160; Smeaton, (a), 109; Russell, 324). He made Edinburgh a City; knighted the Provost; was entertained to dinner in the Castle; and was crowned at Holyroodhouse (Wilson, I, 163; Grant, II, 2).
1641 Charles I visited the city for the last time (Grant, I, 227).
1650 Charles II proclaimed King of Scotland (Grant, I, 227).
1650 Charles II landed at Leith and rode to Edinburgh (Grant, III, 151).
1822 George IV landed at Leith on a visit to the city (O.E.C., XVII, 123; Grant, I, 166; III, 208; Maxwell, 276; Geddie, 167; Smeaton, (a), 136), the first monarch to visit Edinburgh since Charles II.
1842 Queen Victoria visited Edinburgh and stayed at Dalkeith Palace (Geddie, 102; Smeaton, (a), 139).
1850, 1872, 1887 Queen Victoria stayed at Holyroodhouse (Smeaton, (a), 234).
1859 Prince of Wales (later Edward VII) stayed at Holyroodhouse (Smeaton, (a), 234).
1903 Edward VII stayed at Holyroodhouse (Smeaton, (a), 234; 239).
1911 George V held a State Banquet at Holyroodhouse.
Since then the Royal Family has visited Edinburgh regularly,

staying at Holyroodhouse, while many foreign sovereigns, most recently King Olaf of Norway (1962) and King Gustav of Sweden (1975) have stayed in the city.

Royal Scottish Academy, Mound

1826 Royal Scottish Academy founded, and held its first exhibition in Waterloo Place (Keir, 867) in 1827.

1837 Royal Scottish Academy received its Charter.

1859 Royal Scottish Academy shared the building with the National Gallery (q.v.) in the Mound (Keir, 871).

1911 Royal Scottish Academy took over the Royal Institution building at the foot of the Mound (Keir, 871).

Royal Scottish Museum, Chambers Street.

Originally called the National Museum of Science and Industry.

1861 Prince Consort laid the foundation stone (Grant, II, 274; Smeaton, (a), 142). The Flodden Wall ran through the site of the building.

1866 Museum opened (Smeaton, (a), 317).

1871-4 Museum extended (Grant, II, 274).

Royal Society of Edinburgh

1783 Royal Society of Edinburgh founded by Principal William Robertson under Royal Charter (Grant, II, 86; Creech, 72; Carlyle, 590; Keir, 921; 936). and was originally housed in the Royal

Royal Scottish Academy.

Institution at the Mound (see Mound).

19th century Society became predominantly a scientific body with a fine library (Keir, 921).

1906 The Society moved to George Street (Keir, 922).

Royston Castle

c.1544 Royston (or Granton) Castle built (O.E.C., VIII, app. 4).

It was the seat of the Hopes of Granton, a family founded by the son of Sir Thomas Hope, King's Advocate to Charles I (Smeaton, (b), 386).

1794 The Castle was still occupied (Cruft, 95).

1854 "An open and roofless ruin" (Grant, III, 311).

1920 Castle demolished (Cruft, 96).

Royston House see Caroline Park.

St. Andrew Square

1768 Andrew Crosbie built the first house (No. 35) on the east side of the Square (O.E.C., XV, app. 12; R.C., 188).

1773 Sir Laurence Dundas's house (No. 36), designed by William Chambers, built on the site earmarked for St. Andrew's Church in Craig's plan (O.E.C., XXIII, 21; R.C., 188). It later became the Excise Office and is now the Royal Bank.

1775 Sir Adam Fergusson of Kilkerran built No. 34 (Gray, 53), now rebuilt as modern offices for the Norwich Union Insurance Company.

1777 Dun's Hotel (No. 39) opened (O.E.C. XIV, 138; Malcolm, (b), 50, says 1776).

1781 John Young's house (No. 37) built (O.E.C., XXIII, 22).

1781 Square entirely built (Youngson, 81).

1805 Crosbie's house became Dumbreck's Hotel (Gray, 83; R.C., 189).

1808 British Linen Company moved into No. 37 (C. A. Malcolm, *The British Linen Bank,* 1746-1946, 168).

1819 Dumbreck sold the building to the Royal Bank of Scotland (R.C., 189).

1821 Melville Monument to the first Viscount Melville, designed by William Burn, sculptor Robert Forrest, erected in the gardens (O.E.C., XV, 207-213; Grant, II, 171; Cockburn, 259).

1828 Royal Bank, having bought No. 36, sold No. 35 as Douglas's Hotel (Scotsman, 21-8-1942).

1832 Sir Walter Scott lodged briefly in this hotel during his last illness (Gray, 87; Grant, II, 170).

1834 Hopetoun Monument, designed by Thomas Campbell, unveiled in the Royal Bank forecourt (O.E.C., XXII, 28-37; Grant, II, 171, says 1835).

1847-51 British Linen Company (Bank) building, designed by David Bryce with figures by A. H. Ritchie, built on the site of Young's house (No. 37) and adjacent houses (Nos, 38 and 39) (C. A. Malcolm, *The British Linen Bank, 1746-1946* 170).

1884 Statue of Alexander and Bucephalus, by John Steell, presented to the city and erected at the west side of St. Andrew Square facing along George Street.

1917 Gladstone Memorial erected at the west side of the Square in place of the statue of Alexander which had been moved to the City Chambers (W. Forbes Gray, *Edinburgh Miscellany,* (1925), 69).

1955-6 Gladstone statue, whose designer was Pittendrigh Macgillivray, was moved to Coates Crescent (Evening News, 15-3-1978).

1977 Crosbie's house is now a branch of Barclay's Bank.

St. Andrew's House, Regent Road.

1937 Built to the design of Thomas Smith Tait on Dow Craig, Calton Hill, after the demolition of Calton Jail and the Bridewell (O.E.C., XXIII, 53). It housed the offices of the Secretary of State for Scotland and his government departments (q.v.).

1971 New St. Andrew's House erected north of St. James's Square to give greater facilities for the civil service.

St. Anthony's Chapel see Arthur's Seat.

St. Anthony's Preceptory, Leith.

1435 Preceptory founded (Arnot, 255; Wilson, II, 267; Grant, III, 215; Russell, 104; Geddie, 169; R.C., lvii, says work began in 1419).

1560 Preceptory largely ruined by gunfire during the Siege of Leith (Grant, III, 216).

1779 Preceptory wantonly destroyed (Arnot, 256; Wilson, II, 268).

1822 Ruins entirely removed (Russell, 117).

St. Bernard's Well, Dean Valley.

1760 A mineral spring discovered in the Water of Leith (R.C., 239).

1789 Well built, designed by Alexander Nasmyth (Grant, III, 75; Smeaton, (a), 297; Catford, 219). It contained a statue of Hygeia (R.C., 240).

1887 Well restored by William Nelson and to the design of Thomas Bonnar (*Edinburgh — An Architectural Guide*) and a new statue of Hygeia by G. W. Stevenson added (R.C., 240).

St. Catherine of Siena

1511-12 John Craufurd founded the Chapel of St. John the Baptist (Grant, III, 51) on a site near the present Sciennes House Place, from which a lamp burned constantly (Smith, I, 6).

1516-17 Ladies decided to form a religious community (Smith, I, 7) and
Craufurd annulled his foundation of the Chapel deposing it for
founding the Convent of St. Catherine of Siena (Smith, I, 8; Fraser,
60; O.E.C., X, 54; 98; Maitland, 176; Arnot, 251; Wilson, II, 274;
Cockburn, 3). The Convent lay between the present Tantallon
Place and St. Catherine's Place where there is a plaque at No. 16
(Smith, I, 8). The nuns made an annual pilgrimage to the Balm Well
of St. Catherine (O.E.C., XXXIII, 137) at Kaimes (off Howden
Hall Road and bearing the date 1563) where the water was reputed
to cure skin diseases because oil was said to flow out of the ground
in 1539 (Fraser, 60). The Well was wrecked as idolatrous by
Cromwell's troops in 1650 (O.E.C., XXXIII, 139).

1544 Nunnery burned during Hertford's raid (Grant, III, 54; Smith, I, 10).

1559 Convent destroyed by vandals (Smith, I, 10).

1567 Possessions passed into the hands of laymen and the sisters were
evicted (Grant, III, 54). The buttresses and doors were used for
building Greyfriars Church, contemplated in 1602 (Smith, I, 11),
but not begun until ten years later.

St. Cecilia's Hall, corner of Niddry's Wynd and Cowgate.

1762 Built by Robert Mylne for the Musical Society of Edinburgh (see
Edinburgh Musical Society) after the style of the Opera House at
Parma. It contained a fine organ. The oval hall seated 500 people
(Arnot, 379; Chambers, 249; Wilson, II, 207; Grant, I, 251;
O.E.C., I, 19; Cockburn, 129; Williamson, 312). The hall had a
"concave elliptical ceiling and was remarkable for the clear and
perfect conveyance of sounds without responding echoes."
(Chambers, 252).

1802 Hall became the property of the Baptist Church (Harris, 34).

1809 Purchased by the Grand Lodge of Scotland for the Freemasons' Hall
(Harris, 34).

1812 An additional hall was built by the Freemasons on the south side
(Harris, 35) and bears the date.

1844 Bought by the Town Council for Dr Bell's School (Harris, 36).

1945 Used as a dance hall.

1960 Restored for use as the University of Edinburgh's School of Music
(Stewart, 15).

St. Cuthbert's Church, Lothian Road.

Erected on the site of Culdee Church of St. Cuthbert, supposed to
have been built in the 8th century, and dedicated to St. Cuthbert,
Bishop of Durham (died 687) (Grant, II, 131). It was mentioned in
David I's Charter of 1127 (*History of St. Cuthbert's Church*). The
present church was known as the West Church (Kirk) after the
Reformation (Keir, 432).

1689 Church almost ruined during the siege of the Castle (Wilson, II, 271).

1775 Church rebuilt (Grant, II, 134; Smeaton, (a), 262; R.C., 185, says 1774). The steeple was added in 1789 (*History of St. Cuthbert's Church*).

1834 Up to this date almost the whole of Edinburgh was in St. Cuthbert's parish.

1892-4 Church rebuilt and the foundations of "at least six earlier churches" disclosed (*History of St. Cuthbert's Church*).

St. Giles Church

Once called St. Giles Cathedral, now the High Kirk of St. Giles.
   "It seems probable that some Benedictine follower of St. Giles (died 451) brought the name from the south of France to Edinburgh." (Williamson, 140; Grant, I, 138, says St. Giles died in 721; Cochrane, 92, says 541).

854 Mention of a church in Edinburgh (Williamson, 140; Grant, I, 139).

1120 Original building replaced by Alexander I (O.E.C., X, 9; Williamson, 141; Smeaton, (a), 39).

1243 Church formally dedicated (R.C., 26) by Bishop David de Bernham of St. Andrews.

1355 Church suffered in the Burnt Candlemas (Wilson, II, 225; Maxwell, 35).

1380 Additional Chapels built (Wilson, II, 218; Grant, I, 139).

1385 Church burned and largely destroyed by Richard II's army.

1387-1416 Church rebuilt — North aisle, Albany (1409), and St. Eloi chapels built (Grant, I, 139; Smeaton, (a), 185; (b), 37).

1460 Choir lengthened and King's pillar erected as a memorial to James II (Williamson, 142; Smeaton, (a), 185; Wilson, II, 218 and Grant, I, 139, say 1462).

1466 Preston Aisle completed (Smeaton, (a), 186) in memory of William Preston who had brought from France an arm bone of St. Giles in 1454 (Grant, I, 140; Fraser, 32). Fraser (71) says that this bone vanished about 1557. The other arm bone of St. Giles is in St. Giles Church, Bruges (Grant, I, 140).

1466 Erected into a Collegiate Church by a Charter from James III (O.E.C., III, 208; Maitland, 271; Arnot, 268; Wilson, II, 220; Grant, I, 139).

1477 No further burials in the Church; a churchyard formed to the south in the manse garden (O.E.C., III, 209; XI, 129, f.n.).

c.1500 Lantern (Crown) tower built (Fraser, 47).

1502 Gavin Douglas appointed Provost (i.e. Dean) of St. Giles.

1513 Chepman Aisle, in memory of James IV and his Queen, dedicated (Smeaton, (a), 187).

1556 Forty-four altars, gifted by merchants, craftsmen, and many neighbouring lairds, destroyed (Arnot, 20; Fraser, 71; Wilson, I, 77; Grant, I, 147, says 1559).

1558 College of St. Giles in procession for the last time (Wilson, II, 223); Grant, I, 140; Smeaton, (a), 76).

1559 John Knox preached in the Church for the first time (O.E.C., III, 213).

1560 Reformation. Last Mass said in the Church.

1560 Western part formed into the new Tolbooth Church.

c.1570 Church divided by partitions.

1572 Knox buried in the churchyard (Grant, I, 150).

1579 Earl of Athole, Chancellor of Scotland, buried (Grant, I, 143).

1581 St. Giles again divided into four churches, Choir, South-west, Middle and North-west, each with a central pulpit.

1585 Clock from Abbey Church of Lindores in Fife bought by the Town Council and placed in the tower (Grant, I, 146).

1596 'Tumult of St. Giles' — a dispute between James VI and leaders of the Church party (O.E.C., III, 214; Grant, I, 144).

1628 Booths built around the Church (Chambers, 110).

1633 Church made into an Episcopal Cathedral and partition walls removed (Wilson, II, 234; Grant, I, 144).

1637 Jenny Geddes threw her stool at Dean Hanna who attempted to conduct an Episcopal Service (Maitland, 71; Arnot, 108; Maxwell, 162; Chambers, 105; Wilson, I, 120; II, 234; Grant, I, 144; Smeaton, (a), 110).

1639 Episcopacy abolished and partition walls rebuilt.

1644 Sir John Gordon of Haddo imprisoned in tower near the north door (see Haddo's Hole).

1648 Crown tower rebuilt (Wilson, II, 237).

1655 Mid Church divided, western part (i.e. Tolbooth) became a church. There were four churches — High (choir), Old (transepts), Tolbooth (part of nave), and New North (rest of nave).

1660 Alterations to Church (O.E.C., XVI, 59).

1661 Remains of Marquis of Montrose buried (Chambers, 108; Wilson, I, 132; Grant, I, 143).

1689 Episcopalians left St. Giles on account of their Jacobite sympathies (see Old St. Paul's Church). Presbyterianism established as the form of worship.

1798 Norman doorway destroyed (Wilson, I, 17).

1817 Krames (q.v.) cleared away.

1829-33 "Sacrilegious misdeeds" known as "restoration" of the Church to the design of William Burn (Wilson, II, 216; Grant, I, 144; Smeaton, (a), 180). Except for the tower the whole exterior dates from 1829.

1872-83 Plans of Sir William Chambers to restore the Church (Chambers, 108, f.n.; Wilson, II, 219; 235; Grant, I, 147; Smeaton, (a), 187) by public subscription.

1878 Organ placed in Church (Grant, I, 147).

1878 Last of partitions removed (Scott-Moncrieff, 47).

1883 Flags of all Scottish regiments hung in Church (Cochrane, 96).

1883 Church assumed its present form after refacing and renovation.

1909 Excavations for the Thistle Chapel (O.E.C., II, 225; III, 242).

1911 Thistle Chapel, designed by Sir Robert Lorimer, opened and dedicated, and two Knights installed by George V. The order of the Thistle was "almost certainly" founded by James VII (II) in Holyrood Abbey in 1687 (Keir, 159) although some ascribe it to James III.

1912 Old clock removed from the tower; the new one has no dials.

1977 Appeal for £2m. for restoration and development.

St. James's Square, Princes Street — east end.
St. James's Square was traditionally a Jacobite nest (R.C., 211).

1773 Designed by James Craig on crest of Multrie's Hill (q.v.) (Youngson, 98).

1775-90 Square built by Walter Fergusson who had acquired the site in 1762 (Chambers, 335).

1787 Robert Burns stayed in No. 2 St. James's Square (later renumbered No. 30) (Scotsman, 3-3-1938).

1971 Square demolished except for a small area which is approached by the modern James Craig Walk (on the site of East Register Street), and the area is rebuilt as what many citizens regard as the eyesore of St. James's Centre. An old stone, engraved 'St. James's Square, 1779' is mounted in the forecourt.

St. John Close, 188 Canongate — south side.
St. John Close led into St. John Street.

1736 Lodge Room of Canongate Kilwinning Masonic Lodge, the oldest masonic lodge room in the world, is still in use after a major renovation. It contains an organ built in 1757.

1966 Close entry demolished.

St. John Cross, Canongate.

1633 Charles I knighted the Provost of Edinburgh at the Cross (Chambers, 301). The Cross formed the extremity of what was Edinburgh's territory along the south side of the Canongate, and it was to here that the Town Council came to greet royal visitors (Catford, 82).

Its position is marked in the causeway at the entrance to what was St. John Close and is now St. John Street.

St. John Street, Canongate — south side.

1768 Street built (O.E.C., XI, 13; Wilson, II, 91; Grant, II, 26). Here lived Tobias Smollett, Earl of Dalhousie, Earl of Hyndford and Lord Monboddo (Chambers, 302).
1835 Royal Maternity Hospital opened (Grant, II, 27).
1882 Old Church from St. Giles built in St. John Street and closed during Moray House development. The old houses were demolished in the 1950's and 1960's for the enlargement of Moray House College of Education. The building over the entrance to St. John Street from the Canongate, where Smollett lived above the opening for St. John Close, was erected in 1755 and restored in 1955.

St. Leonards
The district between Clerk Street and the Salisbury Crags, it was the terminus of the Edinburgh–Dalkeith railway (see Railways). St. Leonards contained a coal depot.
1271 Hospital and Chapel of St. Leonards was in existence, belonging to Holyrood Abbey and standing on a site now occupied by James Clark School (R.C., 217).
1528 Chapel was the scene of a meeting of the Douglases in a conspiracy to murder James V (R.C., 217).

St. Margaret's Convent see White House.

St. Margaret's Well
There are two St. Margaret's Wells in Edinburgh, the less well known being one of the springs of water in the west face of the Castle Rock (Grant, I, 49). The other is better known —
St. Margaret's Well, dedicated to the wife of Malcolm III, stood near the south side of the Forest of Drumselch (q.v.) by the side of the path to Restalrig. It was of similar design to St. Triduana's Well (q.v.). The Well was engulfed by a railway station during the construction of the North British line, and the building was transferred in its entirety in 1862 to the north face of the Salisbury Crags (Grant, II, 313; III, 129; Fraser, 40, says 1859).

St. Mary's Cathedral see also Easter Coates House.
1870 The Walkers of Coates left money to build a Cathedral (Wilson, II, 7; Grant, II, 211).
1874 Foundations laid in Palmerston Place for the Cathedral designed by George Gilbert Scott (Grant, II, 211; Smeaton, (a), 143).
1879 Nave opened for services (Grant, II, 212).
1891 Chapter House gifted (Cruft, 72).
1915-17 Spires added.
1933 Walpole Hall completed.

St. Mary's Wynd, High Street — south side.

The Wynd contained St. Mary's Cistercian Chapel and Hospital (Grant, I, 297) thought to have existed from the 14th century, and dedicated to St. Mary of Placentia. R.C. (126) says that the Hospital was not founded until 1438.

The Wynd was situated at the Netherbow Port and was replaced in 1867, under the Improvements Act (q.v.), by St. Mary's Street, which, like the Wynd, leads to the Cowgate.

St. Roque's Chapel

St. Roque (died 1327) was the patron saint of those who suffered from pestilence, and the name was given to the grounds of the mansion of St. Roque in Grange Loan (O.E.C., X, 167; Grant, III, 47; Smeaton, (b), 366).

1501-4 St. Roque's Chapel built to the south of Grange Loan area for plague-stricken citizens (O.E.C., X, 167; Maitland, 176; Arnot, 250; Cockburn, 3). Its situation lay in the grounds of the present Astley Ainslie Hospital.

1562 Many pilgrimages made from the town to seek aid against the plague (Smeaton, (b), 366).

1791 Chapel demolished (R.C., 249).

St. Thomas's Hospital, adjoining Watergate (q.v.).

1541 Hospital founded by George Crichton, Bishop of Dunkeld (Wilson, II, 115; Grant, II, 39).

1617 Hospital rebuilt (Maitland, 154; 176; Arnot, 250; R.C., 184).

1634 Hospital given over to the poor of the Canongate (Maitland, 155).

1747 Hospital converted into coach houses (Maitland, 156; Arnot, 250).

1778 Hospital buildings demolished (Arnot, 250).

St. Triduana's Well, Restalrig Churchyard, Restalrig Road South.

c.710 St. Triduana came to Scotland with St. Rule (Grant, III, 130; Russell, 145). Her shrine was sought by pilgrims seeking a cure for eye diseases, but the date of building the Well is unknown.

St. Triduana's Chapel, with inset of St. Triduana offering her eyes to the messenger.

1907 Restoration of the Well (R.C., 253; Fraser, 38) by the Earl of Moray showed it to be enclosed in a stone shrine with a central pillar and a decorative rib-vaulted roof.

c.1944 St. Triduana's Chapel restored by the Ministry of Public Buildings and Works.

'Salamander Land', High Street — south side.
An enormous black tenement, so named because it escaped from the great fire of 1824 (Grant, I, 242). Through an archway in Salamander Land lay the Old Fishmarket Close (q.v.).

1848 Removed for building the Police Office (Grant, I, 242; Scotsman, 23-2-1848).

Salisbury Crags, Arthur's Seat.
Named after the Earl of Salisbury, commander of Edward III's invading army of 1336, and husband of the Countess in whose honour the Order of the Garter was instituted (Smeaton, (b), 261); or from the old form of Salisbrae, suggestive of the French *saule* — a willow. The eastern slopes of Arthur's Seat are the present Willowbrae area (Malcolm, (a), 79). The depression between Salisbury Crags and Arthur's Seat is called Hunter's Bog.

Sanctuary, Holyrood Abbey see also Abbey Lairds.
"A Sanctuary for crime of all kinds until the Reformation [i.e. 1560] and afterwards for debt only . . . Those who sought refuge in the Sanctuary could go out without fear of capture between midnight on Saturday and midnight on Sunday." (Williamson, 104).

The old Sanctuary line is marked by three letters 'S' in the road at the Abbey Strand (q.v.).

The area of Sanctuary included several taverns and extended over what is now Holyrood Park (Catford, 99). Most of the houses were demolished between 1850 and 1860 when Queen Victoria made Holyroodhouse an occasional residence (Scott-Moncrieff, 28).

1128 The greatest Scottish sanctuary was that of Holyrood Abbey (O.E.C., XV, 55-98).

1373 Canons forbidden by Parliament to protect murderers (Malcolm, (a), 66).

1469 Law against protection of murderers renewed (Malcolm, (a), 66).

1535 Act against church aid to certain offenders against the State (Malcolm, (a), 68).

1560 "The forces of the Reformation . . . swept away all right of ecclesiastical sanctuary." (O.E.C., XV, 62).

1687 Act against evasion of war service in sanctuary (Malcolm, (a), 70).

1796-9 Comte d'Artois (brother of deposed Louis XVIII and later

Charles X) in Holyrood Sanctuary (O.E.C., XV, 95; Grant, II, 76; Maxwell, 250).

1830-32 Charles X of France in Sanctuary (O.E.C., XV, 96; Grant, II, 78; Maxwell, 251).

1835 Thomas De Quincey in Holyrood Sanctuary (O.E.C., XV, 97) on several occasions (Catford, 102).

"No Act of Parliament has ever repealed the privilege of sanctuary within the girth of Holyrood Abbey . . . In 1880 imprisonment for debt was in most cases abolished. The Bankruptcy (Scotland) Act, 1913, practically ended the need for it." (O.E.C., XV, 98).

Smeaton ((a), 233) noted that in 1904 the privilege of sanctuary still existed, but Catford (107) records that the last entry in the court book of the Bailie of Holyrood, under whose care the debtors lived, was dated 1880.

Saughton House

1537 Saughton acquired by the Watson family from the Abbey of Holyrood when the lands passed to the Earls of Morton (Geddie, 66).

1623 Saughton House built (Grant, III, 319; Geddie, 66) for Patrick Ellis (but this may be a confusion with Stenhouse (q.v) unless he had the house and the mill built for him in the same year).

The house was demolished some 30 years ago, but the grounds and rose gardens were acquired by the city and are open to the public.

1908 Scottish National Exhibition held in Saughton Park.

Saughton Prison

1925 Saughton Prison built on the demolition of Calton Jail (Keir, 1008).

Schools

Some schools will be found under their own names, especially those of historic interest, e.g. Royal High School and George Heriot's; or those which have occupied various sites, e.g. the Merchant Company Schools of George Watson's, Mary Erskine (under the original name of Merchant Maiden Hospital), Trades Maiden Hospital and James Gillespie's School. Others, e.g. Royal Blind School and the School for the Deaf will be found under Hospitals.

During the time when the Royal High School was unopposed for what is now called secondary education, primary 'English' or 'vulgar' schools taught the 'three Rs'. Among these were the Charity schools, c.1700, at Castlehill and Canongate; the Society for the Propagation of Christian Knowledge Schools, c.1743, in

World's End Close and Forester's Wynd; Session schools run by the Kirk Sessions of some churches; and, from c.1833, George Heriot's free day schools under the Heriot Trust. Schools which taught non-classical subjects (the classics being the perquisite of the Royal High School) were called 'Adventure schools' each run by a master who ventured his capital to teach French, German, mathematics, history etc., e.g. Louis Cauvin who taught French in Bishops's Close.

The following list is by no means exhaustive, and is confined to larger or older schools —

1806 Leith High (or Grammar) School, later Leith Academy (Grant, III, 265; Russell, 456); moved to Duke Street in 1931.

1823 Morningside School, Morningside Road; closed in 1892 but the tiny building remains (Smith, I, 149).

1823 Edinburgh Academy founded; opened in 1824 in Henderson Row in building designed by William Burn (Grant, III, 85; Cockburn, 415; Keir, 779).

1825-28 John Watson's Hospital, Belford Road, designed by William Burn, (O.E.C., XXIX, 164; Grant, III, 68). Closed in 1975 and building recently acquired for National Gallery of Modern Art.

1827 Loretto School, Musselburgh (Keir, 784).

1832 Edinburgh Institution (Keir, 782). It was in No. 59 George Street; in No. 8 Queen Street (Grant, II, 153); in Melville Street from 1920 during which time the name changed to Melville College; joined in 1972 with Daniel Stewart's as Stewart's-Melville College.

1832 Dr Bell's School, Leith (O.E.C., XX, 67; Grant, III, 251, says 1839; School History gives 1838). It occupied St. Cecilia's Hall in 1844 (Harris, 36). Now a Resource Centre under Lothian Regional Council in Junction Place, Leith.

1833 Merchiston Castle School, Colinton Road in the grounds of Merchiston Castle (q.v.) (O.E.C., XV, app. 24); moved to Colinton in 1930 (Keir, 785).

1833 Louis Cauvin's will founded a school for the sons of teachers and farmers at Willowbrae crossroads (Grant, II, 318).

1844-45 Four Evening Schools open (Robertson, 308).

1845 Church of Scotland Normal School, Johnston Terrace (Grant, I, 295).

1847 Dr Guthrie's Original Ragged Industrial School, held at first in Tolbooth Parish School and later an adjacent building in Ramsay Lane was erected (Grant, I, 87; Robertson, 311). Moved to Liberton in 1887.

1847 Industrial School, Blackfriars Street (Grant, I, 264; Smeaton, (a), 141). There was also one in the West Port area.

1849-53 Daniel Stewart's Hospital (College), designed by David Rhind, in Queensferry Road (Grant, III, 67); opened 1855 (O.E.C., XII, app. 32); amalgamated with Melville College in 1972 as Stewart's-Melville; proposed primary school conjunction with Mary Erskine in 1979.

1855 St. Denis School for Girls, Great King Street; 1858 Royal Circus; 1915 Chester Street; 1932 Ettrick Road (Keir, 789).

1863 Ministers' Daughters' College (Esdaile) (Keir, 174); now closed.

1865-70 Fettes College, designed by David Bryce, Fettes Avenue (Grant, III, 82; Smeaton, (a), 299; Keir, 785).

1872 Education Act placed the responsibility for schooling on the School Board of the Town Council (Keir, 798).

1873 Cargilfield Preparatory School, Trinity; moved to Barnton in 1899 (Keir, 786).

1873 School Board started Evening Continuation Classes (Robertson, 311).

1876 Portobello School (Keir, 799); now in Duddingston Road.

1886 St. George's School for Girls opened in Melville Street in 1888 (Keir, 789); moved to Garscube Terrace in 1912; recently incorporated Lansdowne House School (opened in 1879).

1890 St. Margaret's School, East Suffolk Road.

1892 South Morningside School.

1893 Trinity Academy, Newhaven Road (Keir, 799).

1904 Boroughmuir School (Keir, 799) opened on Bruntsfield Links site (see James Gillespie's Hospital) and moved to Viewforth in 1914.

1905 St. Thomas of Aquin's R.C. School, Chalmers Street (Keir, 800).

1907 Holy Cross R.C. Academy, Craighall Road (Keir, 800).

1909 Broughton School, Broughton Road (Keir, 798); moved to Carrington Road in the early 1970's.

Sciennes

The name is derived from St. Catherine of Siena (q.v.).

1741 Sciennes House built, opening from the Meadows (Grant, III, 54) and it was demolished in 1867.

1741 Sciennes Hill House built on the site of the Chapel of St. John the Baptist (see St. Catherine of Siena) (O.E.C., X, 101). It became the home of Adam Ferguson, the historian and philosopher, and the only meeting between Sir Walter Scott and Robert Burns took place in the house in 1786 (Grant, III, 55). There is a plaque on the back wall of a flat in 7/9 Sciennes House Place (formerly Braid Place) recording the meeting. This may be seen by going through the common entry into the back garden of the block of flats (Pennycook, 75).

Scots Pint

In 1621 the standard pint for all liquids was the measure of three pounds Scots of water from the Water of Leith. Williamson (300) said that it equalled two quarts (English measure), while Robertson and Wood (284) noted that it represented three modern pints.

Before 1707 the Scottish measures were 4 gills = 1 mutchkin; 2 mutchkins = 1 chopin; 2 chopins = 1 pint.

Scottish Assembly
A measure, still undecided at the time of writing, aimed at devolving certain powers from London to Edinburgh, while still retaining the Secretary of State for Scotland whose office has existed as a member of the Westminster Cabinet since 1885. The proposed site for such an Assembly is the Royal High School building on Calton Hill, which is being converted for this use.

Scottish Land Court, Grosvenor Crescent.
1911 This Court was created by statute to take over the functions of the Crofters' Commission of 1886; to cope with problems of over-population and consequent competitive rents for small holdings; to revalue holdings and determine fair rents; to deal with dispossession of tenants and with questions relating to boundaries (Keir, 197).

Scottish Mint, see Cunzie House.

Semple's Close, Castlehill — north side.
Contains the house bought by Lord Semple in 1736 which bears the date 1638 and the inscription 'Praised be the Lord, my God, my stength and my redeemer', and a neighbouring doorway, also dated 1638, with the motto 'Sedes Manet optima Coela'.

Sett
1. The sett was the municipal constitution of the town (Robertson and Wood, 179; 195), first proposed in 1583 by a committee set up by James VI to consider a dispute between merchants and tradesmen.

2. A sett is the name given to a block of granite used for making the streets, and is still to be found in certain streets of the city.

Seven Hills
The seven hills associated with Edinburgh are generally regarded as being the Castle Rock, Arthur's Seat, Calton Hill, Blackford Hill, Braid Hills, Craiglockhart Hill and Corstorphine Hill.

There was an old rhyme about the seven hills —
> "Abbey, Calton, Castle grand,
> Southward see St. Leonard stand,
> St. John's and Sheens as two are given
> And Multrie's makes seven."

Shakespeare Square
Shakespeare Square was the site at the north end of the North
Bridge where the General Post Office now stands. It was largely
taken up with the Theatre Royal together with lodging houses,
taverns and oyster shops.
1768 Theatre Royal founded (O.E.C., XXIII, 16; Wilson, II, 91; Grant,
I, 341; Maxwell, 242; Smeaton, (a), 225).
1778 Shakespeare Square completely built (Youngson, 94).
c.1815 The north-east side of the Square removed for building Waterloo
Place and the Regent Arch.
1860 Theatre Royal and the rest of the Square pulled down when the
General Post Office was to be built (Grant, I, 353).

Shoemakers' Land, 213-217 Canongate — north side.
Through this property a passage led to Shoemakers' Close which
contained the Hall of the Incorporation of Cordiners, erected in
1682. The frontage was reconstructed in 1725 by which time the
Hall had disappeard. The building was taken down and rebuilt in
1882 (R.C., 179). Some regard this as synonymous with Bible Land
(q.v.), but R.C. (177) gives different numbers in the Canongate to
each.
1677 Shoemakers' Land built (Grant, II, 10; R.C., 177) by the
Incorporation of Cordiners.
1954-58 Town Council rebuilt the property, but there is no plaque to
show that it belonged to the shoemakers.

Shops or **Booths**, see also Luckenbooths.
1484 Booths, six or seven feet square, were rented at £4 Scots per annum
(i.e. six shillings and 8 pence stg. or 33p.) (Smeaton, (b), 47).
    The word booth is derived from the Norse for a stall, and is
found in several books of the Old Testament (Genesis, Leviticus,
Nehemiah, Job and Jonah) meaning a shelter.

Short's Observatory, see Outlook Tower.

Shrubhill, Leith Walk, see Gallow Lee.

Signet Library, Parliament Square.
1722 Library set up in Writers' Court (Grant, I, 186; O.E.C., XII, 28,
says 1699) as a legal library for the Society of Writers to H.M.
Signet (q.v.) (Scotsman, 23-1-1978).
1778 Decision to enlarge this into a general library (Keir, 915).
1825 Library built adjoining the County Hall (q.v.) (Smeaton, (a), 176),
and to the east of it (Grant, I, 123) and north of the Advocates'
Library (q.v.). Robert Reid designed the exterior as part of his

façade for Parliament Square, and William Stark was responsible for the interior. Keir (916) gave the date of building as 1816, and stated that in 1826 the Upper Library was bought from the Faculty of Advocates.

To reduce the cost of upkeep of the very large library 40,000 general books were sold in 1960, and the sale of a further 50,000 general books was planned for 1978-9 thus reducing the size of the library to some 70,000 books. In both sales the National Library had the first choice of books (Scotsman, 23-1-1978).

Silvermills, near Stockbridge.
Formerly a village of silversmiths and tanners on the Water of Leith (Wilson, II, 204; 208; Smeaton, (b), 318), "for the sake of which, as an access to the city, Gabriel's Road (q.v.) existed." (Chambers, 367).

Slateford
1745 Prince Charles slept at Gray's Mill (Geddie, 71) before entering the city (Grant, III, 326).
1822 Aqueduct built for the Union Canal (q.v.).
1910 Corn and cattle markets in New Market Road (Keir, 1008) (see Markets).

Societies, see also Clubs.
1701 Society for the Propagation of Christian Knowledge founded (Maitland, 471; Arnot, 426; Wilson, II, 53).
1728 First Society of amateur musicians formed (Maitland, 167; Arnot, 379; Chambers, 161; Grant, I, 251).
1731 Philosophical Society formed (Arnot, 427; O.E.C., II, 10, says 1739).
c.1735 Royal Medical Society founded (Grant, III, 311; Stewart, 6, says 1737) originally met in the Land of the Black Friars near the Surgeons' Hall; later in Melbourne Place (1852-1966); now in the University of Edinburgh Students' Centre.
1736 Grand Lodge of Scotland created (Wilson, II, 288) (see Freemasonry).
1737 Society for Improving Arts and Sciences (Maitland, 355).
1754 Select Society formed (Maxwell, 234; Carlyle, 311) and was recognised in the following year as the Society for Encouraging Arts, Science and Industry (Maitland, 258; Graham, 115). It met in the Advocates' Library.
1760 Scottish School for Design (Grant, II, 86).
1764 Speculative Society (O.E.C., V, 163-190; Arnot, 430; Creech, 71; Cockburn, 74).
1779 Caledonian Hunt (Arnot, 363).

1780 Society of Scottish Antiquaries (Wilson, II, 215; Creech, 72).

1782 Harveian Society, a medical society to honour William Harvey, the discoverer of the circulation of the blood in 1628 (H. L. Watson-Wemyss, *Record of the Harveian Society,* (1933)).

1783 Royal Society of Edinburgh (q.v.) which grew out of the Philosophical Society of 1731.

1834 Edinburgh Geological Society.

1884 Royal Scottish Geographical Society (Smith, II, 455).

Society

So called from the Land of the Society of Brewers (1596), but previously belonged to the Convent of Siena, at the west end of the present Chambers Street (Robertson and Wood, 264). It sloped down to the Cowgate east of Candlemaker Row and was planted with trees (Grant, II, 268).

1598 First brewers at Society (O.E.C., II, 70, f.n.; Wilson, II, 152; Grant, II, 268).

1871 Society removed for the building of Chambers Street.

Society of Solicitors in the Supreme Courts

1797 Society formed (Keir, 203).

1892 Library opened.
    Members use the initials S.S.C.

Society of Writers to H.M. Signet, see also Signet Library.

In the 15th century they were clerks in the Secretary of State's office (who was Keeper of the King's Seal or Signet) (Youngson, xv).

1532 Writers to the Signet became members of the College of Justice (Youngson, xv).

c. 1600 Writers to the Signet formed a Society (Youngson, xv) presided over by the Keeper of the Signet, a Crown appointment combining the office of Lord Clerk Register (Keir, 203).
    Since the 18th century the Society has been "the principal and most numerous body of solicitors in Scotland" (Youngson, xv).
    Members use the initials W.S.

Sou' (South) Gate, see Cowgate.

South Bridge

1786 "A bridge to the south, over the Cowgate street, was built, and the area for building shops and houses on the east and west side of it sold higher than perhaps was ever known in the city." (Creech, 64).

1788 South Bridge opened, a series of nineteen arches (O.E.C., V, 83; Grant, I, 374).

Southern Districts
Expansion of Edinburgh south of Telfer's Wall began in the 1760's
with the building of Bristo Street, Nicolson Street, George Square
etc. and the area, as far south as Preston Street, was divided in 1771
into eight districts, each supplying five commissioners. This body
could impose rates and represent to the Town Council the needs of
the southern suburbs in regard to lighting, policing, water supply
and cleaning. The districts were Teviot Row and Lauriston,
Potterrow and Bristo, George Square, Nicolson Park,
Crosscauseway, Gibbet (Preston) Street, Causewayside, and
Tollcross (Grant, II, 345).
1820 The Southern Market was set up to sell butcher-meat, poultry, fish
and vegetables near the Chapel of Ease in Buccleuch Street (Grant,
II, 346), but this lasted only a few years because shops opened
nearby.
1856 Southern Districts abolished.

South Gray's Close, 40 High Street — south side.
1574 Cunzie House (q.v.) built at the foot of the Close (Chambers, 260;
Maitland, 182; Wilson, II, 131; Grant, I, 267; Smeaton, (a), 208;
Dunlop and Dunlop, 50) and this gave the Close the alternative
name of Mint Close.
1746 Birthplace of Henry Erskine, Lord Advocate (R.C., 99) and his
brother Thomas (in 1750) who became Lord Chancellor of England
(Steuart, 72).
1771 Episcopal Church, the 'Cowgate Chapel' built at the foot of South
Gray's Close (Arnot, 283; Grant, I, 268; II, 247).
1856 R.C. Church of St. Patrick took over the 'Cowgate Chapel' (Grant,
I, 278).
        The Close still leads from High Street to Cowgate.

South Loch or **Borough (Burgh) Loch**
The South (Borough, Burgh) Loch, or Straiton's Loch after John
Straiton who leased it, covered most of the Meadows.
1575 Brewers to use water from the South Loch (Maitland, 34; 175;
Smith, I, 20, says 1596).
1612 Loch partly drained by Town Council (Smeaton, (b), 356).
1621 Water supply from Loch discontinued (O.E.C., X, 256).
1653 Drought in city; water from the loch used again (O.E.C., XVI, 39).
1657 Plan to drain Loch (O.E.C., X, 257; XVI, 49).
1658 Drainage begun and completed in 1740 (R.C., xxxvi). This was
during the time of John Straiton's lease (Daiches, 173).
1722 Thomas Hope of Rankeillor began reclamation of the Meadows
(O.E.C., X, 258; Maitland, 173; Grant, II, 347). William Burns,
father of the poet, took part in this scheme c.1749 during Hope's 57

years' lease (O.E.C., X, 259).

1743 Middle Meadow Walk opened.

1850 Pillars at western entrance to Meadows (Robertson, 165).

1859 Melville Drive opened (Gilbert, 130).

1860 Meadows opened as a pleasure ground.

1881 Messrs. Nelson erected pillars at the east end of Melville Drive (Grant, II, 355).

1886 International Exhibition of Industry, Science and Art held in the Meadows. The sundial in West Meadows commemorates this (the brass-founders column which formed part of the sundial is now in Nicolson Square). Octagonal columns were built by the master craftsmen of Edinburgh and erected in Melville Drive at the western entrance to the Exhibition.

1886 The Jaw Bones at the Jaw Bone Walk were presented by the Zetland Fair Isle Knitting stand at the Exhibition.

Sports

Archery, bowls, golf, horse-racing, ice-rinks and tennis are mentioned separately.

1764 Riding school (the Royal Menage) in Nicolson Street (O.E.C., XX, 122; Arnot, 424; Grant, II, 334; Scotsman, 24-5-1828).

1776 Charter for riding school (Grant, II, 335).

1829 New riding school built on site of present Caledonian Station Hotel (O.E.C., XXX, 144) the former building having been sold for the Surgeons' Hall.

1832 Grange Cricket Club formed (Keir, 535).

1835 Royal Eastern Yacht Club formed (Keir, 540).

1870 Royal Forth Yacht Club at Granton (Keir, 540).

1870 Powderhall New Year professional athletic sprint begun (Keir, 536). This continued until mid 1960's and is now run at Meadowbank.

1873 Scottish Rugby Union formed.

1874 Heart of Midlothian Football Club formed (Keir, 532).

1875 Hibernian Football Club formed (Keir, 532).

1920's Speedway racing ('Dirt track')at Old Meadowbank, transferred to Powderhall in 1977.

1927 Greyhound racing at Powderhall, previously at Stenhouse until the 1930's.

1950 Edinburgh Croquet Club formed (Keir, 538) using the lawn at Lauriston Castle (q.v.).

1964 Car racing at Ingliston.

1969 Royal Commonwealth Swimming Pool, Dalkeith Road, opened for the Commonwealth Games.

1970 Meadowbank Sports Centre, London Road, opened for the Commonwealth Games in that year.

1977 Upkeep of sports facilities costs Edinburgh District £1.3m annually.

Stamp Office Close, see Old Stamp Office Close.

Stenhouse
Grant (III, 339) says that this is a corruption of Stonehouse or Place of the Stones, and refers to a hamlet near Burdiehouse. This was a different place from the present Stenhouse district of Gorgie.

　　Stenhouse was formerly Stenhope and the mansion was Stenhope Mill (Geddie, 69). The Stenhopes intermarried with the Watsons of Saughton (q.v.).

1623 Stenhouse Mansion (or Mill) built (O.E.C., XVII, app. 22) for Patrick Ellis, the City Treasurer (Geddie, 69). (See note on Saughton House).

1920's Greyhound racing track at Stenhouse.

1938 Garden gifted to National Trust for Scotland by Greyhound Racing Association. It is now used for industrial work.

1964 Mansion restored for the National Trust for Scotland, and leased to the Department of Environment as a conservation centre.

Stent
Stents were local taxes ingathered by officials known as 'stent-masters' (Robertson and Wood, 189).

'Stinking Style', see Luckenbooths.

Stockbridge
Formerly called Stokebridge. The name may mean 'wooden bridge', a stock meaning a stick or timber (*Edinburgh Weekly*, 21-10-1966).

　　The old village had a china factory. Stockbrige was the birthplace of the artists Sir Henry Raeburn (1756) and David Roberts (1796).

1826 New Town markets at Stockbridge (Cockburn, 434), the remains of which may still be seen.

Stock Exchange
1844 Stock Exchange formed in Princes Street (Keir, 586).

1846-88 Stock Exchange occupied various rooms in St. Andrew Square (Keir, 587).

1888 Stock Exchange built in North St. David Street (Keir, 588).

1960's New building in North St. David Street to house new machinery, but this edifice showed structural faults and the Stock Exchange office has moved to Dublin Street, the Exchange now being linked with London.

'Stoppit Stravaig'
1639 At the White Horse Close (q.v.) "the Royalist nobles were intercepted on their way to join the King [i.e. Charles I] at Berwick, Montrose being the only one who managed to carry out his purpose. This was known as the 'Stoppit Stravaig'." (Williamson, 121).

Storms etc.
1659 Violent storm in the city (O.E.C., XVI, 52). "A signal manifestation of the Divine wrath at an impost of eightpence Scots upon the pint of ale sold in the city."

1739 Three months of hard frost from December (Arnot, 210; Grant, III, 51; Carlyle, 62).

1740 Bad harvest (Maitland, 124; Arnot, 210).

1744 Great thunderstorm (Keir, 967, quoting from the Caledonian Mercury).

1797 Violent storm destroyed Newhaven pier (Grant, III, 302).

Worst recorded gale, 1868 (Keir, 962).

Greatest rainfall in one day, 1787, − 4.20 inches; in one month, August, 1948, − 9.40 inches, the worst since September, 1785 (Keir, 964).

Most severe snowfall, 1795 (Keir, 964).

These figures are based on the continuous recordings of weather by a series of observers from 1764 until the Scottish Meteorological Society was formed in 1855 (Keir, 959).

Street Cleanliness
1505 Town bellman ordered to keep High Street clean.

1519 Magistrates ordered streets to be kept clean (Grant, II, 239).

1553 Council ordered dunghills and swine to be removed from the streets (Maitland, 14; Grant, I, 193).

1554–89 "The attempts of the Council to keep the main streets and vennels free from middens, stones and swine were praiseworthy, though crowned with small success save on the great occasions of royal entries." (O.E.C., XV, 7; Smeaton, (b), 100).

1606 Town executioner to clean middens out of the High Street.

1619 Each inhabitant to keep clean that part of the street before his own bounds (Grant, I, 199).

1636–1775 "It is not easy to convey a true impression of the state of the streets without offending modern susceptibilities: but a few extracts from the writings of contemporary travellers may . . . enable the reader to trace out the cause of the periodic visitations of the plague by which the Scottish capital was afflicted." (Maxwell, 202). The accounts of some of the contemporary travellers will be found in Hume Brown, *Early Travellers in Scotland,* (1891).

1686 Magistrates responsible for cleaning the streets by an Act of Parliament (R.C., xlix).

1705 Joseph Taylor, commenting on the offensive state of the streets wrote, "We were forc't to . . . take care where we trod for fear of disobliging our shoes." (*Journey to Edenborough,* (1705), 1903 edition, 134).

1726 The main street cleaned by scavengers early every morning except Sundays (R.C., lii).

1727 Daniel Defoe commented that the difficulty of obtaining an adequate water supply to a town built upon a high ridge was the principal casuse of the filth in the streets, rather than the uncleanliness of the inhabitants. (*A Tour through Great Britain* (1727), vol. 3, *A Description of Scotland,* 31-2).

1750 "In the middle of the eighteenth century vagrant swine went as commonly about the streets of Edinburgh as dogs do in our day." (Chambers, 276).

Edinburgh "had the disadvantage, shared by few Scottish towns, of being built upon neither a river nor the sea . . . On the north side . . . wynds and closes drained into the Nor' Loch. But on the south side everything ran into the Cowgate, and nothing but torrential rain could have washed that street clean." (O.E.C., XXIII, 96).

1752 Street rakers employed.

1774 As a result of improved water supply "in the morning the streets are so clean, that foot-passengers walk in the middle of them." (Topham, 152).

1786 Cleaning put into the hands of police commissioners.

1817 Manure collected from the streets was sold and the revenue used to pay for lighting the city.

1848 Thirty additional scavengers were employed and 500 tons of filth and rubbish were cleared (Scotsman, 25-10-1848). Cholera in the city was ascribed to filth in the poorer quarters of the West Bow and Cowgate (Scotsman, 28-10-1848; 1-11-1848).

1850 Effective drainage established in Craig's Close, opposite the Cross, extending from the High Street to the main drain in Market Street (Scotsman, 20-3-1850).

1856 Town Council resumed responsibility for cleaning.

1865 Every street had a sewer.

1960's Total street mileage of 490 miles (800km) was cleaned by 7 mechanical sweepers, 30 pedestrian controlled electric trucks and 79 orderlies (Keir, 344).

1977 Lothian Regional Council estimate an annual expenditure on drainage at over £9m., working out at 18.4p in £1 of the rates, while the District Council anticipate an expenditure of over £5m. for cleansing.

Street Lighting
(See Wood *et al.*, 170 *et seq.*)
1498 Citizens to carry lanterns after nightfall.
1554 Council ordered lanterns to be hung in the streets at night
(Maitland, 14; Wilson, I, 75; Grant, I, 193).
1557 Nobody allowed out after dark without a light on account of crimes
(Fraser, 71).
1564 Citzens to hang out lanterns.
1582 Lanterns at Netherbow Port.
1653 Lanterns to be outside houses from 5 p.m. until curfew.
1684 Lamps to be hung by citizens in the High Street (O.E.C., XVI, 134;
Maitland, 105). This practice did not last long.
1688 Town Council empowered to place lanterns where they thought
fit.
1785 Lighting in charge of Town Council, and an Act for lighting in the
New Town.
1817 Edinburgh Gas Light Company formed (Gilbert, 64) and by the
following year shops and some streets were so lit (Anderson, 336).
1820 Gas lighting in the High Street (Grant, I, 203).
1822 Princes Street lit with gas (Malcolm, (b), 74; Gilbert, 72).
1856 City lamps under the charge of the police commissioners.

Street Lighting. After lighting the way through the
darker streets the boy extinguishes his torch in Charlotte
Square link horn.
(The link horns are still there.)

1895 Electric lighting introduced (Grierson, 8; Malcolm, (b), 74) from a power station in Dewar Place.

Strichen's Close, 66 High Street — south side.
Formerly called Rosehaugh's Close, the name being changed when Lord Strichen, a relative by marriage of the descendants of George Mackenzie of Rosehaugh, lived here in the eighteenth century (Grant, I, 254).
1526 Town residence of the Abbot of Melrose (Chambers, 223; R.C., 94).
1677 Home of George Mackenzie of Rosehaugh ('Bluidie MacKingie', q.v.) (Chambers, 223; R.C., 94).
1857 Bookbinding firm of William Hunter founded in the Close (University of Edinburgh Journal, June, 1977, 58).
   The Close no longer exists, having disappeared in the demolition between Niddry Street and Blackfriars Street.

Stripping Close, Castlehill — south side.
The Close in which prisoners removed their clothes before being whipped in the High Street. There were nine whipping places in the Old Town, the last public whipping taking place in 1822 (R.T. Skinner, *The Royal Mile*, (1947), 11).

Sugarhouse Close, Canongate — south side.
1752 Earl of Dunkeld's house acquired by a company to refine sugar (O.E.C., XII, 117).
   The Close does not now exist.

Summerhall
An eighteenth century village east of the Meadows whose buildings were demolished in 1912 for the erection of the Veterinary School (q.v.) (Cruft, 45).
   Summerhall was noted for its brewery (Grant, III, 51).

Tailors' Hall, 137 Cowgate.
"Apart from St. Giles Church and the Magdalen Chapel, the Tailors' Hall is the most important building now surviving in Edinburgh" (R.C., 105).
1621 Tailors' Hall built (O.E.C., XI, 125-171; Wilson, II, 144; Grant, II, 258). The entrance is now difficult to find, being in the south-east corner of a private car park.
1638 "It would . . . appear that the National Covenant was not only approved in the Tailors' Hall but was actually signed there by several ministers." (O.E.C., XI, 161). "An assembly of between two and three hundred clergymen . . . to consider the National

Entrance from the Cowgate to Tailors' Hall (now demolished), showing the insignia of the tailors. A "rag-wife" crosses in front of a brewer's dray. "Rag-wives" are still to be seen in the Cowgate.

Covenant." (Chambers, 346, f.n.).

A draft of the Covenant was approved in the Hall (R.C., 106).

1656 Cromwell's Scottish Commission met in the Hall (Williamson, 256).

1733–47 Tailors' Hall used as a theatre (O.E.C., XI, 162; Chambers, 346; says 1727–53; Nimmo (177) also says 1727).

1757–1800 Alexander Kincaid, the printer, in the lands of Tailors' Hall (O.E.C., XI, 138).

1800 Brewery in the Hall (O.E.C., XI, 138).

Tam o' the Cowgate

The nickname of Thomas Hamilton, 1st Earl of Haddington, who died in 1637 (O.E.C., XIII, 139, f.n.; Chambers, 244; Grant, II, 259). He had studied law in Paris, was President of the Court of Session and Secretary of State. The nickname of Tam o' the Cowgate was bestowed on him by James VI whose friend he was (Chambers, 246; Williamson, 252; Dunlop and Dunlop, 126). Thomas Hamilton of Priestfield was Lord President of the Court of Session, 1592; Lord Advocate, 1596; Earl of Melrose, 1619; Earl of Haddington, 1627; an acute judge who collected legal decisions and amassed much wealth (Wilson, II, 147; Smeaton, (b), 269). He lived in the Cowgate on a site "now occupied by the southern piers of George IV Bridge" (Chambers, 244) near the corner of Candlemaker Row. The house was later used as the Merchants' Hall and the Excise Office, and was demolished in 1829 when George IV Bridge was built.

Tanfield Hall, Canonmills.
1825 Erected as an oil gas-works (Grant, III, 87).
1843 Housed the first General Assembly of the Free Church (Grant, III, 87; Smeaton, (b), 318). (See Assembly Hall).
1847 Housed a meeting to form the United Presbyterian Church (Grant, III, 88; Smeaton, (b), 318).
        Now a warehouse which is reached from Tanfield Lane and which bears a commemorative plaque.

Taverns, see Inns.

Tea
1681-2 Tea tasted for the first time in the city (Smeaton, (b), 112).
1720 Tea drinking in vogue (Graham, 89, f.n.; 91).
1801-32 Price was 12 shillings (60p) to 15 shillings (75p) per pound.
1833 Price dropped to 8-10 shillings (40-50p) per pound with the end of the monopoly of the East India Company.

Telephones
1847 Alexander Graham Bell, the inventor of the telephone, was born in South Charlotte Street.
1879 First telephone exchange in St. Andrew Square owned by the Scottish Telephonic Exchange Limited (Keir, 254).
1889 National Telephone Company (Robertson, 176; Keir, 254).
1896 Trunk service transferred to the Post Office (Keir, 254).
1912 Post Office controlled the whole service (Keir, 254).

Templar (Temple) Lands
The lands belonging to the Knights of the Temple, or Knights Templar, were distinguished by having iron crosses on their fronts or gables (Chambers, 50, Grant, I, 321). They were at the foot of the West Bow and on the south side of the Grassmarket, and dated from the 16th century. Grant (I, 321) states that an iron cross was still visible on one house in 1834, and a photograph in Cruft (15), dated 1855-6, shows such houses in the Grassmarket after the property had passed, on the dissolution of the Order, into the hands of the Knights of St. John of Jerusalem (R.C., 126). This site is now rebuilt for the Bank of Scotland.

Tenement
The area of ground upon which a land (q.v.) was built in the 16th
century.

Tennis
Royal tennis was played in Leith in the 12th century (Marshall, 11),
and at Holyrood where the tennis court was just outside the
Watergate (q.v.) The Royal Tennis Court was formerly called the
Catchpel, a name derived from 'Cache', a game which gave rise to
Fives, and which was a favourite in the reign of James IV
(Chambers, 344).

The Royal Tennis Court was used as a theatre (q.v.) and later
became the Hall of the Incorporation of Weavers which was burned
down in 1771.

Royal, or Real, tennis was superseded by Lawn tennis in 1870
with the invention of the rubber tennis ball, and a court was opened
in Raeburn Place in 1874. There are nearly 150 public lawn tennis
courts in the city, and in 1962 (Keir, 535) there were 28 private lawn
tennis clubs in the city affiliated to the East of Scotland Lawn Tennis
Association.

Theatre
"The earliest Edinburgh theatre was probably the Tennis Court in
the Watergate, down by Holyrood Palace. The occasional touring
London company played there, and Mary of Guise visited it in
1557." (Nimmo, 177). This appears to be improbable as the theatre
was not then created, but she saw *The Pleasant Satyre* at Greenside
in 1554. Chambers (344) says that plays were staged in the theatre at
the tennis court between 1681 and 1710, and James, Duke of York,
(later James VII (11)), attended the tragedy of *Mithridates, King of
Pontus* at the Tennis Court in 1681 (Sitwell and Bamford, 134).

"The first known appearance of the post-reformation theatre
in Edinburgh was in the reign of King James VI, when several
companies came from London, chiefly for the amusement of the
Court, including one to which Shakespeare is known to have
belonged, though his personal attendance cannot be substantiated.
There was no such thing, probably, as a play acted in Edinburgh
from the departure of James in 1603 till the arrival of his grandson,
the Duke of York, in 1680." (Chambers, 344).
1714 *Macbeth* staged before an audience of nobility (Nimmo, 177) at the
   Tennis Court Theatre (Sitwell and Bamford, 160).
1727 Tailors' Hall, Cowgate (q.v.) used a theatre (Nimmo, 177;
   Chambers, 346, says 1727-53; O.E.C., XI, 162, says 1733-47).
1737 Allan Ramsay's Playhouse, Carrubber's Close (q.v.), opened and
   was rapidly closed (O.E.C., I, 50; XI, 163; Chambers, 15; Graham,

94; Wilson, II, 43).

1747 Playhouse in Old Playhouse Close (q.v.) (O.E.C., XII, 115; Maitland, 212; Chambers, 347; Wilson, II, 86; Grant, II, 23; Smeaton, (a), 224).

1756 First performance of John Home's *Douglas* in Canongate Theatre, Old Playhouse Close (Arnot, 377; Chambers, 347; Grant, II, 24; Carlyle, 243; 325; Graham, 95).

1768 Theatre Royal, Shakespeare Square (q.v.) founded (O.E.C, XXIII, 16; Grant, I, 341; Wilson, II, 91; Maxwell, 242; Smeaton, (a), 225).

1769 Theatre in Old Playhouse Close closed.

1784 Mrs Siddons appeared at the Theatre Royal (Maxwell, 228; 242; Graham, 122).

1809 Henry Siddons, Mrs Siddons' son, took a twenty-one years' lease of the Theatre Royal (Steuart, 221).

1809 Corri's Rooms, Broughton Street, fitted as a theatre, called the Caledonian Theatre and later the Adelphi Theatre (Grant, II, 178).

1819 Scott's *Rob Roy* on the Theatre Royal stage (Grant, I, 349).

1830 R. H. Wyndham took over the lease of the Theatre Royal (Steuart, 222).

1853 Adelphi Theatre burned (Grant, II, 179) and was rebuilt as the Queen's Theatre and Opera House.

1859 Theatre Royal demolished (Grant, I, 353).

1865 Queen's Theatre burned (Grant, II, 179).

1875 Little Theatre of Varieties (originally called the Gaiety Theatre) in Chambers Street (Grant, II, 276) — later demolished.

1876 Theatre in Broughton Street rebuilt (Grant, II, 179) and later was called the Theatre Royal.

1883 Lyceum Theatre built (Gilbert, 161).

1892 Empire Palace Theatre, Nicolson Street, built; was rebuilt after a fire in 1911, and reconstructed in 1928 (Keir, 1008). It is now a Bingo Hall.

1906 King's Theatre opened (Keir, 1008).

1946 Theatre Royal burnt down and not replaced (Keir, 861).

1953 Gateway Theatre, Leith Walk opened; closed 1965 (Keir, 866).

1962 Traverse Theatre, West Bow, opened (Keir, 865).

1965 Churchhill Theatre in previous Morningside Free Church (Smith, I, 108).

Three Steps, see Piershill.

Time

1848 Greenwich mean time adopted in the city, and clocks were set forward 12½ minutes (Scotsman, 29-1-1848).

'Timmer Lands', see Early Houses.

Tipperlinn, Colinton Road, near Churchhill.
An old village of weavers which has now disappeared (Catford, 244; Smith, I, 179).

Tirling Pin, see Risp.

Tolbooth, High Street — south side.
The booth at which tolls were paid (O.E.C., XII, 98). A bell rang out from the Tolbooth when goods were to be sold, when there was to be a civic meeting, and to sound the curfew (Fraser, 28). A ten o'clock curfew was imposed on citizens in 1583 (Maitland, 42).
1369 A praetorium or town hall may have stood on the site to be occupied by the Tolbooth, and may have been destroyed in 1385 (R.C., xl).
1386 Charter for building Old Tolbooth or Bell-house (O.E.C., IV, 78; XIV, 7-24) on the same site. This date is marked on brass bricks on the location.
1403-30 Tolbooth probably built (O.E.C., XIV, 11) north-west of St. Giles Church, the site now being marked on the road.
1438 The Tolbooth was the likely place for an assembly of Parliament to deliberate on measures rendered necessary by the assassination of James I (Chambers, 83).
1480 Prison included in the Tolbooth (Catford, 35).
1532 Court of Session met in the Tolbooth.
1561 Mary, Queen of Scots, required the Town Council to take down the dilapidated Tolbooth (O.E.C., IV, 9; Maitland, 21; Wilson, I, 92; Fraser, 76).
1562 Town Council erected a new Tolbooth instead to the south-west of St. Giles Church (O.E.C., III, 221; Smeaton, (a), 176) and this was the locus for meetings of the Scottish Parliament until Parliament Hall (q.v.) was built in 1639.
1575 Tolbooth's west gable repaired (O.E.C., XIV, 10).
1610 Building of tower and west gable (O.E.C., XIV, 11; Wilson, I, 241). This date is marked in brass bricks on the site.
1640 Old Tolbooth used only as a jail (Arnot, 297). The 'Guidman of the Tolbooth' was the Governor of the prison (Dunlop and Dunlop, 85).
1650 Marquis of Montrose's head set on a pinnacle of the west gable (Williamson, 68) following his execution (O.E.C., I, 31; Arnot, 129; Wilson, I, 123; II, 100; Grant, II, 13).
1657 Tolbooth records began (O.E.C., IV, 75-144).
1678 Annexe added to west of the Tolbooth (O.E.C., XIV, 18). This date is marked on brass bricks on the site.
1736 Captain Porteous removed from the Tolbooth by a mob and hanged in the Grassmarket (Catford, 40). (See Porteous Riots).

1785 First hanging at the west end of the Tolbooth (Grant, II, 231).

1787 Shops formerly on the north side of the Tolbooth converted to a guardhouse for the Town Guard (q.v.) (Chambers, 84).

1788 Deacon Brodie hanged on gallows he had previously designed (Chambers, 92).

1811 New Tolbooth demolished (Catford, 36).

1817 Old Tolbooth demolished (O.E.C., IV, 86; XIV, 12; Cockburn, 241; Smeaton, (a), 176).

The site of the Tolbooth is marked by causeway stones in the form of a heart, while brass plates follow the outline of the building west of St. Giles Church. "The Tolbooth of Edinburgh is called the Heart of Midlothian." (Scott, *Heart of Midlothian*, chap. 1).

Town Council, see also Lord Provost.

"By the beginning of the fifteenth century municipal power was a monopoly of the merchants and trades of this burgh." (Robertson and Wood, 171).

1296 First mention of an Edinburgh magistrate (Maxwell, 28).

1377 First recorded Provost of Edinburgh (Maxwell, 39).

1469 Act providing "(1) that office-bearers and members of Council should only hold office for a year; (2) that the retiring Council should choose their successors, the new Council; (3) that the retiring Council and the new Council together should choose the office-bearers for the coming year — namely, Alderman, Dean of Guild etc.; and (4) that, in the election of office-bearers, one deacon from each of the trade incorporations should vote along with the old and new Council." (Robertson and Wood, 177).

"The close corporation . . . had a career of more than three and a half centuries." (Robertson and Wood, 184).

Of the trade incorporations (q.v.) fourteen were allowed one representative or Deacon, but of these only six attended each Council meeting, the other eight attending occasionally, so that the merchants effectively controlled the Council.

1487 First use of the title of Lord Provost (Robertson and Wood, 175).

1551 Town Council minutes survive from this date.

1583 Decree Arbitral by James VI laid down a definite scheme for the election and government of the burgh — the 'sett' (q.v.) of the burgh (Wood *et al.*, 281).

1610 James VI gifted gowns to be worn by Provost and Magistrates (Maitland, 58; Grant, I, 199).

1627 Charles I presented the Sword to be carried before the Provost, and this is still used.

1633 Charles I knighted the Provost at St. John Cross (Grant, II, 2).

1667 Charles II granted the title of Lord Provost to the city (Wilson, I, 187; Grant, II, 281).

1700 First reference to a Chamberlain "to act as assistant to the Treasurer in the collection and management of the city revenues." (Robertson and Wood, 185).

1718 Salary of £300 per annum to the Lord Provost in lieu of gratuities (Arnot, 203; Maitland, 120; Robertson and Wood, 187).

1771 Salary increased to £500; to £800 in 1805; to £1000 in 1817 (Robertson and Wood, 187).

1771 Act for lighting, watching and cleaning of Edinburgh's southern suburbs (q.v.).

"The [Council] chamber was a low-roofed room [it was a Laigh Council House in the Tolbooth], very dark, and very dirty, with some small dens off it for clerks. Within this Pandemonium sat the town-council, omnipotent, corrupt, impenetrable. Nothing was beyond its grasp; no variety of opinion disturbed its unanimity, for the pleasure of Dundas was the sole rule for every one of them. Reporters, the fruit of free discussion, did not exist; and though they had existed, would not have dared to disclose the proceedings. Silent, powerful, submissive, mysterious and irresponsible, they might have been sitting in Venice. . . About the year 1799 a solitary schism amazed the public, by disclosing the incredible fact that the town-council might contain a member who had an opinion of his own. A councillor. . . electrified the city by a pamphlet shewing that the burgh was bankrupt. Time has put it beyond all doubt that he was right. . ." (Cockburn, 95-6). The consequences of Bailie Thomas Smith's action are recorded in Robertson and Wood, 228-232.

1800 The Council consisted of 33 members, including four bailies, Dean of Guild, Treasurer, old bailies, old Dean of Guild, old Treasurer, and certain merchants and trades councillors (Robertson, 147).

1812 Act to concentrate under the police commissioners the whole of watching, lighting and cleansing of the city (Robertson, 193).

1833 Parliamentary Reform Act to elect by public franchise.

1833 Council made a representative body under the Burgh Reform Act which established elections by inhabitants on the basis of the new parliamentary franchise (Wood et al., 312). There were five wards in the city and 31 councillors.

1856 Until this year the city possessed only four bailies (Robertson and Wood, 174) and the Council only had responsibility within the Flodden Wall. The Edinburgh Municipality Extension Act enlarged the town to 15 wards.

1900 Act providing that the Town Council should take over the powers possessed by police commissioners (Robertson and Wood, 198).

1900 Town Council consisted of 50 members, three for each of 16 wards with the Dean of Guild and the Convener of Trades (Roberson, 169).

1920 Council of 71 members, three for each of 23 wards with Dean of Guild and Convener of Trades. There were eleven Magistrates — the Lord Provost and ten bailies (Robertson and Wood, 201).

1975 Under Local Government Reorganisation the duties were shared between District and Regional Councils. Edinburgh District Council now has 64 electoral divisions, each electing one representative for three years, and presided over by the Lord Provost who is Chairman of the District Council.

   The Edinburgh District Council is responsible for planning, housing, parks, sports centres, baths, museums, art galleries, libraries, halls and theatres, cleansing, laundries, public health, and burial grounds. The Lothian Regional Council controls education, social work, highways, drainage, transport, police, fire services, and water supply.

Town Guard (City Guard)
In early times watching was carried out by burgesses in rotation.

1514 Origin of the Town Guard (Maitland, 12; Maxwell, 211).

1648 Town Guard of 60 men under a captain (Arnot, 505; Maxwell, 211).

1682 Town Guard increased to 108 men (O.E.C., XVI, 114; Maxwell, 211; Cockburn, 197; Robertson, 262). They were known as the 'Town Rottens' (Town Rats) (Cockburn, 339) or 'Toon Rattens' (Dunlop and Dunlop, 145).

1689 Town Guard raised for the defence of the city.

   The Town Guard were armed with musket, bayonet and Lochaber axe. The Guard House was in the centre of the High Street, originally at the Tolbooth. It "was a long, low, ugly building which . . . might have suggested the idea of a long black snail crawling up the middle of the High Street." (Scott, *Heart of Midlothian*, chap. 6).

1875 Guard House removed (Grant, I, 135; Dunlop and Dunlop, 145).

1787 Shops on the north side of the Tolbooth converted into the Guard House (Chambers, 84).

1805 Town Guard reduced from 126 to 37 men. Police introduced (Robertson and Wood, 192; Robertson, 262).

1812 Foundation of police system (q. v.).

Town Guardsmen.

1817 Town Guard disbanded (O.E.C., XIV, 170; Wilson, II, 38;
218; Cockburn, 197; 339; Smeaton, (b), 206; Robertson, 263). The
police establishment "was the first example of popular election in
Scotland." (Cockburn, 199).

Town Walls

1450 First wall round the town, the King's Wall (O.E.C., III, 210;
Maitland, 137; Arnot, 234; Wilson, I, 24; II, 76; Grant, II, 80;
Smeaton, (a), 29; Fraser, 30, says that "nothing in the civic records
suggests that any wall was built that year."). "It began about
half-way down the south side of the Castle bank . . . eastwards
along the steep slope above Grassmarket and Cowgate . . . until it
came nearly where St. Mary's Street crosses the High Street. There
it turned at right angles across the High Street ridge and dropped
into the valley on the north." (Catford, 17). The Nor' Loch (q.v.)
was created as part of the defences. Vestiges of the King's Wall may
still be seen in the Castle Wynd, which leads from the upper end of
Castlehill to the Grassmarket, and in Tweeddale Court (Catford,
17).
1513 Flodden Wall begun (O.E.C., II, 61-79; Maitland, 12; 138; Arnot,
236; Wilson, I, 47; II, 172; Maxwell, 89). This wall defined the
limits of the Burgh for 250 years. It began at the east end of the Nor'
Loch, went uphill to cross the High Street at St. Mary's Street, then

The Vennel, showing the Town Wall
and Castle.

downhill to the Cowgate, uphill parallel to the Pleasance, west along Drummond Street and College Street, through the site of the present Royal Scottish Museum to enclose Greyfriars Church and Kirkyard, but excluding the site of Heriot's Hospital, and north down the Vennel to the Castle Rock. There were six gates or ports (q.v.), New, Netherbow, Cowgate, Potterrow, Bristo and West (Catford, 18). The wall may be seen in the Pleasance and the Vennel.

1618-20 Telfer's Wall built (O.E.C., II, 78; XVIII, app. 31; Maitland, 61; 139) and in 1636 it extended the Flodden Wall around George Heriot's Hospital (O.E.C., XVIII, 155; Catford, 20). Traces of this wall exist in the Vennel (Catford, 20).

In the mid–eighteenth century the wall was breached at all parts in the outward expansion of the city.

Trades Maiden Hospital

1704 Founded by Mary Erskine in Argyle Square (q.v.), west of Horse Wynd (q.v.) (O.E.C., XXVIII, 5; Maitland, 463; Arnot, 564; Grant, II, 272). This building was eventually cleared during the construction of Chambers Street and the Museum (O.E.C., XXVIII, 5).

1855 School moved to Rillbank, Sciennes (O.E.C., XXVIII, 29). A 17th century replacement of the 'Blue Blanket' (q.v.) (Fraser, 43) was preserved within the Trades Maiden Hospital (Grant, III, 55), and has been in its possession for over a century.

1892 Rillbank property bought for Royal Hospital for Sick Children and Trades Maiden Hospital moved to Grange Loan (O.E.C., XXVIII, 42).

1971 Moved to Melville Street where it offers a home for girls whose parents live outside the city, and for partially handicapped girls, all of whom attend schools in the city. The 'Blue Blanket' is still on display.

Transport, see also Railways and Air Transport.

1610 Stage coaches between the town and Leith (Smeaton, (a), 105; (b), 98).

1633 Noblemen began to use private carriages (Smeaton, (b), 103).

1658 A stage coach between London and Edinburgh once in three weeks (R.C., li).

1660 Hackney carriage between the city and Leith (Grant, III, 151; R.C., li).

1661 First recorded sedan chair in the city (O.E.C., IX, 184).

1673 First hackney coaches in the city (Maitland, 338; Arnot, 597).

1678 Edinburgh-Glasgow coach drawn by six horses performed the double journey in six days (Grant, I, 354). Smeaton ((b), 111) said that the roads were so bad that the project had to be abandoned.

1687 Six sedan chairs on the city streets for public hire (O.E.C., IX, 186).

1702 Four hackney coaches plied between the city and Leith (Grant, III, 151).

1712 Stage coach to London took 13 days at a fare of £4-10-0 (£4.50) (O.E.C., XIV, 126; Maxwell, 189).

1753 Ninety sedan chairs in the city (O.E.C., IX, 204).

1763 Two stage coaches (of three horses) plied every hour between the city and Leith (Grant, III, 152; Creech, 67).

1773 Post coach to London in four days, fare £4-14-6 (£4.72) (O.E.C., XIV, 137).

1780 Fifteen coaches left every week for London (Maxwell, 236).

1783 Five or six stage coaches to Leith every half hour (Creech, 68).

1817 Hackney carriages registered.

1824 Six stage coaches plying between the city and London (Gray, 21).

1825 Sedan chair gave place to horse coach in the city (O.E.C., IX, 222).
Between the sedan chair and the four-wheeled cab, taxi services were undertaken by what were popularly called the 'Noddy' and the 'Minibus'. The 'Noddy' was so balanced on two wheels that on going uphill passengers were tilted backwards violently and baggage might fall on them, while on going downhill over irregular roadways passengers might be precipitated on to the horse. The 'Minibus' had a rear door, necessitating backing and manoeuvring to deposit the passenger at his destination (Catford, 204; Scotsman, 23-4-1950).

1846 Four-horse coach with four passengers led direct to Newcastle and thence by train to London (Scotsman, 1-8-1846).

1846 Coach to Dumfries left daily from Princes Street (Scotsman, 9-5-1846).

1850 Coach with 22 passengers to Perth via Queensferry at a cheaper cost than train (Scotsman, 15-6-1850).

1850 Sedan chairs had practically disappeared (O.E.C., XIV, app. 10). "By the time the sixties came in . . . the sedan chair business was entirely at an end." (O.E.C., IX, 234).

1871 Horse tramcars on the city streets (Grierson, 12), and before long some rails were laid to ease the work of the horses in winter.

1878 Roads and Bridges Act. Before this date there were tolls on all roads out of Edinburgh except to Leith where tolls were abolished in 1835 (Grierson, 12).

1891 Edinburgh Corporation acquired cable tramcars (Gilbert, 173); Daiches, 221, says 1893).

1897 Cable tramcars replaced horse cars (Malcolm, (b), 74; Grierson, 12), but the last horse tram ran in 1907 (Minto, 96).

1905 Electric tramcars in Leith (Keir, 406).

c.1906 Motor char-a-bancs with solid wheels for longer trips under the Scottish Motor Traction Company (Keir, 407).

1907 First motor taxi–cab registered in Edinburgh (Minto and
Armstrong, 56).
1910 First electric tramcar in Edinburgh (Evening News, 28-6-1978) ran
from Ardmillan Terrace to Slateford.
1919 Electric tramcars on many routes (Keir, 406).
1919 Motor buses introduced (Keir, 407).
1922 Electric tramcars throughout Edinburgh (Keir, 406); cable cars
ceased in 1923 (Daiches, 222). There is a short length of tramcar
rails maintained at the west end of Waterloo Place after motor buses
became established in 1956 (Keir, 408).

Trinity
Named from Trinity Mains, part of the lands belonging to the
Incorporation of Mariners of Trinity House, Leith.

Trinity College Church, site covered by Waverley Station.
1462 Church founded by Mary of Gueldres, Queen of James II (O.E.C.,
XIII, 80; XVI, app. 9; Maitland, 207; 480; Arnot, 271; Wilson, II,
239; Grant, I, 290-303; Maxwell, 68; Cockburn, 437; Smeaton, (a),
37; (b), 34; R.C., 36, says 1460).
1463 Mary of Gueldres buried in the Church (Maxwell, 68; Smeaton, (a),
37; (b), 34).
1531 Building ceased (R.C., 36).
1567 Sir Simon Preston gave the Church to the town (Maitland, 210).
1580 Church taken into Protestant use.
1848 Church sold to the North British Railway Company (Wood *et al.,*
51) and removed for building Waverley Station (O.E.C., XV,
128). The Church, one of the most beautiful churches in the city,
was "one of the finest models of Gothic architecture that this
country has to boast of." (*Edinburgh Advertiser*, 1815). "Many of
the stones were carefully preserved and numbered, and these, after
a lapse of about thirty years, were utilised in connection with the
building of the present Trinity College Church in Jeffrey Street."
(O.E.C., XVI, app. 9). Many of the marked stones, which had
been dumped on the Calton Hill, had disappeared in the intervening
years.
1871-2 "Erection of the present Trinity Church in Jeffrey Street, a
building in Gothic of a different period from the original, but
constructed largely of the stones laid in 1462." (Maxwell, 69).
1872-77 Church rebuilt (O.E.C., XV, 127; Grant, I, 290; Gray, in
Scotsman, 15-5-1948) and was designed to serve the north-east of
Edinburgh (R.C., 37).
1959 Building ceased to be used for worship, the congregation joining
Lady Glenorchy's South to form Holy Trinity (Keir, 174). The
Altar-pieces from Trinity College Church are on display in the

National Gallery in the Mound.
1977 The apse was used as a Corporation Reading Room, opening from Chalmers' Close, but is presently closed from lack of staff. The remainder of the church has been pulled down and is concealed behind a modern Government Department building.

Trinity Hospital, beside Trinity College Church.
1479 Trinity Hospital built (O.E.C., XI, 10; Arnot, 247; Smeaton, (a), 38) having been founded by Mary of Gueldres in 1462 (Cockburn, 437).
1578 New Hospital completed (Wood *et al.*, 35 *et seq.*).
1585 Town Council bought the Hospital (Arnot, 562).
1587 Considerable alterations (Cockburn, 437) the Hospital being moved to a nearby site (R.C., 36).
1645 All residents died of plague.
1728 Hospital in a state of disrepair from lack of funds.
1730 Rebuilt with individual rooms. A description of the Hospital in 1828 by Cockburn (436-444).
1845 Hospital buildings sold to the North British Railway Company and demolished (O.E.C., XV, 132; Grant, I, 307; Smeaton, (a), 39).
1940 Remains as the Trinity Fund, Edinburgh's oldest charity, under the administration of the Town Council as Governors of Trinity Hospital, and is joined to other pension funds giving a small annuity to 900 pensioners.

Tron
A tron was a public beam for weighing goods, a weigh-house. There were two in Edinburgh.
 The Butter tron was at the head of the Lawnmarket opposite the Upper Bow (Steuart, 23). It was destroyed in 1384; in use in 1561; rebuilt in 1614; destroyed in 1650 (R.C., 127); rebuilt in 1660 (Wilson, I, 205) and finally removed in 1822 before the visit of George IV (Wilson, I, 126).
 The Salt tron was in the High Street near the present Tron Church (Wilson, II, 39).
1817 Act for the erection of weighing machines in certain streets.

Tron Church, High Street — south side.
Formerly Christ's Church at the tron (i.e. the salt tron).
1635 Town Council resolved to build Church, designed by John Mylne (O.E.C., V, 74), after St. Giles was changed to an Episcopal Cathedral.
1637 Building begun (Smeaton, (b), 207).
1642 John Mylne undertook to complete the mason-work (R.C., 35).
1647 Church open for worship (O.E.C., XI, 14; Arnot, 274; Maitland,

Tron Church spire burning in the Great Fire of 1824.

165; Wilson, II, 284; Grant, I, 187; Smeaton, (a), 203; (b), 207).

1663 Church completed (Maitland, 166; Smeaton, (b), 207).

1671 Steeple added.

1785-7 Church shortened for building of North Bridge and Hunter Square (R.C., 35).

1788 East transept cut short and west transept removed to allow construction of South Bridge (Scotsman, 27-7-1977).

1824 Spire burned in great fire (Smeaton, (b), 207).

1828 New spire built (Grant, I, 188). Bell added (Scotsman, 1-11-1828).

1888 Interior remodelled (Scotsman, 27-7-1977).

1952 Church closed for worship and has not been used since (Catford, 33). The congregation were "transported to Moredun" (Keir, 174).

1969 Bought by Secretary of State for Scotland and gifted to Edinburgh Town Council who were to maintain it.

1974 Diggings inside the Church disclosed Marlin's Wynd (q.v.) which had led from the High Street to the Cowgate.

1975-7 External renovation, but the function has not yet been determined (Scotsman, 27-7-1977).

Tron Square, Cowgate.

1897 Built as a planned housing scheme of four-storey flats (Keir, 53). It is reached from High Street and Cowgate by Stevenlaw's Close, probably named after Stephen Loch, an adherent of Mary, Queen of Scots (Grant, II, 242).

Trunk's Close, High Street north side.
1795 Archibald Constable set up his shop and published *Edinburgh Review* in 1802 (Steuart, 66).

Tulzie (Tuilzie)
A tulzie or tuilzie was a quarrel, struggle, skirmish (Chambers, 37); a brawl, combat, street conflict (Grant, I, 195; Robertson, 138).

Turnpike Stair
A turnpike stair is a spiral flight of steps. Straight flights of steps were known as 'scale stairs' (Arnot, 246, f.n.).

Tweeddale Court, 14 High Street — south side.
1572 Tweeddale House built by Lady Yester (Wilson, II, 71).
1645 Home of the first Marquess of Tweeddale (Wilson, II, 71).
1792 Occupied by British Linen Company (Wilson, II, 72; Grant, I, 279), later the head office of the British Linen Bank (Scott-Moncrieff, 65) — but the Bank was not so named until 1906.
1806 Murder of William Begbie, Messenger of the Bank, in the Court (Chambers, 280; Wilson, II, 72; Grant, I, 280; Cockburn, 226; Smeaton, (a), 209).
1806 Became the printing office of Oliver and Boyd (Grant, I, 281; Keir, 56).
1978 The house is overgrown and derelict, but the entrance still contains a fragment of the King's Wall of 1450 (Catford, 17).

Twelve Apostles' House, Liberton's Wynd.
Twelve Apostles were carved on the pediment on the west wing of the house.
1829 House removed for building George IV Bridge (Dunlop and Dunlop, 14).

Umquhile
Umquhile means former or deceased.

Union Canal
To link Edinburgh with the Forth and Clyde Canal at Falkirk (Grant, II, 215; Catford, 227), for the conveyance of coal, goods and passengers (Youngson, 30). The principal Edinburgh terminus was Port Hopetoun at Portsburgh (q.v.) (Youngson, 179), that for coal was Port Hamilton in Lothian Road and there was a basin at Lochrin.
1818 Building of canal begun and many Irish labourers employed (Gray, 19).
1822 Canal opened (Grant, II, 215).

1848 Taken over by the Glasgow and Edinburgh Railway Company (Scotsman, 13-9-1848; Wood *et al.*, 197, say 1849).

1922 Port Hopetoun, near Lothian Road, drained and built upon.

1977 Canal, described as a 'remainder waterway', owned by British Waterways Board who plan to reopen it in its entirety as a long-term objective should funds permit. Voluntary clearing of dumped rubbish in the Lochrin basin has begun.

University of Edinburgh
(See Grant, III, 8-27; Horn; and, for later building, Stewart).

1558 Bishop of Orkney left 8000 marks Scots to found a College (Chambers, 355).

1561 Town Council resolved on a College.

1562 Mary, Queen of Scots, asked for the use of the site of Kirk o' Field (q.v.).

1566 Kirk o' Field (including Hamilton House of 1554) granted as a site for the Toun's College (Williamson, 245; Stewart, 8).

Old College, University of Edinburgh, with the dome floodlit, as seen from the Surgeons' Hall.

1582 James VI's Charter for the College (O.E.C., II, 8; Maitland, 182; 355; Arnot, 387; Maxwell, 137; Grant, III, 8; Smeaton, (a), 93).

1583 First students entered (Stewart, 8) commonly about fourteen years of age. Lectures began at 6 a.m. in winter and 5 a.m. in summer.

1617 College to be known as King James's College (Grant, III, 10).

1690 Inquiry into teaching staff (O.E.C., VIII, 79-100).

c.1690 Medical classes begun. Chair of Anatomy in 1705.

1693 Divinity classes begun and Chairs of Divinity and Ecclesiastical History established.

1707 Chair of Public Law, followed by those of Civil Law and Scots Law.

1726 Faculty of Medicine established.

1763 500-600 students at the University (Maxwell, 143, f.n.).

1783 1,255 students at the University.

1789 Foundation stone laid for present Old College, designed by Robert Adam and later William Playfair (Grant, III, 22; Cockburn, 6; Creech, 74; Smeaton, (a), 134; Williamson, 247; Stewart, 9).

1791 1,279 students at University (Maxwell, 143, f.n.).

1793 Work on building ceased from lack of funds, and was resumed in 1816, by which date Robert Adam had died.

1821 2,182 students (Maxwell, 143, f.n.).

1834 University building completed (Grant, III, 23; Maxwell, 144; Smeaton, (a), 134).

1860 Reid School of Music erected (Smeaton, (a), 326; Stewart, 11, and *Edinburgh — An Architectural Guide* say 1858). Designed by David Cousin.

1874-84 New College built for Medical Faculty in Teviot Place (Williamson, 247), designed by R. Rowand Anderson.

1883 Students' Representative Council formed, the prototype for the United Kingdom (Stewart, 7).

1884 Tercentenary celebrations; the dome and the 'golden boy' added in Old College (Smeaton, (a), 134).

1889 Scottish Universities Act included a provision for women to graduate (Stewart, 6).

1890's Students' Union built (Stewart, 7; Daiches, 234, says 1899) near the site of the 1793 Edinburgh General Lying-in Hospital.

1897 McEwan Hall (q.v.) built (Catford, 68).

1902 Usher Institute of Public Health, presented by Sir John Usher, built in Warrender Park Road (Stewart, 12).

1906 High School Yards, Infirmary Street, acquired for Department of Natural Philosophy and later Geography (Stewart, 17).

1914 Department of Agriculture sited near the College of Agriculture in George Square (Stewart, 22).

1920 King's Buildings site, Mayfield Road/West Mains Road, acquired and Department of Chemistry built (Stewart, 40).

1920 Women's Union, George Square (Stewart, 22); lasted until Chambers Street Union built in 1948-9.

1926 Minto House (q.v.), Chambers Street, formerly the extramural medical school, acquired (Stewart, 30).

1928-30 Departments of Zoology, Engineering and Animal Genetics opened at King's Buildings (Stewart, 40).

1930 Faculty of Divinity moved to New College at the head of the Mound (Stewart, 18). (See Assembly Hall).

1932 Grant Institute of Geology at King's Buildings (Stewart, 40).

1939-45 Polish Medical School in Medical Buildings.

1947 Adam House, replacing the former home of the Adam brothers, erected in Chambers Street (Stewart, 33).

1948 Pollock Halls of Residence, Dalkeith Road, on site presented by Sir Donald Pollock, accommodates 1800 students (Stewart, 37). Buildings completed in 1973.

1948 New Dental Hospital and School, Chambers Street (Stewart, 30).

1949 Spread of Medical Faculty into George Square, north side.

1960 St. Cecilia's Hall (q.v.) acquired for Faculty of Music (Stewart, 15).

1961 University Staff Club, Chambers Street (Stewart, 31).

1962 Houses in Buccleuch Place, acquired from 1958, used for small units.

1963 7,783 matriculated students at University (Keir, 763).

1977 11,228 students matriculated of whom 1,392 were part-time.

From 1959 further development of King's Buildings, West Mains Road — 1959, School of Agriculture; 1966, Department of Forestry; 1972, Department of Natural Philosophy; 1972, Department of Mathematics and Regional Computing Centre.

From 1963 there has been extensive building in George Square — 1963, David Hume Tower; 1965, Appleton Tower; 1967, University Library (q.v.); 1968, William Robertson Building; 1970, Adam Ferguson Building. The west side and a small portion of the east side still retain the original frontages although the houses are occupied by small departments and offices.

In 1970 the Student Centre was built on the site of Bristo Street and contains a Refectory, Student Health Centre, University Chaplaincy Centre and Royal Medical Society.

University of Edinburgh Halls of Residence
Blackie House, Wardrop's Court (q.v.) (Nimmo, 67) was founded by Patrick Geddes (Keir, 47). It faced on to North Bank Street on which front there is a plaque to Professor J. S. Blackie. It was reconstructed in 1952 (Keir, 1010) and now contains private flats.

Cowan House, George Square, now one of the Pollock Halls (Stewart, 36).

Masson Hall, George Square, now in South Lauder Road (Stewart, 36).

University of Edinburgh buildings in George Square.

Muir Hall, now in Drumsheugh Gardens (Stewart, 36).

Mylne Court, restored 1969-70 for Salvesen and Henman Halls (Stewart, 19).

Patrick Geddes Hall, on the site of the first student Hall of Residence (Lister House) in Mound Place opened in 1887 by Patrick Geddes, restored and reopened in 1978 (Scotsman, 10-11-1978).

Pollock Halls, 1948-73 (Stewart, 36), surround the house of Thomas Nelson, Dalkeith Road.

Ramsay Lodge, Ramsay Garden, founded by Patrick Geddes, now a staff college for a finance company.

St. Giles Hall, St. Giles Place, founded by Patrick Geddes (Keir, 47), demolished in 1937 for the erection of the Sheriff Court.

Blackie House, Lister House, Ramsay Lodge and St. Giles House were formerly owned by the Town and Gown Association, founded by Patrick Geddes.

University of Edinburgh Library
1580 Library founded by Clement Little (Arnot, 414; Grant, III, 330; Williamson, 248) who bequeathed some 300 books.
1626 "It may have been the [legacy of books] by William Drummond of Hawthornden in 1626 which roused the Council to appreciate the need for care in that department of the College." (Extracts from the Records of the Burgh of Edinburgh (1626-1641), xi).

247

1709-1837 The Library received copies of all books published.
1967 The Library moved to George Square with potential
accommodation for 3,000,000 books and with 3,000 reading places
(Stewart, 25).

Upper Baxter's Close, Lawnmarket — north side.
One of three closes leading to property owned by the Incorporation
of Baxters (bakers) (O.E.C., XII, 14). Marked by a plaque at the
entrance to Lady Stair's Close, to the east of which it lay.
1786 Burns' first lodging in the city where he shared the room of his
friend John Richmond (Grant, I, 106; Catford, 126; Scotsman,
3-3-1938).
1796 Acquired by the city (O.E.C., XII, 14).
1800 Lower Baxter's Close to the east was demolished during the
construction of Bank Street, and Upper Baxter's Close is no longer
named.

Upper Bow, Lawnmarket — south side.
Formerly called the Head of the Bow, it formed the upper end of the
West Bow, and is now separated from it by Victoria Terrace (q.v.).

Usher Hall, Lothian Road.
1896 Sir John Usher gifted £10,000 to build a Hall (Robertson, 174).
1913 Usher Hall built (Robertson, 174; Keir, 1008, says 1914).

Vennel
A steep lane leading from Lauriston Place to West Port, running
along the line of the Flodden and Telfer's Walls west of George
Heriot's School. Part of the wall is still to be seen in good condition.

Veterinary College, Summerhall.
Now the Royal (Dick) School of Veterinary Studies. William Dick,
founder of the College, was born in 1793 in White Horse Close
(q.v.) where his father had a blacksmith's forge.
1823 Dick gave veterinary lectures in Clyde Street (now the site of the
Eastern Scottish Omnibus Station) to which the forge had been
moved.
1837 Veterinary College opened in Clyde Street (Smith, II, 453).
c.1880 There was a veterinary college in Gayfield House (q.v.) (Grant,
III, 161).
1917 Veterinary College established in buildings in Summerhall Place
(Stewart, 35).
1934 Veterinary studies embodied within the University of Edinburgh
(Keir, 336), as the Faculty of Veterinary Medicine.
1971 New extension to the School at the expense of Hope Park Church.

Victoria Street and **Terrace,** George IV Bridge.

1835-40 Victoria Street built westwards from George IV Bridge to join West Bow at the angle of the Bow. This, and the building of Victoria Terrace at a higher level above Victoria Street, split the old West Bow. The Upper Bow (q.v.) ends in Victoria Terrace whence steps descend to the junction of Victoria Street and West Bow.

1867 India Buildings erected at the upper end of Victoria Street (Grant, I, 291) and is now used as an additional Sheriff Court.

War Memorials

There are many War Memorials in the city, and apart from those in private buildings, schools, churches etc. and the War memorial clock at Haymarket erected by the Heart of Midlothian Football Club, the following are listed alphabetically —

Black Watch, South African War; Mound.

David Leslie, Earl of Leven, who in 1689 raised a Regiment of Foot whose gallantry at the Battle of Killiecrankie resulted in them, and later the King's Own Scottish Borderers, being permitted to beat drums through the City; Esplanade.

Duke of Albany's Highlanders, Afghanistan, 1878-80; Esplanade.

Duke of York, Commander-in-Chief, British Army, 1877; Esplanade.

Earl Haig, Commander-in-Chief, British Army, World War I; Esplanade.

Ensign Ewart, who captured the standard of the French 45th Regiment at Waterloo, which gave rise to the Eagle Badge of the Royal Scots Greys; Esplanade.

Gordon Highlanders, South African War; Esplanade.

Highland Regiment; Indian Mutiny (1861); Esplanade.

King's Own Scottish Borderers, South African War; North Bridge.

National War Memorial, World Wars I and II; Castle.

Princess Louise Argyllshire Highlanders, 1874; Esplanade.

Royal Scots, First Regiment of Foot, various campaigns; West Princes Street Gardens.

Royal Scots Greys, South African War; West Princes Street Gardens.

Scottish-American War Memorial, World War I; West Princes Street Gardens.

Scottish Horse, South African War; Esplanade.

Scottish soldiers killed in the American Civil War; Old Calton Burying Ground.

Stone of Remembrance, World Wars I and II; City Chambers.

Wardrop's Close and **Court,** Lawnmarket — north side.
Situated beside Upper Baxter's Close (q.v.) near Lady Stair's
House (q.v.). It was the site of Blackie House, a University of
Edinburgh Hall of Residence whose frontage on North Bank Street
shows a plaque of Professor J. S. Blackie, formerly Professor of
Greek at Edinburgh University.

Wardrop's Court was reconstructed as flats in 1952 (Keir,
1010).

Wards see also Town Council.
The earliest wards or districts of the city numbered six in 1805, and
were formed for police purposes (Robertson and Wood, 192).

Modern municipal wards date from 1833. The city was
divided in 1920 into 23 wards, each returning three members to the
Town Council. With the reform of local government in 1975 the
city was divided into 64 electoral divisions, each returning one
Councillor to serve for three years.

Warrender House see Bruntsfield House.

Warriston's Close, High Street — north side.
Formerly called Bruce's Close (O.E.C., XII, 27; Grant, I, 223).
1560-66 John Knox lived in the Close (Catford, 28).
1583 House later owned by Lord Philiphaugh (Grant, I, 223).
1630's Home of Lord Warriston (Grant, I, 226).
1848 Industrial School in the Close (Scotsman, 15-4-1848).
1868 Publishing house of W. & R. Chambers in the Close (Grant, I, 224;
Williamson, 224).
1902 Close demolished for enlargement of the City Chambers (O.E.C.,
I, 7) but there is a modern entrance from the High Street west of the
City Chambers leading to Cockburn Street.

Watchmaking see Clockmaking.

Water of Leith
Rises at Craigengar, Pentland Hills; first house is Colzium Farm;
passes through Harper Rig; crossed by the Drove Road to Linton,
the Lang Whang; Temple House and Hill (Knights Templar
Lands); Balerno with mills for fulling, corn, barley, paper (for 250
years); 80 mills in ten miles in 1793; Malleny; Lennox Castle;
Lymphoy; Currie — old brig, c.1599, snuff mills until 1929; poet's
glen (James Thomson); Juniper Green — paper and snuff mills;
Colinton — Spylaw 'built by snuff'; Dell at Colinton; Redhall Mill;
Boag's Mill — from snuff to chemicals and electricity; leaves woods
at Slateford; Inglis Green; Gray's Mill; Longstone; Stenhouse;

Saughtonhall; Balgreen; Coltbridge; Roseburn; Bell's Mill; Dean Village; Dean Bridge; St. Bernard's Well; Stockbridge; Deanhaugh; Canonmills; Silvermills; Tanfield; Powderhall; Pilrig; Redbraes; Chancelot Mills; Bonnington Mills; Bowling Green Street; Mill Lane; Sheriff Brae; Coal Hill; Leith. (D. Paterson, The Scots Magazine, November, 1946).

Water Supply

The situation of the Old Town on its high ridge and surrounded by flat ground made the supply of water difficult, and until sources could be tapped from the neighbouring hills the water from the Nor' Loch and South Loch was unwholesome, and the town was at the mercy of droughts in hot summers.

1552 Proposal to bring the Water of Leith into the Nor' Loch for water supply (Robertson and Wood, 8).

1575 and 1582 Scarcity of water in the town (Nimmo, 62).

1621 Water supply from South Loch discontinued (O.E.C., X, 256).

1674 Water supplies brought from Comiston, a distance of 3½ miles (5.6km) (O.E.C., II, 10; IV, 12; Arnot, 341; Creech, 87; Grant, I, 82, says 1632 which seems improbable; R.C., lxxi, says 1676; Geddie, 101, says 1681). A German engineer, Peter Brusche (Grant, I, 82) or Brauss (R.C., lxxi) received the contract for a gravitation supply of water from the springs at Comiston to a cistern in Castlehill. From here the water was conveyed in lead pipes, later replaced by elm-wood, to ten smaller cisterns or wells throughout the city from which it was carried to houses at one penny per cask. Some of these wells still remain — at the Lothian Region Buildings in the High Street; at Old Assembly Close in the High Street; near John Knox's House in the High Street; and at the foot of the West Bow in the Grassmarket.

"The water is brought in leaden pipes from a mountain in the neighbourhood to a cistern in Castlehill from whence it is distributed to public conduits in different parts of the city. From these it is carried in barrels on the backs of male or female porters up two, three, four, five, six, seven and eight pairs of steps." (Smollet, 266).

1704 Additional water brought from Liberton and the Pentland Hills (Grant, I, 82; Smeaton, (b), 158).

1720 To increase the supply further, water from Tod's Well was brought to the reservoir in Castlehill, tunnelling through the rock to carry the pipes. This water failed to arrive at the opening ceremony until an air lock in the pipe had been released. Nimmo (63) said that the water had been brought by a Dutchman, Peter Bruschi, who rode out to investigate and never returned. (c.f. the Peter Brusche, a German, who had brought water from Comiston fifty years previously, and the German, Peter Brusche, who was reported by Keir (50) to have stuck lead in Cannonball House in 1609 to show the water level).

1755 Further water shortage resulted in the development of a new source at Swanston (Robertson, 263; R.C., lxxi says 1760) and the bore of the iron pipes, which had replaced lead, was increased in 1772, 1787 and 1790 (Cochrane, 10; Youngson, 241).

1758 An Act of Parliament stated that the city was not "supplied with a sufficient quantity of good and wholesome water." (Youngson, 241).

1767-1819 With the building of the New Town water from the reservoir in Castlehill, supplemented by a new one near Heriot's Hospital built in the 1780's (Youngson, 241) was led by pipes along the North Bridge to a secondary reservoir on Multrie's Hill from where it was taken in pipes along the streets. Water was tapped into cisterns in the basement of houses and had to be carried upstairs. A second supply from Castlehill was led in pipes down the Mound as building of the New Town proceeded westwards.

1790 Elm-wood water pipes were completely removed.

1791 The southern suburbs (q.v), which had public wells, requested the Town Council for piped water.

1810 and 1814 Water shortages in the city (Youngson, 241).

1819 Edinburgh Joint Water Stock Company formed (Gilbert, 67; Youngson, 241), and brought supplies from the Crawley springs at Glencorse until 1869.

1820 Bad state of the water supply (Cockburn, 353).

1847 Water famine in the city (O.E.C., XV, app. 19).

1848 Water from Thriepmuir and Harlaw reservoirs and springs from Bavelaw, Listonshiells and Black Springs (Scotsman, 29-3-1848) collected and conveyed in an aqueduct.

1849 Large reservoir tank on Castlehill to replace the insufficient one (Grant, I, 82; Smeaton, (a), 160; Grierson, 16; R.C., lxxi).

1862 Landlords compelled to install water in houses (Grierson, 17; Wood et al., 27).

1864 Installation of water closets compulsory (Wood et al., 27).

1869 Edinburgh and District Water Trust formed (R.C., lxxii).

1870 Moorfoot scheme (Gladhouse reservoir) inaugurated (Cochrane, 10), completed in 1879 (R.C., lxxii).

1905 Talla reservoir built (R.C., lxxii). The water from these Moorfoot reservoirs was led by wide pipes which were later duplicated to take more water from neighbouring valleys.

1920 Town Council Water Committee assumed control of the water supply.

1946 Comiston water supply discontinued.

1967 South of Scotland Water Board responsible for supply of water and they opened Fruid reservoir in 1969.

1975 Lothian Regional Council responsible for water supply, which cost £1½m. in 1977. Megget valley scheme planned.

The demand for water has risen with a doubled population, a greater awareness of hygiene, and modern industrial consumption, from 8 million gallons (36,000kl) daily in 1871 to 39 million gallons (176,000kl) in 1973. This represents a personal daily usage of 31 gallons (140 litres) in 1871 increasing to 66 gallons (300 litres) in 1973.

Watergate, Canongate — north side.

Watergate is further down the Canongate than the White Horse Close, and it took its name from a large pond for watering horses (Maitland, 156; Wilson, II, 114). It was the principal entrance to the Canongate from the east.

In the 12th century the Royal Tennis Court was near the Watergate (Marshall, 11).

1544 Hertford's army entered the Canongate through the Watergate (Wilson, II, 115).

1681 The first theatre in Edinburgh at the Royal Tennis Court was used from 1681 to 1710 (Chambers, 344).

1822 The Watergate existed as a single arch of wood which was blown down (Grant, II, 22).

Waterloo Place see also Calton Hill.

1815 Waterloo Place constructed through the Old Calton Burying Ground and was designed by Archibald Elliott (Grant, II, 104; Russell, 102; Steuart, 222; Youngson, 144).

1815 Regent Bridge built as a War Memorial, designed by Archibald Elliott (Grant, II, 104).

1815 Governor's House, Calton Jail, designed by Archibald Elliott, built (Youngson, 159).

1821 General Post Office in Waterloo Place (O.E.C., XII, 35; Grant, I, 234; 358). The Excise Office now occupies the building (C. McWilliam, *New Town Guide*, (1978), 16).

1956 When the city transport became entirely by bus a short length of tramcar rails was left at the west end of Waterloo Place.

Waverley Bridge

1872-3 Bridge built (Grant, II, 100; Smeaton, (a), 269; (b), 287).

1894-5 Bridge enlarged (Smeaton, (a), 269; (b), 287).

1978 Now contains Tourist Information Office and Airport Coach Terminal.

Waverley Market

1868 Market, called the Green Market, opened as a vegetable market

(Grant, II, 100; Smeaton, (a), 269; Gilbert, 145; Wood *et al.*, 186).
1877 Promenade erected on top (Grant, II, 100).

     The Waverley Market was also used for exhibition etc. and each year there was a Christmas Carnival. The flower and vegetable markets continued, but part returned to Market Street.
1974 Market closed and was demolished for a proposed Conference Centre (Minto and Armstrong, 23), but it is presently a car park.

Waverley Station see Railways.

Weather see Storms.

Webster's Close, Castlehill — south side.
The residence of Dr Alexander Webster, appointed to the Tolbooth Church (St. Giles) in 1737, "statist and calculator of extraordinary talent . . . [who obtained] the first population returns of Scotland . . . in 1755." (Chambers, 20). The name of the Close, which does not now exist, was changed to Brown's Close, and the Society of Scottish Antiquaries moved there in 1794 (Chambers, 20, f.n.).

Weigh-House see Tron.

West Bow, Lawnmarket leading south to Grassmarket.
The principal entrance to the town from the West Port giving access to Castlehill from the Grassmarket (Wilson, II, 155). Up the West Bow "for centuries did all that was regal, noble and diplomatic advance on entering the city; and down it, for 124 years — between the Restoration and 1784 — went more criminals than can be reckoned to their doom, and many a victim of misrule, such as the luckless and unflinching Covenanters, testifying to the last and glorying in their fate." (Grant, I, 317).

     The part nearest the Lawnmarket was called the Head of the Bow, and latterly the Upper Bow (q.v.).
1450 Archway of the ancient West Port gave its name to the West Bow, because a bow was an arch.
1477 Under James III's Charter the butter and cheese market was at the butter tron at the Head of the Bow.
1566 Lord Ruthven, one of Rizzio's murderers, lived in the West Bow (Grant, I, 316).
1602 Old Assembly Rooms built (Wilson, II, 162).
1670 Major Thomas Weir, hanged and burned for sorcery in 1670, lived at the Head of the Bow (Wilson, II, 157; Grant, I, 311; Chambers, 32; Sitwell and Bamford, 128; Fraser, 118).
1710 First Dancing Assembly (O.E.C., IX, 191; Maitland, 187; Arnot,

381; Chambers, 43; Graham, 97) (see Dancing Assemblies).
1798 Thomas Nelson opened his printing business (Grant, II, 355; Keir, 688).
1835-40 The construction of Victoria Street ended the old West Bow as a continuous street.
1878 The timber-fronted tenements at the Head of the Bow demolished (O.E.C., I, 4; Dunlop and Dunlop, 23; Cruft, 2).
1966 "Most of the shops in the West Bow are old, and include a cord and moleskin shop, three scales merchants, two brushmakers, welders, tool-merchants, and ironmongers where oils and other drysalteries may be sold . . . [and] a shop which still sells horn and woodware." (Keir, 52). Many of these have been replaced by antique shops.

West Port, Grassmarket.
The main entrance to the town from the west.
1513 West Port built as part of the Flodden Wall (Maitland, 139; Wilson, II, 169; Grant, II, 222).
        West Port was also the name given to the nearby suburb (Wilson, II, 169; Grant, II, 219). (See Portsburgh).
1828 The West Port suburb was the scene of grave-robbing and murders by William Burke and William Hare who lived in Tanner's Close near Lady Lawson Street (Wilson, I, 235; Grant, II, 226; Maxwell, 90; Smeaton, (a), 137; 260; Gilbert, 90), and who sold the bodies to Dr Robert Knox, the anatomist. The area of their exploits is now covered by a Government building (Minto and Armstrong, 30).
1844 Chalmers Territorial Church built (Grant, II, 224).

White Friars see Carmelite Friars

White Horse Close, 31 Canongate — north side.
White Horse Close was the 17th century site (R.C., 158) of White Horse Inn (*vide infra*) and William Dick's forge (see Veterinary College).
1889 Partly rebuilt for working-class houses.
1965 Rebuilt by the Town Council as small modern flats while retaining much of the original design.

White Horse Inn, White Horse Close.
Reputed to have been named after a white palfrey ridden by Mary, Queen of Scots, but this may refer to a previous building (Steuart, 108).
1623 Inn built at the north end of the Close, from which travellers set out by coach for London.
1639 'Stoppit Stravaig' (q.v.).
1745 Said to have been the inn where Prince Charles' officers were

White Horse Close, Canongate.

quartered when he stayed at Holyroodhouse.

White Horse Inn, Boyd's Close see Boyd's Inn.

White House, Whitehouse Loan.
The White House was "occupied previous to 1671" (Grant, III, 43).
Smith (I, 44) says that the original house, Quhytehouse, was built
in 1505. John Home is said to have written his *Douglas* (first
produced in 1756) in the White House (Grant, III, 45).
1767 House occupied by MacLeod of MacLeod (Grant, III, 45).
1835 Incorporated into St. Margaret's Convent (Grant, III, 45) which
now contains a private Roman Catholic school for girls.

Whitefoord House, Canongate — north side.
Access is from the old Galloway's Entry, and the frontage of the
present building facing on to the Canongate is marked as the site of
Jenny Ha's Change House, a tavern frequented by the poets John
Gay, Allan Ramsay and others, which existed from 1600 to 1857
(Stuart, 93).
    Whitefoord House was built on the site of the Earl of Winton's
house (Grant, II, 34). In 1565 Lord Darnley occupied Whitefoord
House (Wilson, II, 112; Grant, II, 35). Scott refers to it as "my Lord
Seyton's lugeing in the Canongate" in *The Abbott,* chap. 18.
1806 Dugald Stewart lived in the House (W. Harrison, 23).

The original house is enclosed within the buildings comprising the Scottish Naval, Military and Air Force Veterans' Residence.

Widdy Tree see Gibbet.

Window Duties
Window duties were taxes imposed in 1696 (Smith, I, 79) on the number of windows in each house, and consequently many windows were blocked up to save paying extra duty. The tax was discontinued in 1851 (Scotsman, 1-5-1850 and a note added in 1950).

Wood's Farm
This farm extended from the present Queen Street to Canonmills (Wilson, II, 204; Carlyle, 226, f.n.). Wood was the father of 'Lang Sandy' Wood, a well-known Edinburgh surgeon of the second half of the eighteenth century.

World's End Close, High Street — south side.
Formerly called Stanfield's Close (O.E.C., XII, 87; Grant, I, 281) and Swift's Close (O.E.C., XII, 87; XV, 113), it was the Close that was nearest the Canongate.
    It is now derelict and the buildings are being demolished.

Wright's (Wryttes, Wrychtis) House, Gillespie Crescent.
1339 Wrychtishouse built (Maitland, 508; Wilson, II, 177; Grant, III, 31; Cockburn, 173). The house was frequently added to, and the dates 1376, 1400 and 1513 adorned the building. It belonged to the Napier family and was one of the oldest and most picturesque baronial dwellings in the neighbourhood (Grant, III, 32).
1800 Demolished, after much protestation, for the erection of James Gillespie's Hospital (q.v.) (O.E.C., IV, 55; Grant, III, 34).
1870 Hospital rebuilt on the same site as a school for boys and girls (Grant, III, 35; Keir, 797).
1922 The site of the Royal Blind Asylum workshops (Smith, I, 73).
1975 Pulled down for the building of homes for the elderly, but the Royal Blind Asylum offices remain (Smith, I, 73).

Wright's Houses, Bruntsfield Links.
"A conglomeration of old edifices" (Grant, III, 30). The wrights were the timber wrights who cleared areas of the Drumselch Forest (q.v.) see also Early Houses (Smith, I, 5). They formed a row looking east over Bruntsfield Links, with the Barclay Church at the northern end. The houses have been demolished, but the Golf Tavern ('Established 1476') remains, although the earliest tavern

recorded on the Bruntsfield Links, the Golfhall, was built in 1717 (O.E.C., X, 244; Smith, I, 62).

Writers' Court, High Street — north side.
1688 Designed and built by Robert Mylne with entry from Warriston's Close (q.v.) (O.E.C., XII, 28). It was the original home of the Signet (Writers') Library (q.v.) — hence the name (Grant, I, 186).
    It contained Cleriheugh's Tavern (Grant, I, 120) (see Inns) which was described in Scott's *Guy Mannering,* chap. 36.
1908 The Court was swallowed up in extensions to the City Chambers, but there is a modern opening west of the City Chambers leading to Cockburn Street and Market Street *via* Warriston's Close.

Wynd
A wynd was a thoroughfare open from end to end — c.f. Close. For a description of the origins of the names of the Wynds see O.E.C., XII, 1-156.

York Place
1798 Feuing began (Youngson, 92). No. 32 was the house of Sir Henry Raeburn, while No. 47 was owned by Alexander Nasmyth (Grant, II, 188), and in which in 1810 Andrew Geddes was a tenant (Pennycook, 42).

Zoological Park, Corstorphine.
1840-67 There was a Zoological Garden in Broughton Park (Grant, III, 88).
1909 Zoological Society formally constituted (Keir, 997).
1913 Incorporated by Royal Charter (Keir, 997).
1913 Zoological Park opened, and Corstorphine Hill House became the Society's House (Keir, 998).
1958 Supplementary Charter granted by Queen Elizabeth (Keir, 997).

REFERENCES

Anderson J., *History of Edinburgh from the Earliest Period* (1856).

Arnot, Hugo, *History of Edinburgh* (1779).

Books of The Old Edinburgh Club, vols. I (1908) to date.

Boswell, James, *Journal of a Tour to the Hebrides* (1773) (1963 edition).

Brown, P. Hume, *Early Travellers in Scotland* (1891) (1973 edition).

Carlyle, A., *Autobiography 1722-1805* (Foulis edition, 1910).

Catford, E. F., *Edinburgh — The Story of a City* (1975); London, Hutchinson & Co. (Publishers) Ltd.

Chambers, R., *Traditions of Edinburgh* (1868) (1967 edition).

Cochrane, R., *Edinburgh Castle, Royal Mile and Holyrood* (undated, c.1912).

Cockburn, Lord, *Memorials of his Time* (1856) (1971 edition).

Creech, W., *Fugitive Pieces* (1815).

Cruft, C., *Edinburgh — Old and New* (1975); Wakefield, E. P. Publishing Ltd.

Daiches, David, *Edinburgh* (1978); London, Hamish Hamilton.

Dunlop, J. C. and Dunlop, A. H., *The Book of Old Edinburgh* (1886).

Edinburgh Architectural Association, *Edinburgh — An Architectural Guide* (1964).

Fraser, D., *Edinburgh in Olden Times* (1976); Montrose, Standard Press.

Geddie, J., *The Fringes of Edinburgh* (1926).

Gilbert, W. M., *Edinburgh in the Nineteenth Century* (1901).

Graham, H. G., *Social Life in Scotland in the Eighteenth Century* (1909).

Grant, J., *Old and New Edinburgh* (1884-7, three volumes).

Gray, W. Forbes, *A Brief Chronicle of the Scottish Union and National Insurance Company, 1824-1924* (1924).

Grierson, M. A., *A Hundred Years in Princes Street — the Story of Jenners* (1938).

Guthrie, Douglas, *Extramural Medical Education in Edinburgh* (1965).

Harris, D. Fraser, *St. Cecilia's Hall* (1899).

Harrison, J., *The Company of Merchants of the City of Edinburgh and its Schools, 1694-1920* (1920).

Harrison, W., *Memorable Edinburgh Houses* (1893) (1971 edition); Wakefield, S. R. Publishers Ltd..

Keir, D., *The City of Edinburgh (Third Statistical Account of Scotland)* (1966); Glagow, Collins Sons & Co. Ltd.

Lindsay, Ian G., *Georgian Edinburgh* (1973 edition); Edinburgh, Scottish Academic Press Ltd.

Livingstone, J., (a), *Our Street* (1893).

Livingstone, J., (b), *Some Edinburgh Shops* (1894).

MacKenzie, H., *Anecdotes and Egotisms, 1745-1831* (1923 edition).

Maclean, A. A., *North British Album* (1975); London, Ian Allan Ltd.

Maitland, W., *History of Edinburgh* (1753).

Malcolm, C. A., (a), *Holyrood* (1937).

Malcolm, C. A., (b), *Princes Street* (1938). (A History of the Life Association of Scotland).

Marshall, J. S., *Old Leith at Leisure* (1976); Edinburgh, Edina Press.

Maxwell, Sir Herbert, *Edinburgh — A Historical Study* (1916).

Minto, C. S., *Victorian and Edwardian Edinburgh* (1973); *London, Batsford Ltd.*

Minto, C. S. and Armstrong, N. E. S., *Edinburgh, Past and Present* (1975); *Oxford, Oxford Illustrated Press Ltd.*

Nimmo, Ian, *Portrait of Edinburgh* (1969); *London, Robert Hale & Co.*

Peacock, H., et al., *The Unmaking of Edinburgh* (1976) *Edinburgh, E.U.S.P.B.*

Pennycook, A., *Literary and Artistic Landmarks of Edinburgh* (1973); *Edinburgh, Charles Skilton.*

Robertson, D., *The Princes Street Proprietors* (1935).

Robertson, D., and Wood, M., *Castle and Town* (1928).

Royal Commission, *Inventory of the Ancient and Historical Monuments of the City of Edinburgh* (1951); *H.M.S.O.*

Russell, J., *The Story of Leith* (1922).

Scott-Moncrieff, G., *Edinburgh* (1947).

Sitwell, S. and Bamford, F., *Edinburgh* (1948).

Smeaton, O., (a), *Edinburgh and its Story* (1904).

Smeaton, O., (b), *The Story of Edinburgh* (1905).

Smith, C. J., *Historic South Edinburgh* (1978 — two volumes); *Edinburgh, Charles Skilton Ltd.*

Smollett, T., *Humphry Clinker* (1771) (World Classics edition 1967).

Smout, T. C., *A History of the Scottish People, 1566-1830* (1969) (Fontana edition, 1972); *Glasgow, Collins Sons & Co. Ltd.*

Steuart, M. D., *The Romance of the Edinburgh Streets* (4th edition, 1936).

Stewart, C., *The Past Hundred Years* (1973); *Edinburgh, Edinburgh University Press.*

Stuart, M., *Old Edinburgh Taverns* (1952).

Topham, E., *Letters from Edinburgh* (1776) (1971 editon).

Turner, A. Logan, *The Story of a Great Hospital* (1937).

Weirter, L., *The Story of Edinburgh Castle* (1913).

Williamson, M. G., *Edinburgh* (1906).

Wilson, Sir Daniel, *Memorials of Edinburgh in the Olden Times* (2nd edition, 1891 — two volumes).

Wood, M., et al., *Edinburgh, 1329-1929* (1929).

Youngson, A. J., *The Making of Classical Edinburgh* (1968); *Edinburgh, Edinburgh University Press.*

OTHER BIBLIOGRAPHY

(These books are only referred to occasionally, if at all, in the text, and the name of the author and the book accompanies each reference.)

Barclay, J. B., *Edinburgh from the Earliest Time to the Present Day* (1965).
Bone, J., *The Perambulator in Edinburgh* (1927) — originally issued in 1911 under the title *Edinburgh Revisited*.
Butchart, R., *Prints and Drawings of Edinburgh* (1955).
Chambers, R., *Walks in Edinburgh* (1823).
Chambers, R., *Minor Antiquities of Edinburgh* (1833).
Chambers, W., *Memoir of Robert Chambers* (1872).
Cox, J. T., *Practice and Procedure in the Church of Scotland* (1964 edition).
Crossland, J. B., *Victorian Edinburgh* (1966).
Donaldson, G., *et al.*, *Edinburgh — A Symposium* (1975).
Dunlop, A. H., *Anent Old Edinburgh* (1890).
Extracts from the Records of the Burgh of Edinburgh.
Geddie, J., *Romantic Edinburgh* (1900).
Horn, D. B., *A Short History of Edinburgh University* (1967).
Hornby, G., *Edinburgh* (1912).
Joyce, M., *Edinburgh — The Golden Age* (1951).
Linklater, Eric, *Edinburgh* (1960).
Marshall, J. S., *Old Leith at Work* (1977).
Masson, D., *Edinburgh Sketches and Memories* (1892).
Reid, J., *New Lights on Old Edinburgh* (1894).
Scott, Sir Walter, *Tales of a Grandfather* (1827-30) (1933 edition).
Skinner, R. T., *The Royal Mile* (1928).
Stark, J., *Picture of Edinburgh* (1806).
Stevenson, R. L., *Edinburgh — Picturesque Notes* (1896).
Turner, A. Logan, *History of the University of Edinburgh (1883-1933)* (1933).
Yee, Chiang, *The Silent Traveller in Edinburgh* (1948).
Young, D., *Edinburgh in the Age of Sir Walter Scott* (1965).

Other books of a more specialised nature have been used, and they are mentioned in full in the text, as are references from newspapers, magazines etc.

INDEX

268